THE SAVVY CONVERT'S GUIDE TO CHOOSING A RELIGION

THE SAVVY CONVERT'S GUIDE TO CHOOSING A RELIGION

Created and published by
Knock Knock
1633 Electric Avenue
Venice, CA 90291
www.knockknock.biz

Printed in China

Illustrations by Teri Hendrich

This book is a work of humorous yet exhaustively researched nonfiction meant solely for entertainment purposes. It is not intended to be the last word on anyone's spirituality. In no event will Knock Knock be liable to any reader for any damages, including direct, indirect, incidental, special, consequential, or punitive, arising out of or in connection with the worship of the information contained in this book. If we got something factually wrong, tell us so we can correct it in subsequent editions. If you're offended, get a sense of humor. If you've got a sacred cow, grill it up as a nice steak and wash it down with some Bordeaux. So there.

ISBN: 978-160106034-1
UPC: 8-25703-50000-4

10 9 8 7 6 5 4 3 2 1

THANK GOD(S)

CONTENTS

INTRODUCTION

Choosing a religion is no small task. As a religion consumer, you'll want to determine what you seek in a faith as well as acquire the tools to find it in the religion marketplace.

SPOTLIGHTS

99 RELIGIONS PROFILED: A TO Z

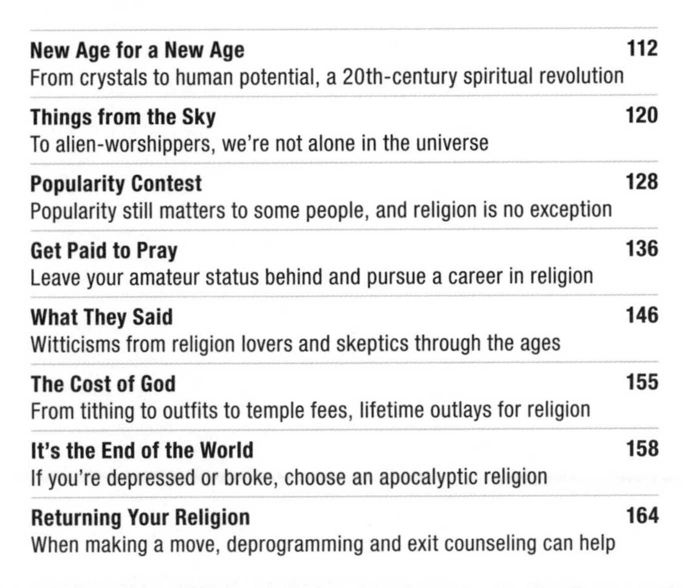

CONCLUSION

Even with 99 religions to choose from, the right fit can elude you. If you're an entrepreneurial seeker, perhaps it's time to start your *own* religion—with these easy, step-by-step instructions.

THE TWENTY-FIRST-CENTURY RELIGION CONSUMER IN THE GLOBAL RELIGION MARKETPLACE

IF ONLY RELIGION SHOPPING WERE AS EASY AS BUYING a car. Houses of worship, lined up like a row of dealerships, would proclaim their tenets from stickers on stained-glass windows. As we experimented, we'd consult and annotate consumer guides listing each faith's pros and cons. We'd carry along a list of preconsidered questions to ask both clergy and followers. After test-driving multiple services, when we were sure we'd seen all the religion marketplace had to offer, we would join the flock of our choice.

Fear of rejection?
DON'T choose a religion that requires missionary work.

Unfortunately, that's not the way most of us come to faith. We accept the traditions of family, geography, politics, or ethnicity, or we want to run so far away from those that we embrace the first pamphleteer to come our way in a weak moment. Others, brought up in secular households, yearn for something more but have no idea where to start.

The purpose of this book is to compare religions side by side so that spiritual seekers everywhere can pick the path that's right for them. Religious choice used to be limited based on where we lived, but in our global economy, access to a world of beliefs is spreading fast, and the religion marketplace has expanded to all corners of the planet. Although there's never been a better time to be in the market for a new religion, with increased choice comes heightened possibility for confusion. In this richly complex arena of options, it's essential to make apples-to-apples comparisons—an opportunity previously unavailable to the religion consumer.

You hold in your hands the first religion guide designed to help you make the right choice based on aspects of faith that really matter in today's lifestyle-oriented consumer culture—time commitment, perks and drawbacks, afterlife promises, and so much more. And "religion consumer" isn't just a sacrilegious metaphor. If you're going to, say, commit 10 percent of your income to tithing, buy new outfits, and pay for extensive conversion coursework, don't you want to know how much it'll add up to and what you'll get in return?

WHAT KIND OF RELIGION CONSUMER AM I?

Maybe you're curious about the temple down the street, or you've always wanted to know what they're chanting in that shrine next to the grocery

Computer geek or technophobe?
DO choose a religion that suits your virtual lifestyle.

store. Perhaps you're wondering what your cousin's meditating is all about or why your neighbor's ex-wife doesn't eat root vegetables. Whatever your particular curiosities, they're informed by your motivations for seeking faith. Often such seeking coincides with life changes like marriage, childbearing, or significant and deliberate shifts in lifestyle. When beginning the search, it's helpful to identify one's seeking type among 4 basic varieties: first-timers, those of lapsed faith, converts, and searchers, each characterized by unique desires that affect the hunt:

1. **First-timers:** First-time seekers were generally raised in a secular family, or perhaps in a religion to which they never connected and in which they never participated. In adulthood, these individuals consider themselves non-religious, so the hurdle from nothing to something (more difficult than the shift from one thing to another) must be surmounted. This group tends to be characterized by any or all of the following:
   - **Looking for Meaning:** Yearning for something more: a connection with humankind; inner peace; a cosmic system of checks and balances.
   - **Loneliness:** Many first-time seekers are unhappy with their current aspiritual sense of isolation and long for community.
   - **Skepticism:** Their internal radar vigorously questions unprovable assertions, part of the reason these intellectually rigorous seekers haven't found religion before.
   - **Embarrassment:** In secular communities, religious beliefs may be disparaged such that desire for faith is repressed or unexpressed.
   - **Commitment to Love:** Among the secular, belief in romantic love has projected itself onto religion or replaced it. The secular have a particularly hard time accepting faith because they believe they must feel it deeply before pursuing it.
2. **Those of Lapsed Faith:** For the formerly religious, many factors may motivate the move away from a former religion:

Generous to a fault?
DON'T let your new religion put you into debt, even if you think the end is near.

- **Discontentment:** For those who never chose their religion, instead sliding into the religion of their parents and community, a poor religious fit may have been confused with the overall unacceptability of religion. In these cases, a new religion can be particularly effective.
- **Rebellion:** Many individuals undergo a period of their lives incompatible with the strictures of religion, so they reject their faiths. At a later date, they may long to return to their original religion, or they may prefer something altogether different.
- **Recovering:** A bad experience with religion can turn people away from religion for a lifetime. Others respond to betrayal by letting their faith lapse, but at some point they're willing to try again.
- **Experience:** Having experienced faith at some point is helpful when the time comes to rejoin a religion or seek a new one. Once exercised, the faith muscle retains at least some of its memory and returns, with varying degrees of work, to its previous state of belief.

3. **Converts:** Given their prior worship experience, converts and those of lapsed faith can have much in common. Converts are generally in current practice but for varying reasons are contemplating a shift:

- **Passivity:** Choosing the religion of family of origin and community is certainly the easy way to go, especially before one realizes there are so many more from which to choose.
- **Evolving:** Sometimes individuals and religious institutions change at different rates. Perhaps the convert's religion hasn't changed with the times, or maybe it's changed too much.
- **Disillusionment:** Whether a pious preacher is caught with his pants down or the UFOs and apocalypse aren't coming according to prediction, it's common for converts to grow frustrated with hypocrisy and lies.
- **Reawakening:** If a follower has never had the opportunity to compare and contrast, the realization that so many religions beckon can be thrilling.
- **Marriage:** For those about to enter marriage, the question of religion looms large. Conversion will make one set of in-laws happy, or a couple can choose an entirely new faith and upset everybody—not to mention get out of family holiday obligations.

Identity crisis?
DO find a religion that will give you a new name.

4. **Searchers:** Searchers are the nomads and omnivores of the religion marketplace. Some switch from belief to belief, while others either create their own blends or worship different gods simultaneously. Some are uniquely open-minded, while others disavow their previous beliefs as soon as they acquire new ones.

    - **Seekers:** Seekers are stimulated by spirituality and constantly explore new ways to understand the world, the cosmos, the soul. They revere few sacred cows and are instead dominated by the desire to ponder, through various belief systems, the meaning of life.
    - **Serial true believers:** These individuals prefer to belong to cohesive communities that provide all the answers but quickly become disillusioned—or differently inspired—and move from one to the next, completely recanting what came before.
    - **Metrospirituals:** They're spiritual, they're urban, they're consumers with a social conscience. These smorgasbord, DIY cool-seekers are rapidly becoming a major force in the religion marketplace. They prefer to blend their spiritual, political, and environmental beliefs into a concoction that strikes them as uniquely their own.

The purpose of identifying yourself among the seeking types is to understand the opportunities and obstacles you may face in your search. For example, if your lapsed faith or desire for conversion is motivated by displeasure with your previous religion, you will want to analyze exactly what you didn't like and seek out faiths that treat these aspects differently. If you're a first-timer who's never believed, recognize your deeply inculcated skepticism and don't expect belief at first worship.

Given that more than 90 percent of us believe in some sort of higher power, however, you're bound to meet like-minded souls as you kick the spiritual tires. In the religion marketplace, *nosce te ipsum* (know thyself) leads to *caveat emptor* (buyer beware), helping to ensure that an informed decision—one you'll be happy with for decades rather than days—is reached.

Adam and Steve?

DON'T choose a religion where you can't ask or tell.

WHAT PURPOSE DOES RELIGION SERVE?

There's no recorded time in history when people did not hold religious beliefs. For millennia, religion ensured community survival by establishing codes of conduct and behavior. Most rules had to do with purity, eating habits, sex, marriage, and family life. Concepts of unity and order kept groups peaceful and organized. A shared culture of stories and rituals was passed down through generations, helping to protect the community's way of life from outside attacks and internal dissension. Leaders such as the pharaohs bolstered their authority by claiming a direct connection to the gods. Religion also gave followers authority. A parent's "Because I said so" could be backed up with "and so do the shamans and the entire cosmos."

Some scholars believe that our minds are geared toward religious belief in the same way that they are wired for speech. Others argue that religion completes us, and that without beliefs we would be unable to lead fulfilled lives. One school of thought asserts that human nature can't grasp that bad things might happen without a reason, leading to the creation of rituals, moral rules, and cosmic systems of checks and balances.

Religion explains the inexplicable, whether it is a child's death or the reason for the sunrise. Now we have psychotherapy, and every day more natural phenomena are met with scientific explanations. In contemporary life, does religion still serve a purpose? The benefits of religion really haven't changed since the days when it actually contributed to our survival (except where it no longer contributes to our survival):

- Religion explains the human soul.
- Religion gives human life value and helps put events into context by asserting that we're here for a reason.
- Religion provides truth, purpose, and goals, and the maps to find and attain them.

Need a little extra help?
DO choose a religion with spirit guides or angels.

- Religion outlines a system of justice, then levels the playing field because anyone who believes and follows the rules can reap the rewards—if not now, then in the afterlife.
- Religion yields hope and comfort through faith.
- Religion unifies like-minded believers, providing an extended family and sense of identity for entire societies—in this life and the next.
- Religion provides a manual for life, from relationships to food consumption to sex to personal dress to bathroom habits.

When so much trouble in the world seems to stem from religious differences, it's easy to overlook the fact that all religions serve comparable functions in their followers' lives—not to mention that, at their roots, individual religions are far more similar to one another than they are different. To nonbelievers, the distinctions that do exist between religions seem so minor that it's almost impossible to understand why people kill each other over them.

RELIGION DEFINED

Religion is a system of beliefs explaining where we come from, why we're here, and what comes next, often involving faith in an unseen, superhuman power and practiced through rituals, traditions, mythology, and prayer or meditation. Religion establishes a moral code and a sense of right and wrong to determine which behaviors are rewarded and which are punished. Followers express devotion to a supreme being or multiple gods through worship and adherence to guidelines or commandments, which are defined in sacred texts and are often directly attributable to a higher power(s).

Born to be wild?
DON'T choose a religion that believes in sin.

ARE ALL RELIGIONS THE SAME?

On the one hand, the fact that major religions, like cars, share many of the same characteristics is good news for the religion consumer: if you're getting just about the same thing no matter what you choose, it's that much harder to make a poor selection. On the other hand, it's more difficult to identify the nuances that distinguish the faiths, and as the saying goes, "God is in the details." (Case in point: the saying also goes, "The devil is in the details.") As you shop around, both the similarities and the differences will help inform your questions.

Religion Similarities:

- Connection to each other and to something bigger than ourselves.
- Belief that all human life has a purpose, and there's a reason we're here.
- Some version of the Golden Rule—showing compassion for one another and rejecting murder, violence, theft, and dishonesty.
- Division of the world and specific behaviors into good and bad.
- Concept of giving thanks.
- Promotion of marriage, or other rules concerning procreation.
- Respect for life.
- Emphasis on charity and forgiveness.
- Importance of family and family obligations.

Religion Differences:

- Supreme beings (quantity, description, role, name).
- Sacred texts; literal vs. interpretive readings; written vs. oral traditions.
- Prophets and messiahs.
- What is sacred: places, people, objects, symbols.
- Rituals and ceremonies.
- Community worship vs. individual enlightenment.

- Creation stories.
- Afterlife beliefs.
- Search for internal truths and divinity within (drives most mystical and Eastern religions), or external truths (God as separate from humans, the focus of many Western faiths); basically, whether the source of divinity is internal or external.
- Whether it's necessary to commune with God through intermediaries (usually in the form of church leaders).
- Views on sex, marriage, procreation; war, suicide, euthanasia, abortion.
- Human role within nature—part of it or separate from it.
- Open to newcomers (evangelical; dependent on belief) vs. closed to newcomers (indigenous; transmitted by birth).
- Hostility to other faiths and outsiders, such as whether or not outsiders are saved.
- Daily lifestyles and conduct: proper behavior, laws, prayer, meditation, the role of women, diet, purity concerns.
- Despite their quasi-religious role in followers' lives, some belief systems don't consider themselves religions but philosophies, and favor rational thought over supernatural powers.

Add in the conflict over interpretation of the same faiths among individual denominations and the proliferation of cults, sects, and new religious movements (NRMs), and the spiritual quest can get complicated.

WHAT WILL RELIGION GIVE ME?

The perks and drawbacks of religion haven't necessarily changed over the course of time—what's changed is whether it's mandatory or optional. Like most things in the contemporary marketplace, we have more choices than we can possibly contemplate. In religion, we can decide whether to abstain or adopt, and if we adopt, there are many faiths vying for our membership.

Conspicuous consumer?
DON'T take a vow of poverty.

RELIGION DESIGNATIONS: DENOMINATION, SECT, OR CULT?

With so many types of religious activities out there, it's hard to keep them straight.

Denomination: Large, often historical division within a larger shared faith, especially Christianity. Generally united by an administrative body and comprising many congregations. For example, the Roman Catholic Church vs. the Baptist Church. Though not generally used for non-Christian religions, *denomination* could be applied to Sunni vs. Shi'a Muslims.

Sect: An offshoot from an established group, often focused on returning to the religion's fundamentals. Frequently used synonymously with *cult.*

Cult: *Cult* has negative connotations and has been largely replaced among scholars by NRM (see below). The connotations of *cult* include coercion, control, brainwashing, totalitarianism, megalomaniacal leaders, questionable fund-raising techniques and distribution of wealth, deceit, insularity from the outside world, and aggressive recruitment and retention. Sociologically, it's a group whose existence causes tension with other, more dominant groups.

New Religious Movement (NRM): Any religious group formed in the past 100 years.

Whether nonmainstream groups are called sects, cults, or NRMs, they tend to promote practices and dogma thought to be outside the mainstream. Cults, sects, and NRMs generally seek new members vigorously and have strong, messianic founders and leaders who claim to have divine powers. And while newer groups are often easiest to join, they may be the most difficult to leave.

WHAT DEFINES A CULT DEPENDS ON WHOM YOU ASK. TO SOME, IT'S JUST A RELIGION THAT HASN'T CAUGHT ON YET:

- A cult is a religion with no political power. —*Tom Wolfe*
- What's a cult? It just means not enough people to make a minority. —*Robert Altman*
- The only difference between a cult and a religion is the amount of real estate they own. —*Frank Zappa*
- The less reasonable a cult is, the more men seek to establish it by force. —*Jean-Jacques Rousseau*
- Nationalism is our form of incest, is our idolatry, is our insanity. "Patriotism" is its cult. . . . By "patriotism" I mean that attitude which puts [one's] own nation above humanity, above the principles of truth and justice; not the loving interest in one's own nation. . . . Love for one's country which is not part of one's love for humanity is not love, but idolatrous worship. —*Erich Fromm*
- I am of a sect by myself, as far as I know. —*Thomas Jefferson*

Potential Religion Perks:

- Faith, hope, spiritual guidance, moral compass, security, conviction.
- Connection to inner self, higher being, humankind.
- Sense of community, acceptance, comfort, peace of mind.
- Framework for life and raising a family.
- Continuity with tradition, path for the future.
- Answers about the unknown, confidence about what happens after death.
- Unconditional love.
- Sense of superiority.
- Potential salvation.
- Social opportunities, whether in a congregation or through online-dating websites such as JDate.com.

Potential Religion Drawbacks:

- Isolation in an insular community, especially if friends and family do not share your beliefs.
- Time-consuming and expensive.
- Adhering to rules and making sacrifices, such as giving up meat, alcohol, sex, movies, music, dancing, popular culture, other beliefs, old friends.
- Separation from nonbelieving family members after death.
- Less control over your own life.
- May turn you into a dogmatic know-it-all.
- Guilt.
- Repression.

But as they say, "When one door closes, another opens," and any worthwhile pursuit entails both sacrifices and opportunities. In 1905, the philosopher George Santayana wrote, "What religion a man shall have is a historical accident, quite as much as what language he shall speak." More than 100 years later, however, it doesn't have to be an accident. If you want to make your religion *your* choice, it's time to get down to selecting the right one for you.

Never learned to share? Light sleeper? Picky eater?

DON'T choose a religion that requires communal living.

HOW DO I IDENTIFY WHAT I WANT FROM A RELIGION?

In today's marketplace, the religion shopper needs to find lasting value. The contemplation of such a big decision can lead to fear of making a mistake. Everybody wants to find a faith that will last a lifetime, but rest assured that in case of a bad fit, you can indeed return or exchange your religion. The first blush of religious exhilaration aside, there's no "perfect" religion for you—instead, you should seek a religion that's good enough, a religion that connects with your belief systems and meets your needs. Any faith, no matter how complementary the match, will at times frustrate you. Like all meaningful relationships, once you've determined that your religion is worthwhile and offers more positives than negatives, you'll need to ride out the inevitable bumps.

To determine a good match, you'll want to address a few considerations and ask yourself some questions. Most religions will get you from point A to point B, but how you travel can make all the difference in your overall spiritual experience. Knowing what you're looking for, where you'll find it, and how much time, money, and emotion you're willing to invest are key factors in successful religion shopping.

1. **First, define your overall goals.** Salvation, enlightenment, spirituality, or nothingness? Active vs. relaxing afterlife, or none? Material wealth in this life, or the ability to transcend a previous life? Harmony with nature and the world around you, or harmony within? Great church potlucks?
2. **Next, narrow your focus.** Do you want to attend services on Saturdays, Sundays, or never? Do you have any phobias that would preclude you from getting the most out of a particular religion, such as a fear of snakes, water, or communicating with the dead? Do you want to have

Mommy track or career gal?
DO choose a religion that's on your path.

a large family, or would you prefer to remain celibate? Can you kneel for extended periods of time? Does spinning make you dizzy? Are you allergic to incense?

3. **Think about what you enjoy doing.** Are there activities at which you excel or skills you'd like to acquire? Faith healing, speaking in tongues, sumo wrestling? What kind of leadership or organizational style do you find the most motivational—patriarchal, hierarchal, communal, or none? Would you like a power animal, angel, or ancestor to accompany you on your spiritual path, or would you prefer to go it alone?

These are just some general principles to get you started in your quest, to put you in the mind-set of the religion consumer. The following questionnaires, however, will take you into the specifics of your deepest desires and determine whether a change is in order, and if so, to what.

Captivated by a charismatic leader?
DON'T forget—false eyelashes may mean false prophets.

QUESTIONNAIRE FOR CONVERTS: ARE YOU HAPPY WITH YOUR CURRENT RELIGION?

1. Do you ever fantasize about other religions?	☐ YES ☐ NO
2. Has your current religion stopped meeting your spiritual needs?	☐ YES ☐ NO
3. Do you question the leadership of your current religion?	☐ YES ☐ NO
4. Do you question your current religion's dogma?	☐ YES ☐ NO
5. Do you believe your current religion's promises?	☐ YES ☐ NO
6. Do you feel your current religion has strayed from its own core beliefs?	☐ YES ☐ NO
7. At services, do you feel like you're just going through the motions?	☐ YES ☐ NO
8. When you read your current religion's sacred texts, do you fall asleep?	☐ YES ☐ NO
9. Do you dislike most of the other followers of your current religion, or feel you have nothing in common with them?	☐ YES ☐ NO
10. Do you ever tire of explaining your religion to outsiders?	☐ YES ☐ NO
11. Does your current religion no longer fit your lifestyle?	☐ YES ☐ NO

Think the man of the house should rule the roost?
DO choose a religion that says who's in charge.

12. Do you need directions to get to your current religion's closest house of worship?	☐ YES ☐ NO
13. Is your current religion no longer convenient?	☐ YES ☐ NO
14. Is your current religion no longer in business?	☐ YES ☐ NO
15. Have you married outside your current religion?	☐ YES ☐ NO
16. Does your current religion require too much of a commitment?	☐ YES ☐ NO
17. Do your current religion's restrictions—wardrobe, diet, sex—interfere with your lifestyle?	☐ YES ☐ NO
18. Have any of your current religion's leaders been convicted of a felony?	☐ YES ☐ NO
19. Have you sunk your life savings into your current religion?	☐ YES ☐ NO
20. Do you suspect members of your current religion would attempt to prevent you from leaving if they knew you were planning to do so?	☐ YES ☐ NO

EVALUATING YOUR ANSWERS:
Count the number of "yes" responses, and proceed as follows:

1–5 Wait for inspiration, but keep an open mind.

6–10 Time to start browsing.

11–15 Go forth and shop!

16–20 Leave immediately, whether or not you have a new religion destination.

Just want to be alone?
DON'T choose a religion in which spirits walk among us.

QUESTIONNAIRE FOR SEARCHERS: WHAT RELIGION IS RIGHT FOR YOU?

In determining your religion choice, there's no easy way to rank or score your responses in order to spit out the perfect faith. Instead, these questions are meant to help you clarify what you're seeking so you'll have a list of preferences when you evaluate individual religions.

PERSONALITY

1. Do you enjoy agitating people, or do you prefer to go with the flow without making waves? Do you consider yourself a renegade, or are you more conventional? An individualist, or someone who likes to stay in the mainstream? In the language of idea diffusion, are you an innovator, early adopter, majority participant, or laggard?
2. Do you like spending lots of time alone? Do you prefer to seek inner truth without scheduled worship services? Or are you social? Are big family holidays important to you? Do you prefer kneeling-room-only worship services?
3. Do you care if your religion is growing, stagnant, or shrinking? Would you try a religion with only a few dozen followers?
4. Are you a one-stop shopper? Do you want your religious and political leaders, your therapist, and your parental figures to be the same people? Or are you skeptical about authority and power?
5. Do you want your religion to accept you with open arms, or do you want it to present initiation hurdles and hard work for entry?
6. Are you looking for a structured religion, or something more independently spiritual?

COMMITMENTS

7. What kind of time commitment are you prepared for? Do you want religion to be an intermittent, scheduled commitment, or a way of life?
8. How much reading are you prepared to do?
9. Can you take time off work for religious observances? Missionary or pilgrimage travel?

10. Would you prefer to pray once a week, 3 times a day, or 5 times a day?

11. What's your religion budget?

12. Do you have a preference for paying voluntary offerings, paying regular membership dues, tithing, or signing your house and checking account over to your religion?

ACTIVITIES

13. Are you an adventurer? Do you want exotic rituals and potential travel? Or do you prefer to stay at home and in your comfort zone?

14. If missionary work is called for, would you feel comfortable doing it? Could you recruit when necessary?

15. Would you rather spend time reading and interpreting scripture, or learning and passing down oral traditions?

16. Do you enjoy uninhibited singing, dancing, and praising, or does that make you self-conscious? How about meditating, reciting, and chanting?

17. Do you want lots of rituals, holidays, and services, entailing elaborate preparations, costumes, and observances?

18. Do you care if others govern such intimate aspects of your life as sex and diet? Is freedom of choice important to you, and if so, in what areas?

MOTIVATION

19. Are you waiting for an internal epiphany before joining, or do you feel that you will come to love and believe in the religion that you choose?

20. Do you want to make the world a better place, or would you prefer to focus on the individual benefits that religion can bestow upon you?

21. Are you looking for a family-friendly religion, or one that will help you meet a mate?

Think 24/6 should be the new 24/7?
DON'T choose a religion that allows work on the Sabbath.

22. Do you want a strict creed or dogma that will direct you in all areas of your life, or are you seeking a set of loose guidelines?

23. Do networking and career advancement matter to you?

24. Do you want something to believe in, or are you looking for something that doesn't require any beliefs at all?

25. Do you believe in multiple gods or in one supreme being? Or is your belief system more broadly spiritual, focusing, say, on the life force within each of us?

26. Are you an optimist who believes in the inherent goodness of humans, or a pessimist who believes we're born sinners? Do you believe humanity will be redeemed by salvation?

27. Do you believe in the concept of good and evil?

28. Do you believe our lives are predestined?

29. Do you believe in karma and reincarnation? Heaven and hell?

30. Do you believe we control our own happiness?

31. Do racism and sexism bother you?

32. Do you like your family enough to worship your ancestors?

33. Do you believe in miracles and angels? Spirit animals?

34. Do you believe in mind over matter and faith healing?

35. Do you believe that everybody should believe what you believe?

36. Are you just in it for the afterlife?

Fear of 40?
DO choose a religion that doesn't celebrate birthdays.

DO I HAVE TO COMMIT TO JUST ONE RELIGION?

No. Whether you prefer religious monogamy, serial monogamy, polygamy, or just plain sleeping around, there are diverse and exciting ways to proceed. For the commitment shy, the world of spirituality offers less structured "religion fusion," the metrospiritualism movement, and religion tourism. After all, we can now have 10 careers in our lifetime—why not 10 religions, whether consecutively or all at once?

RELIGION TOURISM

You spent the summer as a Lutheran, became a Sikh by Christmas, and by the time Vaisakhi rolled around, you were already booking reservations for a sweat lodge. You'd no sooner unpacked your didgeridoo than you were off to meet the Dalai Lama. If you're a serial true believer with a closet full of discarded prayer beads and *kami* statues, or a confirmed dabbler less interested in enlightenment than in Zen garden tips, you're a religion tourist. A perpetual quest to see what everyone else is talking about, religion tourism is a great way to get a feel for different beliefs—it's the spiritual equivalent of seeing the world. Although religion tourism isn't right for everybody, for some people it's the only way.

Pros of Religion Tourism:

- You'll experience a variety of beliefs; if you ever do commit, you'll be secure in your choice.
- You can keep what works for you and disregard the rest.
- You can argue all sides of any religious issue.
- You'll probably never be called on to fight a holy war.

Social drinker? Medicinal pot smoker? Caffeine addict?
DON'T choose a religion that cramps your lifestyle.

- No one will ever be able to guess your political party based on your religious beliefs.
- When someone begins a joke with "A priest, a rabbi, and a monk . . . ," you'll finally get it.
- Every day will be a holiday; Christmas, Hanukkah, Kwanzaa, Winter Solstice, and Diwali will ensure a busy holiday season.

Cons of Religion Tourism:

- It's expensive buying everything you need each time you convert.
- It's hard to make lasting friendships with fellow followers.
- You may accidentally invoke the wrong deities during worship services and rituals.
- Others will consider you a flake.
- With all the time you'll have to take off from work to celebrate multiple holidays, you might never get that corner office.
- Religion tourism is difficult to explain to more conventional followers.

RELIGION FUSION

As you explore different religions, you may find that you relate to certain aspects of 2 or 3 faiths but can't commit to others. If this is the case, you can blend the aspects that resonate into the hybrid religion of your own creation—sort of like declaring an independent-study major in college. For example, if you like the Way of Taoism and the hellfire and brimstone of Baptists, maybe you'd be happy as a Tao-Bap. If you enjoy strict adherence to the commandments of Judaism but feel a kinship with the karma of Buddhism, you could be a Jew-Bu. Take a look at the following list and see if any fusion options appeal to you, or use this book to come up with one of your own.

Thrive on controversy?
DO explore religions that court it.

- **Voo-Moo** (Vodou-Moonie): Conservative spell-casting.
- **Co-Mo** (Confucianist-Mormon): Caffeine-free *I Ching.*
- **Sci-Shint** (Scientologist-Shinto): Celebrity Center origami.
- **Ag-Sham** (Agnostic-Shamanist): Uncertainty about power animals.
- **Ras-Ten** (Rastafarian-Tenrikyo): Weed worship.
- **Penta-Krish** (Pentecostal–Hare Krishna): Chanting in tongues.
- **Jeh-Quak** (Jehovah's Witness–Quaker): Peaceful and outgoing.
- **Ju-Chri-Sci** (Juche–Christian Scientist): Faith healing for the Eternal President.
- **Bah-Pro** (Baha'i-Protestant): Repressed fasting.
- **Cath-Osh** (Catholic-Osho): Guilt-free confessions.
- **Is-ECK** (Islam-ECKist): Praying to ECK 5 times a day.

METROSPIRITUALISM

They're young, they're hip, they're hot: they're metrospirituals. The trendy millennial alternative to the late-20th-century New Age movement, metro-spiritualism provides the ultimate consumerist experience for the religion shopper. It combines the smorgasbord approach of the New Age—a dash of meditation, a sprinkling of yoga, a pinch of environmentalism—with the omnispiritual belief in an unnamed, unspecified divine force that runs through us all. The best part of metrospiritualism is that it then expresses itself in the way we shop: organic produce, free-range chickens, locally grown flowers, scented candles, recycled paper, hybrid cars, natural fibers. It's driving to Whole Foods in your Prius while pulsing to the universal consciousness.

Metrospirituals tend to embrace indigenous and non-Western faiths that stress conscious living, timeless spiritual traditions, mindfulness, healing, and integration. They search for the universal without committing to human-made institutions or formal religions. Disillusioned with dominant paradigms past and present, they want to be part of the solution. Metrospiritualism goes hand in hand with *Cultural Creative*, a term coined by sociologist Paul H. Ray and psychologist Sherry Ruth Anderson, who characterize Cultural Creatives as motivated by "a fertile darkness that lies beneath the masks of certainty and the stale old answers that no longer work." Ray and Anderson state that everything Cultural Creatives do is "part of a whole pattern of their values and worldview and a way of life."

Many metrospirituals identify as Spiritual But Not Religious, the catchall that recognizes a higher power without getting too technical about it. If you identify with those who don't identify, then metrospirituality may be for you.

BUT HOW DO I DECIDE?

By now you should be ready to peruse the 99 religions profiled in this book. Armed with your roster of preferences and deal breakers, you can approach your spiritual quest in the same way you might look for a new career or a school for your kids.

As you go through the book, make a list of potential religions that appeal to you in the Notes section at the back, then develop a game plan for finding out more about each one. This will require a little legwork, but in most cases you should be able to learn quite a bit with just a few clicks of a mouse. In fact, for many NRMs, the Internet may be the only way to find the information you seek. Several exist exclusively online or in remote locations hidden far away from curious townsfolk and the long arm of the law.

For religions with physical structures and an open-door policy, prospective converts should sit in on a few services and interview both clergy and

Dislike your family?
DO choose a religion that won't let you see them.

flock. Ask questions based on your preferences. Take notes. In addition to inquiries based on your beliefs, favorite activities, and time and money commitments, you'll want to find out if they're accepting newcomers and whether it's as easy to quit as it is to join.

Once you've shopped around, made your lists, received answers to your questions, and discussed your options with friends and family, you'll be able to make an informed choice. But remember—in the end, only *you* know what's right for you. After you've considered all the possibilities, have faith and go with your gut!

RELIGION WANTED

Spiritual wanderer seeks meaning of life, moral guidance, and something to believe in. Must-haves include a sense of community and a connection with humankind. Please be ready to provide a list of ceremonies, rituals, and afterlife promises upon request. Qualified applicants may respond through revelations, dreams, or local missionaries. Door-to-door solicitation will not be accepted.

HOW DOES THIS BOOK WORK?

The revelation of this book is that its format allows religion consumers to compare faiths in objective, apples-to-apples fashion. With diverse religions reviewed according to the same standards, it's easy to spot both similarities and differences.

To streamline your initial search, you may want to consult the foldout chart immediately following this introduction. It lists all 99 religions side by side, rated in arenas with significant lifestyle impact.

Varicose veins? Sore knees?
DON'T choose a religion that requires excessive kneeling.

Comprising the bulk of this book are the individual religion profiles, each of which evaluates a single religion according to:

- Conversion difficulty
- Time commitment
- Cost
- New friends (worldwide number of adherents)
- Purpose of life
- Deities
- Key texts
- Afterlife promises
- Where (geographic demographics, in descending population order)
- Category (what tradition the religion is in; see page 33)
- Overall description
- Perks
- Drawbacks
- Activities
- Paraphernalia

COUNTING ADHERENTS

When counting a religion's followers, so many factors come into play that it's difficult to determine an accurate number. Given this complexity, the New Friends demographics included in this book are only estimates and may differ from other sources. Here are some of the factors that went into the calculations:

- **It depends on who's doing the counting.** In polls conducted by atheist organizations, the number of atheists tends to be higher. Polls conducted by religious organizations tend to show that those religions are larger and growing faster than nonaffiliated polls show. Some denominations might identify as part of a mainstream religion but may be considered fringe by that organization and not be included. Politics can also affect reliability, especially in countries where one religion is mandated or where religion is discouraged overall.
- **It depends on who's being asked.** The adherent? The organization? Another institution, or a government?
- **It depends on how a follower is defined.** Is a Catholic, for example, somebody who has been born into a Catholic family, or is it necessary that he choose it for himself as an adult? Do children count? If someone never attends services or participates in a religion but still identifies with that religion culturally, should she be counted?

RELIGION CATEGORIES

Each religion is classified into a category to indicate whether it stems from another tradition, making it easier to see which religions relate to one another. As with all categories, they are broad strokes, sometimes overlapping and not always mutually exclusive. Most categories consist of 2 terms: first the foundation, then its origin belief system. Here are some terms that may be less well known:

Abrahamic: Religions that share a common root in the patriarch and prophet Abraham of the Old Testament book of Genesis, considered to be the start of monotheism. Primarily includes Judaism, Christianity, and Islam.

African Diasporic: Religions of African immigrants, primarily slaves, that stemmed from traditional African beliefs but evolved into new forms after immigration.

Dharmic: Religions originating in India, including Buddhism, Hinduism, and Sikhism. *Dharma* is a complex term with differing interpretations, including such concepts as manner of being, divine and moral law, underlying order of nature, universal truth, and path of righteous living.

Entheogenic: Faiths that employ psychoactive drugs to achieve spiritual vision.

Esoteric: Faiths that rely on the comprehension of special, sometimes secret, knowledge.

Indigenous: Tribal religions with no foundation date, generally preceding organized religion.

Left-Hand Path: Religions privileging magic, occult, and the power and divinity of the self.

Neo: New incarnations of older religions that either died out or were reinterpreted.

Non-Religious: While it might seem contradictory to include non-religions, these traditions not only have devout adherents, they've had tremendous influences on spiritual thought.

Non-Revealed: A religion that stems not from divine revelation but from rational thought or observations of nature.

NRM: New religious movement, started approximately within the last 100 years.

Pagan: Nature-centered spiritual beliefs that look to ancient religions (especially Celtic, Norse, Roman, Greek, and Egyptian) that predate and were generally replaced by the major world religions, especially Christianity.

Revealed: Religions founded on divine revelations from deities to humans.

Syncretic: Faiths that fuse multiple religions or belief traditions.

Taoic: Religions that focus on the Asian concept of Tao ("the Way," as in the way of natural harmony).

Need a good rest?
DON'T choose a religion with an active afterlife.

GO FORTH AND SHOP!

Chances are the perfect religion won't hear your plea and miraculously contact you. It takes research and dedication to identify the right belief system, and by now you should have a pretty good idea what you're looking for in the religion marketplace.

There are new religions and old religions, those that require extensive time commitments and those that require none. Some are difficult to join, and some are even more difficult to leave. Practice can be a way of life or a mere online affiliation. Certain faiths will be good for your social life, whereas others will end it.

Only you know what you're looking for and how much you're willing to commit. This book can serve as a guide for questions you should ask, and it will prepare you for some of the answers you'll receive. The world is now a more tolerant place than it was, say, during the Crusades, when practicing the wrong religion could lead to an untimely death. These days religion consumers have the freedom to shop around, and thanks to 21st-century tools like the Internet, the right match may be only a keystroke away.

The newly minted religion consumer has thousands of beliefs to choose from, and the choices seem to grow more numerous and complex all the time. It's no different from what we see in any other contemporary marketplace, which is why we're a society of comparison shoppers—and now we can use those finely honed plasma TV–seeking skills to make an investment that can last a lifetime (or more).

You hold in your hands everything you need to find a righteous path, so open your mind, leave the skepticism behind, and get ready to hit the mall of spiritual choice!

Memory not what it used to be?
DO choose a religion with repetitive chanting.

99 RELIGIONS COMPARED

When comparing religions to determine whether or not they will suit your lifestyle and spiritual needs, it's helpful to see all of them arrayed in one place, compared in apples-to-apples fashion. In this chart, you'll find the 99 religions profiled in this book rated according to the following standards:

SEX REGULATIONS
Are sex practices dictated or prohibited in any way? Must you wait until marriage, for example?

DIETARY RESTRICTIONS
Is there anything you can't or must eat? Is fasting involved?

TIME COMMITMENT
How much time is required for praying, observing, etc.?

COST
What's the overall expense of such things as membership, accoutrements, and tithing?

CONVERSION DIFFICULTY
Are newcomers, outsiders, or people of diverse races or cultures accepted? Is study or initiation involved?

AFTERLIFE QUALITY
Is paradise promised after death for the faithful? How likely is it that you might go to hell if you slip up? Or, will you reincarnate? Experience nothingness?

TRADITIONAL
How mainstream and conventional is the religion, vs. new and perhaps seemingly odd?

RATE OF GROWTH
Is the number of adherents growing or shrinking?

HOLIDAYS
Are there many holidays to observe, whether fun or obligatory?

AESTHETICS
Are there distinctive elements such as symbols, architecture, garb?

Each religion is rated from 1 to 5, with 5 being the highest or most, according to the following key: ① ② ③ ④ ⑤

Bear in mind that many religions have diverse manifestations—for example, some Protestant congregations are liberal while others are extremely conservative. In those cases, a middle-of-the-road ranking implies an average rather than an absolute. Ultimately these ratings are a soft guide and seekers must determine whether an individual group is right for them.

For prospective adherents who are design oriented, the quality and style of a religion's aesthetic may be a deciding factor in whether or not to convert. Designers, architects, and artists in particular, as well as those who merely enjoy beautiful, visually pleasing surroundings, must not overlook seemingly superficial characteristics that in the long run will affect the religious experience.

While symbols are not the only element of aesthetic style, they are certainly indicators of visual attentiveness. Additionally, followers most likely will find themselves wearing the symbols on clothing or jewelry—or even permanently, as tattoos—at some point, so it's important to feel confident about making such a fashion statement.

Because 29 of the religions contained in this book do not have consistent icons, the symbols included here number only 70. For minimalists or people who prefer not to display any type of branding, the 29 symbol-free religions may prove appealing.

Evident in many of these images is an intriguing evolution over time. Where the icons of older religions may have begun as tribal markings and evolved into symbols, the symbols of recent religions are more like brands, one manifestation of our marketing-infused contemporary culture.

If design and aesthetics are priorities for you, see which of these symbols strikes your eye. Then investigate the rest of the religion's iconography and decor by conducting image searches on the Internet, perusing illustrated books, traveling, and visiting houses of worship. Given your prospective commitment to tchotchkes, garb, and worship environment, it's critical that you appreciate your religion's vision. When you feel at home in a religion's aesthetic, you'll know you've found the right faith.

99 RELIGIONS
PROFILED
A TO Z

AFRICAN INDEPENDENT CHURCHES

QUICK RATINGS:

Conversion Difficulty:

① ② ③ ④ ⑤

Time Commitment:

① ② ③ ④ ⑤

Cost:

① ② ③ ④ ⑤

New Friends:
93 million

PURPOSE OF LIFE

Live in accordance with Christianity without giving up African culture; missionary work

DEITIES

God (Father, Son, Holy Spirit); one group believes founder, Johana Masowe, is savior

KEY TEXTS

Bible, especially Old Testament

WHERE

Africa, primarily western and southern

AFTERLIFE PROMISES

Heaven and hell

CATEGORY

Abrahamic: Christian

WHAT IT IS

Ten thousand Christian churches, founded by Africans since breaking from missionary control in late 1800s. Combines Protestant and Catholic roots with indigenous culture. Responsible for continent-wide spread of Christianity. Three types: Initiated (started in Africa but has outside affiliations), Instituted (founded and expanded in Africa), Indigenous (incorporates local beliefs).

PERKS 

- Fastest-growing Christian movement in Africa
- Diversity of denominations and practices
- Some churches teach faith healing and exorcism, practice polygamy
- Communicate directly with God
- Women often share in leadership
- Inexpensive
- Communally oriented congregations

DRAWBACKS 

- Speaking in tongues difficult to understand
- Baptism water recycled for drinking
- Salvation conditional upon individual's behavior
- Polygamists have as many mothers-in-law as they do wives

ACTIVITIES

- Dancing to drums
- Evangelizing
- Greeting new friends with holy kiss (kiss on cheek; referenced in New Testament)
- Following charismatic leader who communicates directly with God
- Praising Lord with hands held high

PARAPHERNALIA

- Microphones and podiums
- Long gowns
- Insignia of denomination for headdresses

AGNOSTICISM

WHAT IT IS

From Greek *a-* (not) and *gnosis* (knowledge), meaning one "doesn't know" whether God exists. Coined in 1869 by evolutionist T. H. Huxley, who believed it was wrong to claim truth with no proof. Three versions: strong (we'll never know), weak (we might know one day), and apathetic (we don't care). Influential adherents include Voltaire (considered father of agnosticism by some), Charles Darwin.

PERKS

- Sit out "Merry Christmas" vs. "Happy Holidays" debate
- Motto can be "Dunno"
- No collection plate
- No Judgment Day
- New friends include Warren Buffett, Bill Gates, Matt Groening, Jack Kevorkian, Sean Penn, Uma Thurman
- Get to keep an open mind
- Will never be called know-it-all

DRAWBACKS

- Appearance of indecision
- May be mistaken for atheist
- Annoy both believers and nonbelievers
- Lose sleep waiting for proof one way or the other
- Uncertainty could spread until not sure of anything, even agnosticism
- Fundamentalists will want to "save" you
- Many confuse word with *diagnostic*, meaning "don't know times two"

ACTIVITIES

- Exercising powers of critical thinking
- Celebrating 12 Days of Agnostimas, Darwin Day
- Not feeling guilty, not praying, not going to confession
- Explaining why agnosticism is not mutally exclusive with spirituality
- Always being the fly in the ointment

PARAPHERNALIA

- *The Agnostic: A Monthly Journal of Liberal Thought*
- iPods for agnostic podcasts
- T-shirts with *Humanist Network News* logo
- Mugs from Bertrand Russell Society

QUICK RATINGS:

Conversion Difficulty:
① ② ③ ④ ⑤

Time Commitment:
① ② ③ ④ ⑤

Cost:
① ② ③ ④ ⑤

New Friends:
100 million

PURPOSE OF LIFE

None besides not harming society; if one has personal purpose, nothing in agnosticism discourages its fulfillment

DEITIES

None; Jesus admired along with Buddha, Socrates, Abraham Lincoln

KEY TEXTS

Why I Am an Agnostic by Robert G. Ingersoll; *Why I Am Not a Christian* by Bertrand Russell

WHERE

Worldwide

AFTERLIFE PROMISES

If it is proven, agnostics will believe in any kind of afterlife

CATEGORY

Non-Religious

AMISH

RELIGION #3

QUICK RATINGS:

Conversion Difficulty:	① ② ③ **④** ⑤
Time Commitment:	① ② ③ ④ **⑤**
Cost:	**①** ② ③ ④ ⑤
New Friends:	150,000

PURPOSE OF LIFE
Avoid temptation and sin by living apart from outside world; never become arrogant or prideful

DEITIES
God (Father, Son, Holy Spirit)

KEY TEXTS
Bible; *Martyrs Mirror* (AKA *The Bloody Theater*)

WHERE
United States, primarily Ohio, Pennsylvania, Indiana

AFTERLIFE PROMISES
Heaven and hell; if follower leaves faith or is shunned, no admittance to heaven

CATEGORY
Abrahamic: Christian

WHAT IT IS
Way of life geared toward achieving salvation on daily basis. Lifestyle still reflects roots in rural 17th-century Switzerland. Adherents live apart from society, speak German dialect, dress modestly, practice humility, avoid modern technology, "shun" members who stray, and follow *Ordnung*, oral tradition regulating all facets of life. Basic concepts of Christianity provide belief foundation.

PERKS 
- Strong community support
- No need to agonize over decisions; everything covered in *Ordnung*
- Safe from power outages (electrical wires viewed as connection with world)
- More time with family
- Quiet surroundings; no radio or other electronic noise
- No violence allowed
- Good excuse to be conscientious objector during wartime

DRAWBACKS 
- Formal education ends at 8th grade
- Sinning not tolerated; punished by *Meidung* (shunning)
- Strict gender roles
- No ornamentation or finery (dubbed "Plain People")
- Inconvenient lack of electricity, divorce, birth control
- Must learn to speak Pennsylvania Dutch
- Photography prohibited, so no visual life record

ACTIVITIES
- Observing holiness of Christ's birthday on Christmas and celebrating on December 26
- Lengthy wedding ceremonies followed by large feasts
- *Rumspringa*: adolescents "run around," party, and see outside world before adult Amish commitment
- Barn raisings

PARAPHERNALIA
- Horse-drawn buggies
- Manual farming tools
- For women, long-sleeved dresses, black bonnets, white caps
- For men, pants without creases or cuffs, coats without pockets, long beards (after marriage) without mustaches
- Beautiful hand-stitched quilts in somber colors

ANTHROPOSOPHY

RELIGION #4

WHAT IT IS

Founded in 1912 by former Theosophist Rudolf Steiner to bring science and logic to spirituality; means "wisdom of human being." Humans become separated from spiritual selves through attachment to material world; use human (not divine) intellect to reconnect. Steiner claimed access to Akashic record, chronicle of everything since beginning of time, recorded on astral light.

PERKS

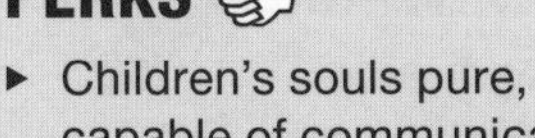

- Children's souls pure, capable of communication with angels, until age 7
- Ability to connect with dreamlike spiritual state lies dormant in everyone
- Can send children to well-regarded Waldorf (AKA Steiner) schools
- Rhythmic massage encouraged

DRAWBACKS

- Some of Steiner's writings appear racist
- Antimaterialism
- Handmade and organic products cost more
- No TV; counterproductive to soulfulness
- Not clear how science and angels go together
- Hard to pronounce

ACTIVITIES

- Attending courses at local Steiner center, ranging from biodynamic farming to astrology
- Meditating on beauty of natural world

PARAPHERNALIA

- Colored scarves for eurythmy, dance movements set to words
- Evergreens and candles for Advent Spiral (vs. Christmas) celebrations

QUICK RATINGS:

Conversion Difficulty: ① **②** ③ ④ ⑤
Time Commitment: ① ② **③** ④ ⑤
Cost: ① ② ③ **④** ⑤
New Friends: 55,000

PURPOSE OF LIFE

Nurture life of soul in both individual and society; establish moral code based on true knowledge

DEITIES

Christ Being mediating between Lucifer and his opposite, Ahriman

KEY TEXTS

Western Approach to Reincarnation and Karma and *An Outline of Esoteric Science* by Rudolf Steiner

WHERE

Switzerland, Germany, United Kingdom, Canada, United States

AFTERLIFE PROMISES

Soul proceeds to astral world and spiritland to prepare for next incarnation

CATEGORY

Esoteric

ATHEISM

RELIGION #5

QUICK RATINGS:

Conversion Difficulty:	① ② ③ ④ ⑤ (1)
Time Commitment:	① ② ③ ④ ⑤ (1)
Cost:	① ② ③ ④ ⑤ (2)
New Friends:	155 million

PURPOSE OF LIFE
Keep church and state separate; fight political influence of religious groups

DEITIES
None

KEY TEXTS
Critical readings of Bible, Qur'an, Torah; *Essence of Christianity* by Ludwig Andreas Feuerbach; "The Necessity of Atheism" by Percy Bysshe Shelley; *The God Delusion* by Richard Dawkins; *God Is Not Great* and *The Portable Atheist* by Christopher Hitchens

WHERE
Worldwide

AFTERLIFE PROMISES
Nothing

CATEGORY
Non-Religious

WHAT IT IS
From Greek *a-* (not) and *theos* (god). Characterized by active disbelief in God, demons, angels, and afterlife. Term first applied to Christians by ancient Greeks. Western atheism dates to 5th-century BCE philosopher Diagoras and Greek Epicurus school. Modern form said to have been born in 1841 with *Essence of Christianity* by Ludwig Andreas Feuerbach.

PERKS 

- No hell
- Sunday mornings free
- Could feel at home in France (30 percent, vs. 4 percent in United States)
- Pleasant assurance of moral relativity
- Perfect crime stays unpunished
- No need to be careful what you pray for if you don't pray
- Convenient way for adolescents to rebel against religious parents

DRAWBACKS 

- No heaven
- Possible persecution by religious right of all faiths
- Historically burned at stake
- Discomfort when others say "under God" during national anthem
- In minority
- Might be banned from public office if unable to swear on Bible
- Often germinates from disillusioning personal tragedy

ACTIVITIES

- Arguing with door-to-door evangelists
- Taking legal challenges to Supreme Court
- Debating fundamentalists on talk radio
- Seeking moral compass in godless universe
- Offending friends and family at religious celebrations

PARAPHERNALIA

- American Atheist pendants, lapel pins, bumper stickers
- Textbooks on evolution
- Philosophical works by Freud, Marx, Nietzsche, Sartre, etc.
- Horn-rimmed glasses, black turtlenecks
- Attitude

TOP 10 PROPHETS OF ALL TIME

A prophet is an individual who speaks the will of God by divine inspiration or instruction. From its Greek etymology, the word literally means "one who speaks for another."

1. JESUS CHRIST
Revered by Christians as the Messiah and son of God, Jesus founded Christianity through his teachings and by performing miracles. Many believe his Second Coming will mark the end of the world.

2. MUHAMMAD
Known as "the Prophet," Muhammad founded Islam after the angel Gabriel appeared to him in a desert cave outside Mecca. He transcribed the word of God into the Qur'an, the holy book of Islam.

3. ABRAHAM
Hailed as a prophet and the patriarch of Christianity, Islam, and Judaism, Abraham was told by God that his descendants would inherit the earth.

4. MOSES
Regarded as a major prophet by Christians, Jews, Muslims, and Baha'is, Moses transcribed the word of God into the Ten Commandments.

5. KRISHNA
Known as the 8th avatar of the Hindu god Vishnu, Lord Krishna is seen as both deity and prophet. Devout Hindus believe that he reveals the wisdom of God in the epic Bhagavad Gita.

6. BUDDHA
Through intense meditation and the practice of asceticism, Siddhartha Gautama of India fulfilled the prophecies of the elders to become Buddha, the Awakened One. His teachings, or dharma, form the basis of Buddhism.

7. JOSEPH SMITH
The founder of Mormonism, Smith transcribed the Book of Mormon from ancient golden tablets he found through visitations from the angel Moroni.

8. GURU NANAK
In 15th-century India, the founder of Sikhism received the word of God to spread a monotheistic religion based on honesty and compassion.

9. BAHÁ'U'LLÁH
This 19th-century Iranian founder of the Baha'i faith proclaimed himself a manifestation of God after receiving a revelation while imprisoned.

10. ISAIAH
One of the Hebrew Bible's "Latter Prophets," Isaiah prophesied the dispersion and persecution of the Jews, the creation of the state of Israel, and the coming of Jesus.

AUSTRALIAN ABORIGINAL

QUICK RATINGS:

Conversion Difficulty:
① ② ③ ④ ⑤

Time Commitment:
① ② ③  ⑤

Cost:
① ② ③ ④ ⑤

New Friends:
7,000

PURPOSE OF LIFE
Respect earth, live peacefully with nature; preserve native skills, ancient way of life; honor gods and ancestors; adhere to "As it was done in Dreamtime, so it must be done today"

DEITIES
Rainbow serpent Waugal, great creator; *wanjina*, creation beings, AKA Totemic Ancestors

KEY TEXTS
None; oral tradition

WHERE
Australia

AFTERLIFE PROMISES
Go to sky; eventually come back to earth (if quickly, to be shaman) or join ancestral world to guide living

CATEGORY
Indigenous: Australia

WHAT IT IS
Faith of first inhabitants of Australia, still practiced by only small number of Aboriginals. Based on reverence for land and sacred sites. Humans belong to network of past, future, and all living things. Dreamtime concept central; place without time or space, home to gods. Commemorated by storytelling and music, with some stories secret, told only to certain groups during special ceremonies.

PERKS 

- Wanjina are all good (though many resemble depictions of aliens, with large heads, big black eyes, no mouths)
- Outdoor survival skills (finding and eating honey, ants, grubs, wombats; herbalism) can come in handy
- Kids enjoy youth-only ceremonies, acting out creation stories to learn ways of tribe
- Cool body and cave painting

DRAWBACKS 

- Legacy of persecution
- Development encroaches on sacred places
- Intense circumcision practices for men, including eating own foreskin and splitting procedure called subincision
- Ritual scarring

ACTIVITIES

- Accessing spiritual powers of Dreaming through ritualized mime, song, trance dancing; when celebrating, festivities called *corroborees*
- Caring for sacred Uluru (AKA Ayers Rock) and its ancient paintings
- Walkabouts (solitary journeys on foot into Australian outback)

PARAPHERNALIA

- *Tjurungas*, sacred, ritual wood or stone objects for initiated males; carried throughout life
- Boomerangs, throwing spears, grinding stones
- Drums, didgeridoos
- Possum-hide footballs for *mam grook* game

WHAT IT IS

Founded in 1863 by Persian nobleman Bahá'u'lláh after revelation in prison that he was prophet foretold by the Báb, head of predecessor Bábi religion. Seeks to unite humanity through oneness of religion; though social laws have separated faiths, God progressively reveals one world religion through manifestations including Buddha, Jesus, Muhammad, and, most recently, Bahá'u'lláh.

PERKS

- Only requirement is belief that Bahá'u'lláh is most recent manifestation of God (but he won't be last)
- World unity (final stage in humanity's evolution), human rights, and equality driving forces of faith
- War, violence unacceptable ways to spread faith
- Practices unification it preaches: no sects exist
- Humans possess essentially good eternal souls
- Resolutions can wait until Iranian New Year, in March

DRAWBACKS 

- Do-it-yourself clergy
- No politics allowed—can vote, but no party joining
- No alcohol, drugs, gambling, gossip; marital, heterosexual sex only
- Though manifestations reveal teachings, God is unknowable
- With so many divine messengers—Abraham, Moses, Krishna, Zoroaster, Buddha, Christ, Muhammad, the Báb, Bahá'u'lláh—heavy reading
- Lots of volunteer work

ACTIVITIES

- Daily prayer
- Daylight fasting for 19 days before Naw-Rúz, Baha'i New Year (at spring equinox)
- Gathering every 19 days for Nineteen-Day Feast, "spiritual feast" of worship, companionship, unity
- Pilgrimages to Shrines of the Báb and Bahá'u'lláh, both in Israel

PARAPHERNALIA

- Temples, 9-sided buildings open to all
- 9-pointed star symbol
- Baha'i calendar, 19 months of 19 days each—4 extra days between 18th and 19th months known as Ayyám-i-Há, a time of gift giving
- Tools for public works, including building, farming, improving water

QUICK RATINGS:

Conversion Difficulty: 1 **(2)** 3 4 5

Time Commitment: 1 2 3 **(4)** 5

Cost: **(1)** 2 3 4 5

New Friends: 7.8 million

PURPOSE OF LIFE

Believe in oneness of God, religion, and humanity; promote harmony and fellowship of humankind; develop spiritually and love God

DEITIES

God, all-powerful and all-loving

KEY TEXTS

The Kitáb-i-Aqdas and other writings by Bahá'u'lláh; writings by the Báb and by Abdu'l-Bahá, son and successor of Bahá'u'lláh

WHERE

Worldwide, especially Asia, Africa

AFTERLIFE PROMISES

Immortal souls travel nearer to or further from God; heaven and hell not real places but states of being

CATEGORY

Syncretic

BRAHMA KUMARIS

QUICK RATINGS:

Conversion Difficulty:	① ② ③ ④ ⑤ (1)
Time Commitment:	① ② ③ ④ ⑤ (3)
Cost:	① ② ③ ④ ⑤ (4)
New Friends:	700,000

PURPOSE OF LIFE
Become free of vice and restore balance between inner self and outer world through meditation and positive thinking

DEITIES
Shiva, the only soul without a body

KEY TEXTS
Murlis, daily aphorisms channeled by Shiva through Brahma Baba and others

WHERE
Worldwide, primarily India, Australia, Kenya, Russia, Europe, United States

AFTERLIFE PROMISES
Soul reincarnates eternally in human form, inheriting dynamics of previous life

CATEGORY
NRM: Hindu Oriented

WHAT IT IS
Established in 1936 by diamond merchant Brahma Baba after divine visions. Raja yoga and positive thinking help realign humans with pure spiritual truth from which they have become disconnected. History consists of 5 repeating stages over 5,000 years; we are in 5th, or Diamond Age, in which widespread calamity precedes rebirth for the devout into pure Golden Age.

PERKS 

- Pro-woman; *Brahma Kumaris* means "daughters of Brahma"; women considered natural spiritual leaders
- Meditation, positive thinking, and stress management ensure next life will be happy
- Self-esteem compulsory
- All courses and seminars free of charge
- Mt. Abu, global headquarters in India, boasts world's largest solar cooker, capable of making 30,000 meals at once

DRAWBACKS 

- Reputation as doomsday cult; date projected for end of Diamond Age has shifted so many times that specific year no longer given
- Celibacy encouraged, even for married couples, in order to focus on loving relationship with Shiva
- White wardrobe stains easily
- *Sattvic* (pure) vegetarian diet required
- No smoking, drinking, or nonprescription drugs

ACTIVITIES

- Daily meditation, listening to murlis, periodic "traffic control" moments (3 minutes of silence)
- Practicing 4 main principles: spiritual study, meditation, practice (fulfilling responsibilities), and service (to humanity)
- Washing body and changing clothing after using bathroom

PARAPHERNALIA

- All-white clothing to signify simplicity, purity, cleanliness, and truth
- Pictures of Brahma Baba for meditation
- Vegetarian cookbooks outlining how "consciousness of cook affects bodies, minds, and emotions of those who eat the food"

CANDOMBLE

WHAT IT IS

Most African sect of Brazilian Macumba religion, originating in 1550s with slave trade. Combines indigenous African and Brazilian traditions with Catholicism. Adherents worship *orixas*, deities that have corresponding Catholic saints. Spiritualist religion; possessed mediums contact spirits, especially through drumming and dancing (*Candomble* means "dance in honor of the gods").

PERKS 

- Tight-knit communities resemble family structure, with each "house" led by high priestess or priest
- Spirit possession results in healing and spiritual evolution
- At birth, each individual assigned (via cowrie-shell divination) personal orisha for protection
- *Baba egum*, spirits of ancestors, help you uphold moral standards
- Get to practice white magic (that which does not bring harm to others)

DRAWBACKS 

- Though legal since 1977, legacy of persecution means many still practice in secret
- Must sometimes consume *jutia,* dried rat powder

ACTIVITIES

- Ritual dancing and drumming to release *axé*, positive energy
- Many colorful ceremonial feasts and celebrations
- Animal sacrifice
- Wearing white on Fridays in honor of Oxala, orixa equated with Jesus
- Detailed pre-ritual and pre-initiation consecration and purification practices

PARAPHERNALIA

- Elaborate costumes, including hoopskirts, headscarves, bead necklaces
- Animal blood for coating medium initiates
- Fresh flowers, food, fruits for offerings to orixas

QUICK RATINGS:

Conversion Difficulty:
① ② ③ **④** ⑤

Time Commitment:
① ② ③ **④** ⑤

Cost:
① **②** ③ ④ ⑤

New Friends:
40 million

PURPOSE OF LIFE

Worship and communicate with orixas and ancestors through ritual, ceremonies, possession; fulfill individual destiny with help of personal orixa

DEITIES

Olorun, sky god, creator of universe; many orixas

KEY TEXTS

None; oral tradition

WHERE

Brazil (especially Bahia), Uruguay

AFTERLIFE PROMISES

Return to earth in spirit form as *egun*, powerful ancestral spirit; more Catholicized followers believe in Judeo-Christian heaven from which baba egum return for visits

CATEGORY

African Diasporic

CAO DAI

QUICK RATINGS:
Conversion Difficulty:   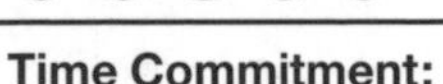
Time Commitment:  
Cost:   
New Friends: 3.2 million

PURPOSE OF LIFE

Unite humanity by promoting universal understanding of Supreme Being to foster peace

DEITIES

Cao Dai, Supreme Being, assisted by divine spirits

KEY TEXTS

Bible, Torah, Buddhist and Taoist works

WHERE

Vietnam, Cambodia, United States, France

AFTERLIFE PROMISES

Karma-based reincarnation cycle until attainment of nirvana; bad karma may result in rebirth on darker, colder planet

CATEGORY

NRM: Syncretic

WHAT IT IS

Self-dubbed universal faith, based on principle that all religions have same divine origin. Established in 1926 after Vietnamese civil servant Ngo Van Chieu received revelation during séance. Incorporates elements of many religions, especially Buddhism, Catholicism, Taoism, Confucianism, and Spiritism. Emphasizes love and justice as paths to God. Vietnamese nationalist flavor.

PERKS

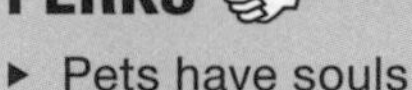

- Pets have souls
- Non-elitist; new friends from all walks of Vietnamese life
- Can become saint via scientific breakthrough or writing great book
- Communicating with deceased is encouraged
- Can admit to truth of other religions without betraying your own
- Get to show kindness to plants
- Ornate temples and outfits

DRAWBACKS

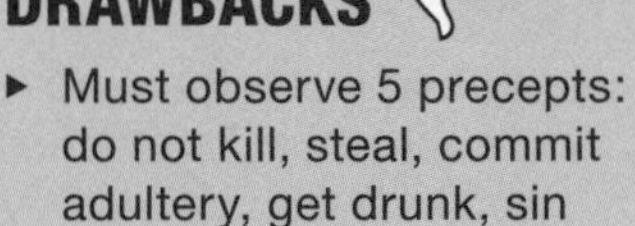

- Must observe 5 precepts: do not kill, steal, commit adultery, get drunk, sin by word
- Lengthy works of Victor Hugo are required reading (no points for seeing *Les Mis*), one of Cao Dai's 3 principal saints
- Vegetarianism required 10 days per month
- Forgoing riches and luxury recommended
- Women can advance only to cardinal, 3rd-highest rank

ACTIVITIES

- Daily prayer at 6 AM, noon, 6 PM, or midnight
- Offering incense, flowers, wine, tea at altar
- Meditating to progressively eradicate "inferior self" and develop divine element within
- Communicating with spirits

PARAPHERNALIA

- Ouija boards and *corbeille-à-bec* (writing device for channeling)
- Pictures of saints such as William Shakespeare, Louis Pasteur, Thomas Jefferson
- Statues of 3 Lords of the Earth, representing Taoism, Buddhism, Confucianism

CATHOLICISM

RELIGION #11

WHAT IT IS

Oldest, largest Christian denomination, originated by apostles of Jesus. Similar to Greek Orthodoxy and Protestantism with addition of pope, saintly intercession, purgatory, and transubstantiation (bread and wine become body and blood of Christ). Weekly ritual-heavy services led by celibate priests. Baptism, sacrament that confers divine grace, is essential for salvation.

PERKS 

- Confessing sins wipes slate clean; no limit to clean-slate frequency
- No dietary restrictions; wine and meat okay
- Can help poor and oppressed, like Jesus did
- Good schools
- All offerings accepted—no contribution too small
- Diversity; at least 10 types practiced globally
- Drinking okay, especially whiskey

DRAWBACKS 

- Papal authority distasteful to independent thinkers
- Study required
- Women can't be ordained as priests
- Men must be celibate to enter priesthood
- Distracting pedophilia scandals
- Birth control, abortion, premarital sex, masturbation, and homosexuality are sins
- Soul-racking guilt

ACTIVITIES

- Feast Days honoring particular saints or miracles, such as St. Patrick's Day
- Abstaining from meat, poultry, or other treats for 40 days of Lent
- Confessing sins as needed
- Novenas, 9-day prayer periods to make special, urgent requests of God

PARAPHERNALIA

- Rosaries, crucifixes, holy water
- Incense, votive candles
- Communion wine, bread
- Patron-saint medals
- Gifts for baptism, First Communion
- Virgin Mary statues
- 3-dimensional portraits of Christ on cross, often hung over bed

QUICK RATINGS:

Conversion Difficulty:
① ② **③** ④ ⑤

Time Commitment:
① **②** ③ ④ ⑤

Cost:
① ② ③ **④** ⑤

New Friends:
1.1 billion

PURPOSE OF LIFE

Seek salvation, made possible by death of Jesus; maintain salvation through sacraments

DEITIES

God (Father, Son, Holy Ghost); Virgin Mary

KEY TEXTS

Bible, including Apocrypha; Catechism of Catholic Church; Code of Canon Law

WHERE

Worldwide, especially South America, Central America, Europe, Philippines, Democratic Republic of Congo

AFTERLIFE PROMISES

Die in state of grace, go to heaven; with venial sins, go to purgatory, then heaven; with mortal sins, go to hell

CATEGORY

Abrahamic: Christian

Religion doesn't always have to be serious. Mock or parody religions, often generated as a backlash against organized religion and fundamentalism, are mostly about having a good time. Some begin as jokes, gain popularity, and develop congregations. Others channel religion into a specific political agenda, such as legalizing cannabis or saving the oceans. Even more hail the godly personae of real humans such as Elvis—and, of course, Bob Saget. Most of all, mock and parody religions provide new opportunities to wear creative T-shirts and engage in open dialogue.

PASTAFARIANISM

After His Noodly Appendage, the Flying Spaghetti Monster, was revealed to 25-year-old Bobby Henderson in a dream, he worried that the FSM's role in creating the universe would not be taught in schools. When the Kansas State Board of Education preliminarily approved the teaching of intelligent design as an alternative to evolution, Henderson threatened a lawsuit if his, among multiple viewpoints, was not heard. Today 10 million Pastafarian followers claim that the FSM created the universe. Basic tenets preach niceness and good behavior among all beings, though Pastafarians have flimsy moral standards (like noodles). Because global warming is directly attributed to the shrinking numbers of pirates, Pastafarians worship dressed as pirates. Fridays are religious holidays, and all prayers are concluded with "RA-men."

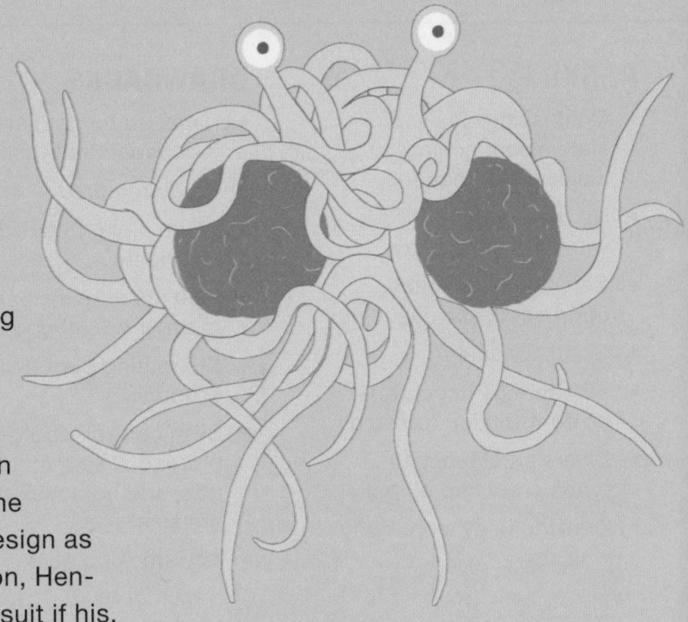

THE INVISIBLE PINK UNICORN

In response to the presence of Christians and other religious naysayers on online atheist discussion forums, the satirical deity the Invisible Pink Unicorn (IPU) was created. The IPU bows her horn proudly in the tradition of philosophers such as Karl Popper, Bertrand Russell, and Carl Sagan who have emphasized the limits of unfalsifiable assertions—especially spiritual beliefs. In his 1952 essay "Is There a God?" for example,

Russell argues that the burden of spiritual disproof should not fall to the skeptic. First revealed to an Internet atheist group in 1990, the IPU has gathered both believers and creed for her ability to embody contradiction (being both pink and invisible) and because her implausibility forces us to examine our belief in the implausible. Her evil nemesis is the Purple Oyster of Doom, her visitations to the faithful frequently take place in the laundry (as demonstrated by pinkness in the wash and holes in socks from the piercing of her horn), and her first commandment is "Thou shalt not use spurs." Most importantly, no one can prove she doesn't exist.

LANDOVER BAPTIST CHURCH

A parody of far-right religious fundamentalism, the primarily Web-based Landover Baptist Church transmits weekly Godcasts preaching that theirs is the only true word of God; those who believe other things will, of course, burn in hell. Billed as "Where the worthwhile worship," LBC claims to have trademarked the word *Christian*. Its 157,286 members limit all consumption to believer-based business, especially such paraphernalia as LBC's "What Would Jesus Do?" thongs. LBC teaches that yoga is a religion for sex addicts and limits masturbation to 7-minute sessions for men over 65. The website's section for children demystifies such questions as why Jesus had long hair like a homosexual. In 2006, the church released its first book, *Welcome to Jesusland (Formerly the United States of America): Shocking Tales of Depravity, Sex, and Sin.*

LAST THURSDAYISM

Last Thursdayism teaches that age and time are an illusion and that the universe was actually created last Thursday, despite some infighting over whether creation might have occurred on Tuesday, Wednesday, or, in fact, 5 minutes ago. Memories are a sham, having only the appearance of age, and were formed at the same time we were. Creator Queen Maeve the Housecat crafted humans to serve and protect her race. When Maeve destroys the world Next Thursday, those nice to cats will become cats in Paradise, evildoers will be condemned to the filthy Eternal Litterbox, and neutral individuals will be the cats' foot soldiers. The church promotes spaying and neutering. Followers offer catnip before Maeve's picture and must give weekly sweet loving to a cat.

CHURCH OF EUTHANASIA

With just one commandment, "Thou Shalt Not Procreate," the Church of Euthanasia seeks to restore balance between humans and the earth's other remaining species. Four pillars are proposed to achieve voluntary population reduction: suicide, abortion, cannibalism, and sodomy (any sexual act that cannot result in procreation). On the church's website, followers can explore suicide methods, why to have an abortion, and how drinking one's own urine helps the world. Those who actively choose not to procreate are instant church members; giving birth results in excommunication. Suicide guarantees sainthood, and the church is happy to be named beneficiary of estates.

CHEROKEE

QUICK RATINGS:

Conversion Difficulty: ① ② ③ ④ ⑤ (5)

Time Commitment: ① ② ③ ④ ⑤ (3)

Cost: ① ② ③ ④ ⑤ (2)

New Friends: 270,000

PURPOSE OF LIFE
Live harmoniously and justly with nature; maintain balance between human and spirit worlds

DEITIES
Many animal, elemental, inanimate, and ancestral spirits

KEY TEXTS
Keetoowah Bible, not words on paper but beads and shells woven into 7 wampum belts; various syllabary manuscripts

WHERE
Oklahoma, North Carolina

AFTERLIFE PROMISES
Good or bad afterlife, depending on actions in life and proper funeral rituals

CATEGORY
Indigenous: Native American

WHAT IT IS
Spiritual beliefs of Native American tribe, based in nature, relationships with animals, and supernatural world. Sacred numbers 4 and 7 infuse rituals and characterize universe. Seven sacred ceremonies mark transitions with dance, song, and fire ceremonies. Strong sense of cosmic justice: good is rewarded and wrongful behavior (disharmony with nature) is punished.

PERKS 

- Personal honor highly valued
- Agreements struck with dangerous animals (such as rattlesnakes) will prevent attacks on humans
- Because language was given written form in early 19th century (in form of syllabary, transcription of individual syllables), spiritual beliefs and medicinal knowledge were recorded for posterity
- Annual ceremonies provide structure and link to changing of seasons

DRAWBACKS 

- Terrifying Raven Mocker witches steal hearts of sick and dying people, killing them
- Little People, spirits that look like humans but are smaller, can be very mischievous
- Legacy of Trail of Tears, forced march from original home in Appalachians to Oklahoma in 19th century; tribe remains split between 2 places
- Christian persecution disrupted spiritual continuity

ACTIVITIES

- Gathering inner bark from east side of 7 trees for sacred fire
- Playing stickball (predecessor of lacrosse)
- Participating in Green Corn Ceremony, Stomp Dance, and Booger Dance
- Naming ceremonies for infants
- Cleansing rituals in rivers

PARAPHERNALIA

- Revered cedar, pine, spruce, laurel, and holly trees
- Symbolic colors: red, blue, black, yellow, white, brown, and green
- Sacred pipes
- Leg rattles for dances
- White deerskin to wrap sacred objects
- 7-sided buildings for ceremonial gatherings

CHRISTIAN SCIENCE

RELIGION #13

WHAT IT IS

Church of Christ, Scientist, founded in 1879 by author and teacher Mary Baker Eddy on a platform of spiritual healing. Only perfect, God-created spirit is real; matter does not exist, we only think it does. Since humans are reflections of God, illness doesn't exist either—instead, it results from sin, fear, or ignorance of God's true nature, so it can be healed spiritually with prayer.

PERKS

- No need to pay for health insurance, doctor bills
- High self-esteem—as images of God, we're perfect
- Low stress: all problems illusory
- Aging and death optional; those who pray and become sin-free escape both
- New posthumous friends include Marilyn Monroe, Milton Berle; Danielle Steel still alive
- Okay to visit dentists and optometrists

DRAWBACKS

- Must battle schools over immunization of children
- Requires hours of study
- No HMO coverage for visits to Christian Science practitioners
- Using prayer in conjunction with modern medicine may worsen condition
- Many skeptics; Mark Twain wrote entire book on subject
- Cannot become a brain surgeon

ACTIVITIES

- Sharing prayer-healing stories at Wednesday night testimony meetings
- Studying religious texts in Christian Science reading rooms worldwide
- Using divine science to help with all of life's issues, even job hunting
- Sunday services

PARAPHERNALIA

- Bible lesson-sermons, distillations of core passages from Bible and *Science and Health*
- Biographies of Mary Baker Eddy
- *Christian Science Monitor* newspaper
- *Manual of the Mother Church,* Eddy's bylaws for organization

QUICK RATINGS:

Conversion Difficulty:

Time Commitment:

Cost:

① ② ③ ④ ⑤

New Friends:
225,000

PURPOSE OF LIFE

Understand God's infinite goodness and "Life, Truth, and Love"; destroy sin, sickness, and death

DEITIES

God the Father-Mother

KEY TEXTS

Bible; *Science and Health with Key to the Scriptures* by Mary Baker Eddy

WHERE

Worldwide, primarily United States

AFTERLIFE PROMISES

Heaven and hell are states of mind; daily choices bring you closer to or drive you further from God

CATEGORY

Abrahamic: Christian

CHURCH OF SATAN

QUICK RATINGS:

Conversion Difficulty:

Time Commitment:

Cost:

New Friends:
Unknown

PURPOSE OF LIFE

"Do what thou wilt shall be the whole of the law"; gratify your id and live life to the fullest

DEITIES

None; Satan, especially as characterized by John Milton and Mark Twain, is concept and ideal rather than divine entity

KEY TEXTS

The Satanic Bible by Anton LaVey; other works by LaVey and by Aleister Crowley

WHERE

United States

AFTERLIFE PROMISES

None; when we die, we rot

CATEGORY

NRM: Left-Hand Path

WHAT IT IS

Inspired by writings of occultist Aleister Crowley, founded in 1966 by former lion tamer Anton LaVey. Foundation is atheism—no God or higher purpose beyond attaining one's fullest human potential. Satan symbolizes rebellion and earthly desires but is not worshipped as divine. Opposes spiritual systems based on abstinence and fear (most religions). Touted as first "carnal" religion.

PERKS

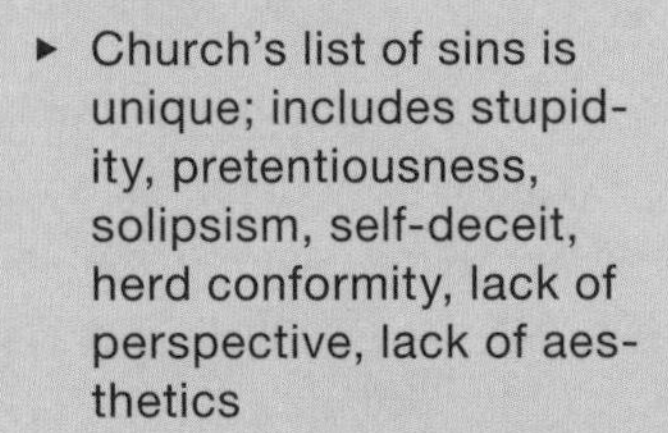

- Church's list of sins is unique; includes stupidity, pretentiousness, solipsism, self-deceit, herd conformity, lack of perspective, lack of aesthetics
- Interpretation of "Do unto others" includes right to seek vengeance
- No kids whine during rituals; membership for adults only
- You are your own god
- Sex—any consenting kind—is encouraged
- No proselytizing

DRAWBACKS

- Satan association controversial; years of bad PR to overcome
- Lengthy application for active membership, including questions about your sex life and feelings toward animals

ACTIVITIES

- Conducting Black Mass to counter blasphemies and oppressive forces
- Casting spells for personal gain and conducting ritual magic to release negative emotions
- Refusing to obey creeds
- Practicing other religions' "so-called sins, as they all lead to physical, mental, or emotional gratification!"

PARAPHERNALIA

- Amulets with Sigil of Baphomet, goat's head on inverted pentagram
- Lots of candles

CHURCH OF THE UNIVERSE

WHAT IT IS

Established in 1969 in Canada by Walter Tucker to celebrate nature, nudity, and Tree of Life (marijuana). Cites biblical passages to support marijuana's sacramental role: "The leaf of the Tree of Life is for the healing of all nations" and "The Lord said to Moses, 'I am going to come to you in a dense cloud.'" Only commandments are "Do not harm yourself" and "Do not harm others."

PERKS 

- According to founder, marijuana is "the most user-friendly plant you could ever smoke"
- Spend less on clothing (nudity shows you have no shame over how God created you)
- Legal defense fund to support members who wind up on wrong side of the law
- All church members are ministers
- If homegrown by clergy, marijuana considered kosher

DRAWBACKS 

- Combination of nudity and potential weight gain from munchies
- Short-term memory loss
- Lung cancer (though danger can be offset by oral ingestion of marijuana via baked goods)
- Legal wrangling
- Original headquarters, Clearwater Abbey—haven of marijuana agriculture (called "cult"), nature, and nudity—no longer accessible to practitioners following forcible eviction

ACTIVITIES

- Ingesting sacrament in group settings or alone for spiritual development
- Nude nature worship
- Providing medicinal marijuana to the ill
- Fighting for legalization of marijuana, promoting hemp usage
- Growing Tree of Life
- Celebrating Cannabis Day (July 1) and solstices

PARAPHERNALIA

- Blankets to be worn around shoulders in court appearances, referencing sole garments of original Clearwater Abbey defendants
- *Canadan*, hemp yarmulkes
- Secluded nature compounds
- Bongs, rolling papers, etc.

QUICK RATINGS:

Conversion Difficulty:
① ② ③ ④ ⑤ (1)

Time Commitment:
① ② ③ ④ ⑤ (3)

Cost:
① ② ③ ④ ⑤ (2)

New Friends:
30,000

PURPOSE OF LIFE

Get close to God through smoking sacramental weed; pursue freedom, nature, and nudity; spread word about benefits of hemp

DEITIES

God and Jesus, though overall religion is universalist and syncretic

KEY TEXTS

Bible; Gnostic scriptures; marijuana-growing guides

WHERE

North America

AFTERLIFE PROMISES

Not discussed but probably entails being nude and high

CATEGORY

NRM: Entheogen Oriented

CHURCH UNIVERSAL AND TRIUMPHANT

QUICK RATINGS:
Conversion Difficulty: **①** ② ③ ④ ⑤
Time Commitment: ① ② ③ **④** ⑤
Cost: ① ② ③ **④** ⑤
New Friends: 40,000

PURPOSE OF LIFE
Dethrone synthetic self and uplift divine self until purified enough for ascension

DEITIES
Divine Consciousness (God); Ascended Masters

KEY TEXTS
Keys to the Kingdom by Elizabeth Clare Prophet; *Climb the Highest Mountain* by Mark L. Prophet and Elizabeth Clare Prophet

WHERE
Worldwide, primarily Montana

AFTERLIFE PROMISES
If karma is balanced and divine destiny fulfilled, soul reunites with God; if not, reincarnation

CATEGORY
NRM: Syncretic

WHAT IT IS
Unites world religions for Age of Aquarius. Developed out of Theosophy and early 1900s "I AM" movement—each person has higher self that is unique individualization of God, evolving through reincarnation. Instruction comes from Ascended Masters (enlightened spiritual beings including Jesus, Buddha, and St. Germain) as dictated through Elizabeth Clare Prophet, church founder.

PERKS 
- Nuclear war to be averted through prayer
- Church already exists in the kingdom of heaven
- Love of God creates magnetized force field of love
- Ascended Masters allow visits to their retreats in the etheric octave (travel occurs on spiritual plane while sleeping)
- Get to intone "OM" as well as pray "Our Father"
- Can pledge membership to Keepers of the Flame Fraternity

DRAWBACKS 
- Encouraged to tithe large amounts in order to receive more abundance
- Ascended Masters called "Great White Brotherhood," though "white" refers to color of their auras, not race
- Run-ins with authorities over underground bunkers, petroleum leakage, weapons stockpiling, tax-exempt status, fraud
- Church currently facing infighting, problems with money and leadership

ACTIVITIES
- Charting your divine self
- Invoking violet flame to purify negative karma
- Attending Summit University, formerly known as Ascended Master University, on beautiful Montana ranch
- Using Science of Spoken Word to "decree"—make positive statements as if they were already true

PARAPHERNALIA
- *Pearls of Wisdom* quarterly, dictation received from Ascended Masters
- Many books, booklets, audio and video recordings, plus online coursework
- Comfortable, straight-backed chairs for decreeing

RELIGION FOR HOBBYISTS

Hobbies provide so much pleasure and fulfillment. Why choose a religion that's incompatible with what you love to do? Instead, choose a faith that will mesh well with your recreational pastimes.

DANCE AND MUSIC

Anthroposophy (eurythmy), Australian Aboriginal, Candomble, Cherokee, Hare Krishna, Lakota, Navajo, Roma, Santeria, Unitarian Universalism (Dances of Universal Peace), Yoruba, Zulu

COMPUTER

Spiritual But Not Religious (Internet dating), Technopaganism (entire religion exists online), Universal Life Church (primarily online)

FAMILY TIME

Catholicism, Eastern Orthodox Churches, Hasidism, Mormonism (families sealed for eternity), Pentecostalism

GARDENING

Amish (farming), Neo-Druidism (tree planting), Self-Realization Fellowship (beautiful gardens), Wicca (tree hugging, herbal healing, and spells), Zen Buddhism (rock gardens and bonsai)

PARTYING

Atheism (anything goes), Catholicism (alcohol), Church of Satan (hedonism), Church of the Universe (marijuana), Discordianism (sin is silly), Judaism (Manischewitz), Native American Church (peyote), Rastafari (marijuana), Universal Life Church (officiate at weddings)

PHYSICAL FITNESS

Australian Aboriginal (walkabout), Falun Gong (tai chi), Gurdjieff (sacred gymnastics), Hinduism (yoga), Jehovah's Witnesses (walking door to door), Masai (roaming with cattle), Neo-Druidism (hiking), Sufism (whirling)

READING

Baha'i (wisdom of all faiths), Christianity (Bible is long), Christian Science (reading rooms, newspaper), A Course in Miracles (3 volumes plus Marianne Williamson), Scientology (founder L. Ron Hubbard was prolific), Sufism (Rumi poetry, etc.), Urantia Brotherhood (central book is 2,000-plus pages)

SCRAPBOOKING

Juche (never too many pictures of Kim Il Sung)

TELEVISION

Discordianism (TV is chaotic), John Frum (they don't actually own TVs but want them), Scientology (Hollywood membership), Technopaganism (into TV, video games)

TRAVEL

Baha'i (very multicultural), Islam (pilgrimage to Mecca), Mormonism (strong global missionary program), Temple of the Vampire (through flying, shape-shifting)

CONFUCIANISM

QUICK RATINGS:

Conversion Difficulty:

① ② ③ ④ ⑤

Time Commitment:

① ② ③ ④ ⑤

Cost:

① ② ③ ④ ⑤

New Friends:
6.5 million

PURPOSE OF LIFE

Improve oneself through virtue, honor family and ancestors, do unto others

DEITIES

No specific gods; worship of ancestral spirits; references to celestial deity and heaven

KEY TEXTS

The Confucian Canon: *Wu Ching* (Five Classics; includes *I Ching*), *Sishu* (Four Books; includes Analects)

WHERE

Primarily China; also Japan, South Korea, Vietnam

AFTERLIFE PROMISES

Ancestors live on as spirits; however, Confucius said, "If we do not yet know about life, how can we know about death?"

CATEGORY

Taoic

WHAT IT IS

Ethical and philosophical beliefs originating in 5th-century BCE China that, with Taoism and Buddhism, provide foundation for Chinese religion. Confucius saw himself as purveyor of ancient wisdom, collecting and interpreting what became the Confucian Canon. Emphasizes *ren* (humanness), self-improvement through virtue, and social and family structure as supported by *li* (ritual).

PERKS

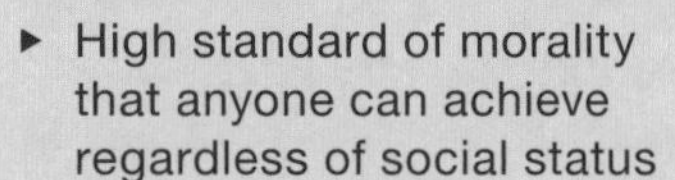

- High standard of morality that anyone can achieve regardless of social status
- Coexists with other religions
- Ability to read deeply into fortune-cookie texts
- Know where you stand: stresses importance of relationship positioning within family and society, and rituals establish guidelines for behavior
- Promotes close family ties and education
- War considered immoral

DRAWBACKS

- Some naysayers allege it's philosophy, not religion
- Must spend time and money honoring dead relatives in order to bring good luck
- No talking in bed or while eating, according to Confucian Analects
- Emphasis on ritual and respect could be distasteful to nonconformists
- Spanking allowed if elders are disrespected

ACTIVITIES

- 6 stages of marriage, from proposal and exchange of astrological information to preparing breakfast for in-laws
- Following childbirth, mother rests for one month, with all needs met
- Wearing coarse clothing, washing body, collecting money from mourners when someone dies

PARAPHERNALIA

- Willow branches for burial rituals
- Incense
- Moon-shaped cookies to announce marriage
- Family altars
- Statues of Confucius
- Books, especially Analects, as well as works interpreting Confucianism

CORE SHAMANISM

WHAT IT IS

Developed by anthropologist Michael Harner in 1960s. Selectively blends indigenous shamanic traditions into one discipline without cultural or tribal affiliations. Unlike ancient shamanism, shamans not born but taught; shamanism practiced for self, not for community; evil not addressed. Attained through drumming, trance states ("journeying") help followers grow spiritually, gain insight.

PERKS

- Feel connected to ancient, nonmainstream ways
- Get to have a spirit animal to help solve problems, find lost things, guide you in other worlds (accessed through holes in earth, trees, or sky)
- By "seeing with your heart," avoid middleman imposed by most religions
- Most religious work is done in dreamlike state, with great deal accomplished in short time
- Get to glimpse things described only in myths

DRAWBACKS 

- Journeys to Lower World, where emotions and memories reside, can be painful
- May get teased by real shamans
- Possible to lose your way in other worlds
- Drumming

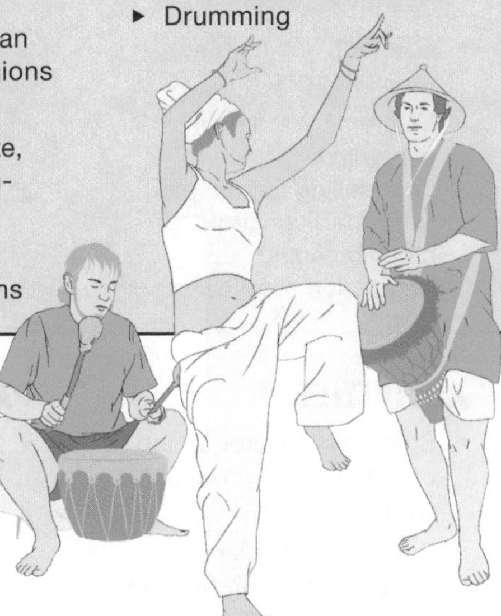

ACTIVITIES

- Participating in drumming circles
- Communicating with spirits
- Interpreting dreams
- Finding lost power through spirit animal
- Weather management, especially rainmaking
- Holotropic breathwork
- Guiding lost souls

PARAPHERNALIA

- Drums, rattles
- For workshops, comfortable clothes, warm socks, pens and notebooks for recording journeys

QUICK RATINGS:

Conversion Difficulty: 1 (of 5)

Time Commitment: 1 (of 5)

Cost: 2 (of 5)

New Friends: 75,000

PURPOSE OF LIFE
Use journeying to improve life, gain insight, solve problems, get in touch with authentic self

DEITIES
Various gods and goddesses referenced, but nothing formal

KEY TEXTS
The Way of the Shaman by Michael Harner

WHERE
Primarily California, Colorado, New Mexico

AFTERLIFE PROMISES
Live as spirit in afterworld, preferably with ancestors in Upper World vs. stuck on earthly plane

CATEGORY
NRM: Neo-Pagan

A COURSE IN MIRACLES

QUICK RATINGS:

Conversion Difficulty:

Time Commitment:

Cost:

New Friends:
1.5 million

PURPOSE OF LIFE
Heal mind through forgiveness, correct errors of Christianity, realize all is love, achieve atonement as Jesus did

DEITIES
God (Father, Son, Holy Spirit)

KEY TEXTS
A Course in Miracles, channeled by Helen Schucman

WHERE
United States

AFTERLIFE PROMISES
Life is heaven (perfect unity of God's will and spirit, with no subject-object duality) after realization that all, including death, is illusory, and only love is real

CATEGORY
NRM: Revealed

WHAT IT IS
Based on text channeled from Jesus through Columbia University psychologist Helen Schucman in 1970s. New Age alternative to traditional Christianity, deleting rules and sin, adding Eastern and psychotherapeutic philosophies. Self-study spiritual path toward understanding universal love and forgiveness; physical world, sin, and death are illusions of ego.

PERKS 
- Racially, nationally, socioeconomically diverse; gays and lesbians welcome
- Study at own pace—no minimum requirement
- Organized community of like-minded individuals, without necessity of church attendance
- Founder was humble, rejected spotlight
- Marianne Williamson, dynamic lecturer and best-selling author, has translated concepts for celebrities and new generation of followers

DRAWBACKS 
- Viewed as heretical by many Christians
- Egotists may not like idea that ego is false identity
- Hard to get up and go to work every day if all is illusory
- Do-it-yourself aspect of study may be difficult for those requiring discipline of rules and regulations
- Text can be dense, unwieldy; indisputably long
- Overly earnest

ACTIVITIES
- Studying alone or in one of 2,000 study groups worldwide
- Submitting prayer requests through Miracle Prayer Ministry
- Forgiving self, others
- Repudiating Christianity's imperatives of suffering and sacrifice

PARAPHERNALIA
- Three-volume *A Course in Miracles* text
- Student workbook consisting of 365 daily lessons
- *The Lighthouse*, quarterly newsletter
- *The Holy Encounter*, bimonthly newsletter
- *Miracles Monthly*, monthly newsletter

DEISM

RELIGION #20

WHAT IT IS

Movement in Europe and United States dating to 17th century. Asserts God created universe, then stepped away, giving humans reason and moral capacity rather than set of rules. Rejects revealed religion and miracles, relying instead on intellect and observation for spiritual knowledge. No personal relationship with God; if God wanted to be worshipped, He would make it known.

PERKS

- Independence: no interference from an active God
- Satan doesn't exist
- New posthumous friends include Thomas Jefferson, Benjamin Franklin
- Curiosity and skepticism welcome
- No one speaks for God; prophets not allowed
- Worship and prayer unnecessary
- Very few taboos beyond not hurting others

DRAWBACKS 

- No churches or community for support
- If you make a mistake, God won't help
- No sense of magic, no miracles
- Concocting rational explanations for everything takes work and effort
- With no Satan or God to blame, must take personal responsibility

ACTIVITIES

- Treating others with dignity and respect
- Participating in annual Thomas Paine essay contest
- Questioning authority
- Studying science to understand life's design
- Explaining differences between Deism and Theism

PARAPHERNALIA

- Clear, rational mind
- Subscription to *Deistic Thought and Action*
- Deist bumper stickers such as "Deism: The Non-Prophet Religion," "God Gave Us Reason, Not Religion," and "I Believe in Life *Before* Death"
- Images of DNA helix used to symbolize design in nature

QUICK RATINGS:

Conversion Difficulty:

① ② ③ ④ ⑤

Time Commitment:

① **②** ③ ④ ⑤

Cost:

① ② ③ ④ ⑤

New Friends:

60,000

PURPOSE OF LIFE

Honor God with reason, live happily without harming others, understand life through observation and logic

DEITIES

God, author of the universe

KEY TEXTS

The Age of Reason by Thomas Paine; *On Liberty* by John Stuart Mill; *Deism: An Anthology* by Peter Gay

WHERE

United States, United Kingdom, France, Germany

AFTERLIFE PROMISES

Differing opinions; however, most Deists believe that if God wanted something done for salvation, He would make it known

CATEGORY

Non-Revealed

DISCORDIANISM

QUICK RATINGS:

Conversion Difficulty:
① ② ③ ④ ⑤

Time Commitment:
① ② ③ ④ ⑤

Cost:
① ② ③ ④ ⑤

New Friends:
Unknown

PURPOSE OF LIFE
Bring order to world through chaos or have fun trying

DEITIES
Eris, goddess of discord

KEY TEXTS
Principia Discordia by Malaclypse the Younger (AKA Greg Hill); *The Honest Book of Truth* by Lord Omar Kayyam Ravenhurst (AKA Kerry Thornley)

WHERE
United States (especially California), United Kingdom, Germany

AFTERLIFE PROMISES
Differing, chaotic views; "Hell is reserved exclusively for them that believe in it"; some believe in paradise of partying for the righteous

CATEGORY
NRM: Hot Dog Oriented

WHAT IT IS
Founded in 1958 following frozen-time revelation in San Francisco bowling alley. Sometimes called the Great Joke. God is "crazy woman": that is, Eris, Greek goddess of discord, who threw golden apple that started Trojan War. Disorder is valid; world is chaotic, and trying to impose harmony makes it worse. Because spiritual imbalance makes us miserable, we should just lighten up.

PERKS 
- Get to experience inner vandal: Operation Mindfuck, "conspiracy without a purpose," mandates sowing disorder with graffiti, pranks, computer viruses, etc.
- Math made easy; Law of Fives stipulates that everything happens as multiple of 5
- Encouraged not to believe anything you read—including Discordian texts
- Emphasis on having fun and joking; even concept of sin is silly

DRAWBACKS 
- Golden apples always have golden worms (first commandment of the Pentabarf, 5 holy laws of Discordianism)
- Life has no purpose: when sacred Chao (cow) was asked, she replied "MU," Chinese ideogram for "nothing"

ACTIVITIES
- Eating hot dogs without buns on Fridays (3rd commandment of the Pentabarf is the hot-dog ritual; 4th stipulates no bun)
- Fighting curse of Greyface, who in 1166 BCE proclaimed that life is serious
- Performing stand-up comedy

PARAPHERNALIA
- Software with glitches
- Clocks that run backward
- Book of Murphy's Law

DRUZE

RELIGION #22

WHAT IT IS

Small, secretive religion in Middle East that began to develop in 11th century from Isma'ilite Islam teachings, incorporating Jewish, Christian, Gnostic, and Greek philosophical elements. Many aspects known only to Druze *uqaal* (initiated class). One God and 7 prophets, including Adam, Moses, Jesus, and Muhammad. Strict moral code and tight community structure.

PERKS 

- Close-knit families and communities
- Only 7 principles to remember, including love of truth, taking care of one another, avoiding the demon, accepting humanity's divine unity
- Humans have free will
- Early proponents of equal rights for women, anti-slavery, and social equality; women considered spiritually superior
- Allowed to outwardly deny faith if life is in danger (e.g., from Muslim persecution)

DRAWBACKS 

- No converts allowed; finite number of Druze souls (continually reincarnated) were created at once
- No intermarriage, alcohol, tobacco, pork, obscenities
- If you're part of *juhhal* (uninitiated) rather than uqaal, you won't be privy to the secrets
- Druze name considered offensive due to treason of namesake; followers call themselves Muwahhidun, but Druze name sticks among outsiders

ACTIVITIES

- Avoiding Muslim rituals and 5 Islamic pillars, which encourage people to sin because they know they'll be forgiven; instead, live in way that constantly pleases God
- Some fasting
- Making pilgrimage to Jethro's tomb
- Striving to live well enough to become uqaal

PARAPHERNALIA

- Black tops, long skirts for women; dark clothing for men
- For uqaal women, white headscarf; for uqaal men, white turban over shaved head
- Long beards for men
- Accoutrements of modest living: simple homes, houses of worship, etc.

QUICK RATINGS:

Conversion Difficulty:
① ② ③ ④ ⑤ 

Time Commitment:
① ② ③ ④ ⑤  

Cost:
① ② ③ ④ ⑤  

New Friends:
250,000

PURPOSE OF LIFE

Live life according to 7 Noahide commandments (refrain from idolatry, immorality, murder, etc.) and Druze moral code

DEITIES

Al-Hakim (God)

KEY TEXTS

Qur'an; *Kitab Al Hikmah* (Epistles of Wisdom), only accessible to uqaal

WHERE

Primarily Syria, Lebanon

AFTERLIFE PROMISES

Body is robe enclosing soul; death is tearing of robe, leading to instantaneous reincarnation until purified enough to reunite with God

CATEGORY

Abrahamic: Islamic

WHERE DO YOU WANT TO LIVE?

One consideration in choosing a religion is geography. Perhaps you are most interested in the Druze faith but cannot relocate to the Middle East because your job and family confine you to your current place of residence. Or maybe you're debating whether Juche or John Frum is the way to go, and the tropical South Pacific island of Vanuatu strikes you as more appealing than North Korea, with its long, bitterly cold winters. Geography can cinch or rule out any life choice, and religion is no exception.

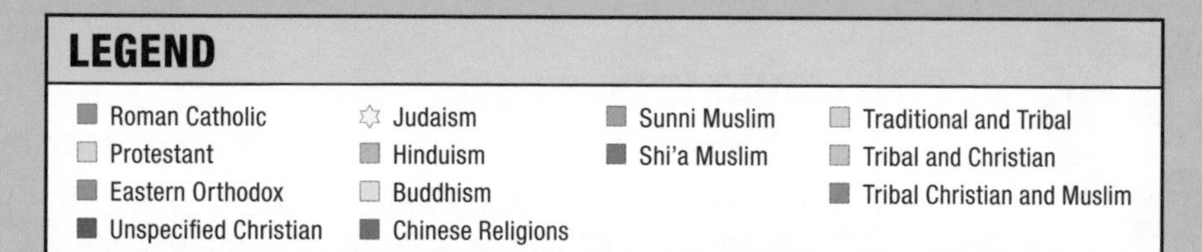
LEGEND
Roman Catholic
Protestant
Eastern Orthodox
Unspecified Christian
Judaism
Hinduism
Buddhism
Chinese Religions
Sunni Muslim
Shi'a Muslim
Traditional and Tribal
Tribal and Christian
Tribal Christian and Muslim

NEO-MANICHAEISM
ROMA
DRUZE
MANDAEANISM
ZEN BUDDHISM
NICHIREN
JUCHE
SOKA GAKKAI
TENRIKYO
SHINTO
UNIFICATION CHURCH
SIKHISM
TAOISM
FALUN GONG
ZOROASTRIANISM
CAO DAI
CONFUCIANISM
BRAHMA KUMARIS
TIBETAN BUDDHISM
OSHO
SATHYA SAI BABA
JAINISM
MASAI
HARE KRISHNA
THERAVADA BUDDHISM
JOHN FRUM
VEDANTA SOCIETY
AUSTRALIAN ABORIGINAL
ZULU

EASTERN ORTHODOX CHURCHES

QUICK RATINGS:

Conversion Difficulty: ① ② ③ ④ ⑤ (3)

Time Commitment: ① ② ③ ④ ⑤ (4)

Cost: ① ② ③ ④ ⑤ (3)

New Friends: 220 million

PURPOSE OF LIFE
Strictly follow Christ's original teachings to reach theosis, state of freedom from all earthly passions

DEITIES
God (Father, Son, Holy Spirit)

KEY TEXTS
Bible; *Philokalia* by Saints Nikodimos of the Holy Mountain and Makarios of Corinth

WHERE
Worldwide, primarily Eastern Europe, Greece, Russia, North America

AFTERLIFE PROMISES
Soul temporarily separated from body; may linger on earth before being judged and going to heaven or hell

CATEGORY
Abrahamic: Christian

WHAT IT IS
Fellowship of individual churches, each governed by autonomous bishop (no central pope). Split from Roman Catholicism in 1014 CE over beliefs, culture, liturgy. Where Catholicism views doctrine as evolving, Orthodox asserts church should remain as established by Christ and apostles. Major denominations include Russian and Greek; services conducted in native languages, not Latin.

PERKS 

- Liturgical choral music is among most beautiful in world
- Ornate churches with Byzantine artwork
- Close-knit communities
- Child friendly; large families encouraged
- Clergy can marry
- Orthodox Christmas celebrated later, during after-Christmas sales

DRAWBACKS 

- Regular fasting and mortification of flesh strongly encouraged
- Worship services last for hours
- Homosexuality and abortion forbidden
- Divorce, though not prohibited, is sin
- Tithing
- No intermarriage; can marry only those who have been baptized
- No visits from pope

ACTIVITIES

- Joining Philoptochos (friends of the poor)
- Greek, Russian, Serbo-Croatian language lessons
- Liturgical choral singing, chanting
- Burning incense in front of saints' pictures
- Big weddings with folk dancing and "upa"-ing

PARAPHERNALIA

- Home altars with personal sacred objects
- Incense in censers (punctured metal vessels swung on chains)
- Icons (small paintings of saints)
- Crucifixes with 2 extra crossbars
- Olive oil–burning vigil lamps

ECKANKAR

WHAT IT IS

Founded in 1965 by self-dubbed 971st ECK Master Paul Twitchell. Claims roots in ancient Egyptian practices but draws on Hindu sound-current yoga. Individual's true identity is soul, independent of body; soul's mission is to discover self through contact with ECK (divine spirit). Souls are connected to God via ECK current. Personal experiences of God arise through sound, light, soul travel.

PERKS 

- *Eckankar* means "co-worker with God"
- No need to give up current religion to participate
- Charitable work not expected
- *Chelas* (students of Eckankar) learn to heed own personal call of ECK as sound and light
- Get to experience past lives and soul travel; also analyze dreams

DRAWBACKS 

- While first initiation often comes in dream, second initiation (by Mahanta, ECK Master) involves traveling to Minnesota
- Might miss nebulous call of God if not paying attention—based entirely on personal revelation
- Leaving Eckankar results in bad karma
- May be considered unoriginal; Twitchell accused of plagiarizing from other religions
- "Ecchh" puns will be irresistible to friends

ACTIVITIES

- Daily 15-minute spiritual exercises (131 exercises total)
- Singing HU (pronounced HYOO) to God
- Leaving body to travel in spirit world
- Keeping dream journals
- Sound-current yoga
- Study groups with fellow ECKists

PARAPHERNALIA

- Literature, audio, video of spiritual exercises and teachings, assigned for different initiation levels
- Writings of ECK Masters, including current Mahanta (spiritual leader) Sri Harold Klemp, former Wisconsin farm boy
- HU music videos

QUICK RATINGS:

Conversion Difficulty: ① ② ❸ ④ ⑤

Time Commitment: ① ❷ ③ ④ ⑤

Cost: ① ② ③ ❹ ⑤

New Friends: 50,000

PURPOSE OF LIFE

Discover self and God by making contact with ECK, divine spirit

DEITIES

Sugmad (God); sound and light of ECK are holy spirit

KEY TEXTS

Shariyat-Ki-Sugmad, sacred scriptures; *Eckankar: The Key to Secret Worlds* by Paul Twitchell

WHERE

Primarily United States

AFTERLIFE PROMISES

Soul reincarnates until it learns enough about God to end cycle and reunite with divine

CATEGORY

NRM: Hindu Oriented

ELAN VITAL

QUICK RATINGS:

Conversion Difficulty:	① ② ③ ④ ⑤ (3)
Time Commitment:	① ② ③ ④ ⑤ (4)
Cost:	① ② ③ ④ ⑤ (3)
New Friends:	250,000

PURPOSE OF LIFE
Use 4 Knowledge techniques to achieve inner peace

DEITIES
None specified, though Maharaji used to call himself Lord of the Universe

KEY TEXTS
None; Maharaji communicates through audio and video

WHERE
United States, India, Germany

AFTERLIFE PROMISES
Unspecified

CATEGORY
NRM: Hindu Oriented

WHAT IT IS
Established in early 1980s by scion of Divine Light Mission, Prem Pal Singh Rawat (AKA Maharaji), groomed in India by father to be guru; started preaching inner peace to audiences by age of 3. After Divine Light schism and creation of Elan Vital, Maharaji narrowed focus to regular meditation techniques called Knowledge, transmitted via video and teaching engagements around world.

PERKS 

- Names of meditation techniques now easier to remember: were called Light (applying pressure to eyelids to discover 3rd eye), Sound (cupping hands over ears to hear heavenly music), Word or Name (breathing regulation), and Nectar (positioning tongue to taste nectar of life); now called 1st, 2nd, 3rd, and 4th
- Although daily practice of all 4 types of meditation takes at least 2 hours, possible to compress into 1 hour if necessary

DRAWBACKS 

- Meditation techniques must be learned directly from Maharaji, but must prepare for 3 to 5 months beforehand by studying the 6 Keys, 5 of which are available on video
- Followers known as "premies" after Maharaji's given name
- Ex-premies publicize terrible things about Maharaji
- Though Maharaji claims he earns no money from organization, lavish lifestyle remains unexplained

ACTIVITIES

- Obtaining Knowledge certification and Smart Card by completing Knowledge coursework
- Attending Maharaji events around world: small donations, large audiences; big donations, intimate encounters
- Daily Knowledge practice
- Maintaining secrecy of Knowledge

PARAPHERNALIA

- Smart Cards, permanent microchipped event credentials with identifying photographs of Knowledge graduates
- DVD players, stereo systems, cable TV to play and receive Maharaji's messages
- For Maharaji himself, Gulfstream V private jet, helicopters, yacht, multiple mansions

EPISCOPALIAN

RELIGION #26

WHAT IT IS

American version of Anglicanism, movement initiated by King Henry VIII in 1534 because Catholic Church wouldn't allow divorce. Despite split, shares many similarities with Catholicism: baptism, Eucharist, penance, unction, rites of matrimony; celebration of saints; apostolic ordainment of clergy; and monastic orders. However, encourages social diversity, equality, justice.

PERKS

- Blessing of same-sex unions a possibility
- Clergy free to marry
- Activism on behalf of poor and oppressed
- Weekday and online worship services leave weekends free
- Plenty of time to change mind: confirmation classes can take months or years
- All pluses of Catholicism without the guilt

DRAWBACKS

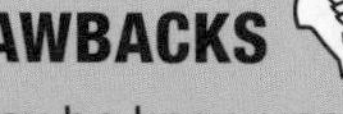

- May be known as "God's frozen people" due to perceived lack of warmth
- Squabbling over women and gay clergy polarizes many congregations

ACTIVITIES

- Liturgy-inspired dance and music
- Chanting, singing, readings
- Feast Days honoring church heroes
- Community outreach and mission work
- Observance of religious holidays: Ash Wednesday, Lent, All Saints' Day, etc.

PARAPHERNALIA

- Wine, wafers, chalices
- Clerical and laity vestments: albs, cassocks, chasubles, stoles
- Advent wreaths

QUICK RATINGS:

Conversion Difficulty:

① **②** ③ ④ ⑤

Time Commitment:

① **②** ③ ④ ⑤

Cost:

① **②** ③ ④ ⑤

New Friends:

3.5 million

PURPOSE OF LIFE

Live according to teachings of Jesus Christ contained in Catechism and Book of Common Prayer, partaking in sacraments

DEITIES

God (Father, Son, Holy Spirit)

KEY TEXTS

Bible; Book of Common Prayer; Apostles' Creed; Nicene Creed

WHERE

United States

AFTERLIFE PROMISES

Heaven and hell not physical places but states of being

CATEGORY

Abrahamic: Christian

ETHICAL CULTURE

QUICK RATINGS:

Conversion Difficulty:	① ② ③ ④ ⑤ (1)
Time Commitment:	① ② ③ ④ ⑤ (2)
Cost:	① ② ③ ④ ⑤ (1)
New Friends:	2,500

PURPOSE OF LIFE
Create more humane and ethical society; discover new potentials, implement realistic solutions, become self-responsible; decrease suffering, increase creativity

DEITIES
None, though no objections to members' believing in deities

KEY TEXTS
An Ethical Philosophy of Life by Felix Adler

WHERE
North America

AFTERLIFE PROMISES
None

CATEGORY
Non-Revealed

WHAT IT IS
Inspired by Immanuel Kant, movement established in 1876 by professor Felix Adler to assert that importance of moral behavior does not have to be justified by existence of a supreme being. Original goals were to promote sexual purity, assistance to the poor, and intellectual development. Now seeks to create global network of respectful relationships to improve human condition.

PERKS 
- Dogma-free; followers can come up with own answers to life's mysteries
- Committed to education and self-improvement
- Seeks common ground for cooperative action among people of all faiths
- Open-mindedness encouraged
- Can also believe in other religions
- Dedicated to improving world, especially environment, civil rights, plight of the poor

DRAWBACKS 
- Too loosey-goosey for some
- Republicans may find environmentalism and liberal sensibility hard to stomach
- Internal pressure to always do the right, or ethical, thing—no cutting in line, road rage, etc.
- No saints or miracles
- Mystery of life still a mystery

ACTIVITIES
- Attending 5-session course, "The Foundations of Ethical Culture," after joining
- Sunday morning meetings
- Taking ethical action: "Working for a better world for ourselves and our children and proclaim[ing] our belief in the worth and potential of all human beings"

PARAPHERNALIA
- Monthly newsletter from local chapter
- Energy-efficient lightbulbs, old Volvos
- Psychoanalyst
- Free time for community service
- Large library of books

FALUN GONG

WHAT IT IS

Founded in 1992 in China by Li Hongzhi during post-Mao boom in faith, one of many NRMs centering on *qi* (vital energy) breathing exercises. Falun Gong is largest such movement, prescribing daily practice of 5 tai chi–like qigong exercises to promote health, moral development, inner peace, and supernatural, alien-fighting powers by awakening *falun* (wheel of dharma) in lower abdomen.

PERKS

- Exercises promote wellness, lower stress and blood pressure
- Can cure cancer and turn white hair black
- Might be able to levitate like, according to Li Hongzhi, David Copperfield
- Underlying Buddhism-themed messages emphasize *zhen* (truthfulness), *shan* (compassion), and *ren* (forbearance)
- Can be practiced individually, at own pace, for free

DRAWBACKS 

- Outlawed as evil cult by Chinese government
- Demonic aliens taking over humans via machines, cloning
- Qigong–induced psychosis recently coined as psychiatric disorder

ACTIVITIES

- Informal group exercise sessions, often outdoors in parks, to recorded voice of Li
- Attending international conferences
- Participating in peaceful protest marches and sit-ins against Chinese human-rights abuses
- Guerrilla theater performances reenacting torture

PARAPHERNALIA

- Texts and recordings of Li's teachings
- Yellow, loose-fitting clothing for exercise

QUICK RATINGS:

Conversion Difficulty: ① ② ③ ④ ⑤ (1 shaded)

Time Commitment: ① ② ③ ④ ⑤ (2 shaded)

Cost: ① ② ③ ④ ⑤ (1 shaded)

New Friends: 30 million

PURPOSE OF LIFE

Through 5 exercises, develop *xinxing* (mind character) and *gong* (cultivation energy) to free self from worldly state

DEITIES

Li Hongzhi

KEY TEXTS

Zhuan Falun and *Falun Gong* by Li Hongzhi

WHERE

China

AFTERLIFE PROMISES

Reincarnation as human, rock, or animal, depending on karmic debt

CATEGORY

NRM: Dharmic Oriented

SEEKING GOD THROUGH DRUGS

Ganja, hashish, peyote, psilocybin, LSD, coca leaves. You might think you're reading a list of illegal drugs, but they actually constitute some of the ways worshippers have gotten closer to God throughout history. Just as dancing, spinning, fasting, davening, intense prayer, meditation, and plain old self-torture have been used to achieve altered states and open what Aldous Huxley called "the doors of perception," so have psychoactive drugs been one method of inviting the universal creative force into one's heart.

In 1979, the term *entheogen* was coined to describe drugs used to achieve spiritual vision, derived from the Greek *entheos*, which means "god within" or "inspired by God." The ethnobotanists and mythology scholars who devised the term felt it was necessary to distinguish such drugs from those used recreationally as well as to move away from the term *hallucinogen* and its etymological association with insanity. "In a strict sense," the group stated, "only those vision-producing drugs that can be shown to have figured in shamanic or religious rites would be designated entheogens."

Evidence of hallucinogenic mushroom cults in Siberia dates back to 5000 BCE, while mescal seeds carbon-dated to 8000 BCE have been found at South American religious sites. Some of the oldest religious texts in the world contain hymns to a mysterious plant called soma, which most anthropologists agree was some type of hallucinogen. These hymns form the foundation for both Zoroastrianism and Hinduism, and although the plant's identity is now a mystery, archaeologist Victor Sarianidi believes early devotees drank soma and sat hallucinating in specially built white rooms. Modern Zoroastrians and Hindus still practice soma rites, but with symbolic placebos.

Using non-narcotic stimuli such as dancing to create altered states of mind appears to go back even further. Paleolithic-era religious cave paintings depict visions achieved by early shamans in the throes of hallucinogenic dance frenzies. The work of J. D. Lewis-Williams, now the foremost cave-art historian, suggests that the ubiquitous grid, parallel lines, dots, and zigzag patterns seen in cave art around the world document "entoptic" hallucinations, visions thought to be derived from patterns within the nervous system itself, such as those seen when the closed eyelid is vigorously rubbed. These patterns, scholars say, are remarkably similar to those experienced by drug users everywhere.

Why then have entheogenic practices vanished? Although they live on in vestigial forms, their mainstream obsolescence is a result of Western Judeo-Christian-Islamic bans. The ruling class of priest-elites rendered taboo the use of God-communing intoxicants, forcing followers to use the priests as intercessors and thus ensuring their hold on the social power structure.

Outside the reaches of the Abrahamic faiths, however, the religious use of narcotic ecstatic agents continues, particularly in India and South America:

- **AFRICAN:** Some indigenous religions use intoxicants, including the roots of the iboga tree and the juice of the amaryllis plant.
- **HINDUISM:** Almost every form of intoxication is permitted, including hashish, powerful hallucinogens like the datura plant, and constant and sanctified smoking of ganja by Hindu sadhus, ascetic holy men.
- **NATIVE AMERICAN:** The native religions of South America and Central America are the world leaders in shamanic entheogen use, with hundreds of varieties, including peyote, hallucinogenic mushrooms and cactuses, psychedelic snuff and eyedrops, the powerful *ayahuasca* drink, and even psychoactive toad venom, sometimes ingested by licking a toad's skin.

For the savvy religious shopper interested in entheogens, however, 2 questions are paramount. Can altered states lead to true religious experiences? And if so, are they better than drug-free religious experiences? Because they achieve their effect without "artificial" stimulants, there's little debate that altered states induced by chanting or dancing qualify as authentic religious experiences.

A series of experiments by the Harvard Divinity School found that profound religious experiences achieved with and without psilocybin were indistinguishable. Some neurologists have argued that there's no difference between spiritual insights created by the body's increased production of tryptophan, associated with religious experiences, and those created by ingesting hallucinogens. These conclusions fly in the face of those who have experienced these types of entheogens as well as millennia of shamanic rituals. God, as they say, sometimes works in mysterious ways.

THE FAMILY

QUICK RATINGS:

Conversion Difficulty:
① ② ③ ④ ⑤

Time Commitment:
① ② ③ ④ ⑤

Cost:
① ② ③ ④ ⑤

New Friends:
10,000

PURPOSE OF LIFE
Accept Christ as Lord and Savior and lead others to salvation; live life in accordance with interpreted biblical teachings and "Mo Letters" (founder's writings, from chosen name, Moses David)

DEITIES
God (Father, Son, Holy Spirit)

KEY TEXTS
Bible; "Mo Letters"; Love Charter

WHERE
Primarily North America

AFTERLIFE PROMISES
New Jerusalem for those who have accepted Christ as Savior; not for relaxation but for continuing God's work and helping those on earth

CATEGORY
NRM: Christian Oriented

WHAT IT IS
Formerly Children of God, hippie, free-love, apocalyptic version of Christianity founded in 1968 by David Brandt Berg in California. Berg encouraged disciples to live with his family, evolving into communal living as movement grew through sex-based recruitment practices such as Flirty Fishing. Known for sexually abusing children, though practice was officially banned in 1987.

PERKS 
- Guilt-free sex with any adult (sex called "sharing"; members encouraged to share)
- Child rearing is collective responsibility
- Get to live communally, separate from rest of world
- Access to God's Lending Library of saints: ghosts, angels, and spirits to help you when called upon
- Famous alumni include the Phoenix family (River, Joaquin, et al.)

DRAWBACKS 
- Risks entailed in joining religion that gave rise to first anti-cult and deprogramming organization, FREECOG
- Must homeschool kids
- World will end

ACTIVITIES
- As soldier in God's Army, engaging in spiritual warfare to turn people away from Satan and to God
- Evangelism and recruitment: the Family claims to have converted one person every 45 seconds for 26 years
- Lots of prayer, reading scripture, fellowship, group chores

PARAPHERNALIA
- *Good News* and *Activated!* magazines, *Endtime News*
- Guitars and tambourines for Music with Meaning

GNOSTICISM

WHAT IT IS

Ancient mystical religion that has assumed many forms and influenced many faiths (especially Christianity). Evil lesser god, Yehovah of Old Testament, created earth (real God would not have created an imperfect world). Within humans, however, God's spark remains; goal is to become intuitively aware of that inner essence and thus know God (*gnosis* means "knowledge").

PERKS

- Get to take credit for Christianity, which was codified in rebellion against Gnosticism
- Diverse: can choose from among many Gnostic traditions, including Mandaean and American/ European Gnostic revival
- No sin, atonement, or church authority
- God has feminine side, Sophia
- Compelling story about true nature of universe and its creation

DRAWBACKS

- Life on earth was horrible mistake, regrettable to God
- Can't rely on church rituals, scripture, personal actions, or reason to know God; must come in unplannable, unforceable revelation
- Some Gnostics are celibate
- Still labeled heretical by most of Catholic Church and many Christian groups

ACTIVITIES

- Accepting dualism (light vs. dark, male vs. female) and finding truth in opposites
- Experiencing unique versions of baptism and Eucharist
- Chanting "Hail Sophia"
- Friday night services and Sunday Mass with Gnostic twists

PARAPHERNALIA

- Emblems of the Dove (representing innocence) and the Serpent (wisdom and knowledge), Gnosticism's primary duality
- Images of Mani, Persian prophet and founder of Manichaeism
- Bumper stickers such as "Gnosis: It's Not What You *Think*!"

QUICK RATINGS:

Conversion Difficulty:

Time Commitment:

1 **2** 3 4 5

Cost:

1 2 3 4 5

New Friends:

500

PURPOSE OF LIFE

Achieve enlightenment by awakening dormant inner knowledge of God

DEITIES

Monad (God; hermaphroditic); feminine side of God, Sophia, mother of Yehovah; Yehovah, akin to Satan, who rules over earth

KEY TEXTS

Nag Hammadi Library, 4th-century gospels discovered in Egypt in 1945

WHERE

North America, Europe

AFTERLIFE PROMISES

Gnostics with secret knowledge will reunite with Pleroma, God's realm above cosmos

CATEGORY

Esoteric

GURDJIEFF

QUICK RATINGS:

Conversion Difficulty:	① ② ③ **④** ⑤
Time Commitment:	① ② ③ **④** ⑤
Cost:	① ② ③ **④** ⑤
New Friends:	20,000

PURPOSE OF LIFE

Reach 3rd and 4th levels of consciousness, self-remembering, and awareness of eternal truth

DEITIES

Great Unknowable (God); can be reached only in progressively closer steps through those more spiritually evolved

KEY TEXTS

All and Everything by G. I. Gurdjieff; *The Fourth Way* and *In Search of the Miraculous* by P. D. Ouspensky

WHERE

North America, France, United Kingdom

AFTERLIFE PROMISES

Limited reincarnation; finite chances to get it right

CATEGORY

NRM: Esoteric

WHAT IT IS

Spiritual movement also called the Fourth Way, founded by G. I. Gurdjieff in 1920s. Most of humanity exists in state of waking sleep, lack of spiritual awareness. Universe depends on spiritual energy, so humans have obligation to progress from instinct to spirit. Laws of Three, Four, Seven, and Nine, represented in Enneagram, outline elements to be balanced, accomplished through the Work.

PERKS 

- Triads easy to understand: active, passive, reconciling (forces); intellectual, emotional, instinctive (brains); bread, air, impressions (food); Ways of Fakir, Monk, Yogi (paths)
- Be part of elite "5 of 20 of 20": only 20 percent of humankind is open to higher realities; only 20 percent of these pursue matter; only 5 percent of these make progress
- Enneagram (chart to explain universe and diagnose personality) is cool

DRAWBACKS 

- Gurdjieff's writings difficult to understand and encompass math and quantum physics
- Not good for procrastinators or quitters: all possibilities exist for short window of time, and it's worse to start, then stop, the Work than never to start
- Only the spiritually advanced can access God directly
- Can be humiliating; group exercises, including "Toast of the Idiots," place students in tense situations

ACTIVITIES

- Ritual dances: the Movements (AKA sacred gymnastics) to connect with Law of Seven (Octave) vibrations
- Self-remembering, 3rd level of consciousness, recalling own true sense of being
- Saying "I AM" once per hour, taking note of state of feeling and state of sensation

PARAPHERNALIA

- Organ Kundabuffer, implanted by angels in humans at dawn of time to cloak our spiritual selves
- Chief Feature of our personalities, which keeps us in state of sleep
- Enneagram charts
- Gurdjieff's recordings and books
- Harmonium, instrument played for the Movements

HARE KRISHNA

WHAT IT IS

International Society for Krishna Consciousness (ISKCON), founded in 1966 by Swami Srila Prabhupada. Based on Vedic scriptures and 16th-century Caitanya movement, which developed devotion based on chanting names of Krishna. Guided by gurus, devotees practice Hindu, *bhakti* yoga for spiritual fulfillment as well as *sankirtana*, chanting of God's names.

PERKS

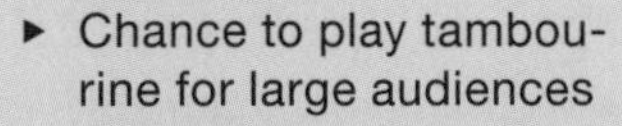

- Chance to play tambourine for large audiences
- Proselytizing great way to make new friends
- Trendsetting, from anti-cult movement to songs by George Harrison and John Lennon

DRAWBACKS

- Strict vegan diet, though Sunday Feasts quite tasty
- No intoxicants, caffeine, tobacco, gambling
- Fashion sense
- Monotonous chanting for several hours per day
- Sex only within marriage, only to procreate
- Solicitation at American airports banned in 1992
- Elaborate cleanliness rituals; toilet paper prohibited, feet vilified, many daily showers

ACTIVITIES

- Rejecting materialism
- Preparing food for Krishna
- Chanting the Maha Mantra: "Hare Krishna, Hare Krishna, Krishna Krishna"
- Marking forehead daily with clay as reminder that body is Krishna's temple

PARAPHERNALIA

- Tufts of hair, *sikha*, in shaved head for men, sign of spiritual surrender
- Dhotis (robes) for men; saris for women
- *Japa* prayer beads worn in sack around neck

QUICK RATINGS:

Conversion Difficulty:

Time Commitment:

Cost:

New Friends:
250,000

PURPOSE OF LIFE

Achieve *moksha* (escape from reincarnation) and return to Krishna consciousness via bhakti (ISKCON rituals and surrender to God)

DEITIES

Krishna

KEY TEXTS

Bhagavad Gita; Vedas; *Bhagavad Gita As It Is* by Swami Prabhupada

WHERE

Worldwide, primarily India, United States, Germany, United Kingdom

AFTERLIFE PROMISES

Soul doomed to *samsara*, endless reincarnation, until reaching Krishna consciousness and uniting with God

CATEGORY

NRM: Hindu Oriented

HASIDISM

WHAT IT IS

Jewish movement, begun in 18th-century Eastern Europe. Moved emphasis of Jewish worship away from intellectual examination of Torah to emotional, personal experience of God. Made esoteric teachings of Kabbalah accessible to all, not just scholars. Prayer provides constant 2-way connection between individual and God. God is in all things, influencing even smallest aspects of life.

QUICK RATINGS:

Conversion Difficulty:
① ② ③  ⑤

Time Commitment:
① ② ③ ④ 

Cost:
① ② ③  ⑤

New Friends:
650,000

PURPOSE OF LIFE
Recognize the omnipresence of God in all things, cultivate piety, serve God in all words and deeds

DEITIES
G-d, the unspoken and unwritten

KEY TEXTS
Tanakh (AKA Torah or Old Testament); Talmud

WHERE
United States, Israel

AFTERLIFE PROMISES
Gilgul, transmigration of soul to repair itself and world: into lower states if one behaved badly; for pious, progressively higher levels in relationship with God

CATEGORY
Abrahamic: Judaism

PERKS 

- Rabbi is free life coach with whom to consult on every aspect of life
- Mating by matchmaker
- No leg shaving or bad hair days thanks to heavy tights, long skirts, and wigs or headscarves for married women
- Wine every Friday night
- First 4 kids take care of next 3.9 (average Hasidic family in United States has 7.9 children)
- Tight-knit community to meet all social needs

DRAWBACKS 

- Insular
- Full-time commitment, with rituals for just about everything and daily prayer services at synagogue
- No touching or being alone with opposite sex except spouse and certain family members
- Keeping kosher is time-consuming and limiting
- Sex only within marriage, tightly regulated with respect to positions, frequency, timing, etc.

ACTIVITIES

- Praying multiple times daily over specific activities (eating, washing, etc.)
- Cooking for Sabbath and frequent holidays
- Ritual *mikveh* baths, daily for men, monthly for women
- For men, curling *payot* (long sidecurls), because Torah prohibits shaving corners of the head

PARAPHERNALIA

- For men, black or fur hats, black or dark clothing, long beards, tzitzit (fringes hanging from corners of prayer shawls)
- Mezuzot, tiny Torah scrolls inside cases attached to doorframes
- Walking shoes for getting to synagogue on Sabbath (no driving)

TOP 10 GURUS OF ALL TIME

A term adopted from Sanskrit, *guru* is a spiritual teacher, especially one who leads a group of followers. Gurus are often seen as conduits to the divine who can guide adherents to self-realization.

1. MARTIN LUTHER
Frequently called the Father of Protestantism, and certainly the founder of Lutheranism, the German theologian's writings and teachings galvanized the 16th-century Protestant Reformation.

2. POPE JOHN PAUL II
The 2nd-longest-serving Roman Catholic pope of the modern era, Pope John Paul II traveled to more than 100 countries, spurring the explosive growth of Catholicism in the developing nations.

3. LAO-TZU
This ancient philosopher's magnum opus, the *Tao-te Ching*, is the primary text of Taoism and vitally significant to Chinese thought.

4. BODHIDHARMA
Traveling from South India, this monk brought the concept of Zen Buddhism to 6th-century China. Zen later flourished in Japan for centuries before making its way to the United States and Europe.

5. CONFUCIUS
Confucianism, regarded as both a philosophy and religion, stems from this 5th-century Chinese sage's teachings.

6. DALAI LAMA
The current (14th) incarnation of the Dalai Lama was the first to travel globally on behalf of Tibetan Buddhism. In 1989, he received the Nobel Peace Prize for his "Free Tibet" advocacy.

7. NICHIREN
The founder of Nichiren Buddhism, this 12th-century Japanese monk taught that enlightenment could be attained only through chanting.

8. BILLY GRAHAM
Arguably the most influential evangelical Christian of the 20th century, Graham advised presidents and led scores of worldwide religious crusades for more than 50 years.

9. BRIGHAM YOUNG
The successor to Joseph Smith as head of the Mormon Church, Young also served as the governor of the Utah Territory, helping Mormonism gain a foothold in the 19th-century American West.

10. NORMAN VINCENT PEALE
A minister and author of *The Power of Positive Thinking*, Peale inspired millions of Americans and influenced religious leaders with his optimistic radio and television sermons.

HEALTHY HAPPY HOLY

QUICK RATINGS:

Conversion Difficulty: ① ② ③ ④ ⑤ (2)

Time Commitment: ① ② ③ ④ ⑤ (4)

Cost: ① ② ③ ④ ⑤ (4)

New Friends: 8,000

PURPOSE OF LIFE

Honor God daily through devotions; overcome lust, anger, greed, worldly attachments, pride; practice healthy habits

DEITIES

One supreme God who cannot take human form but is present in everything

KEY TEXTS

Adi Granth (AKA Guru Granth Sahib), Sikh holy book

WHERE

Worldwide, primarily North America

AFTERLIFE PROMISES

Law of karma governs reincarnation; spirit improves until it can become one with God

CATEGORY

NRM: Sikh Oriented

WHAT IT IS

Founded on principle that "happiness is your birthright" by Yogi Bhajan in 1969. Blends Hinduism, Islam, Sikhism; AKA Sikh Dharma. Healthy lifestyles to improve spiritual awareness, including "technology" of kundalini and tantric yoga, meditation, vegetarian diet. Through practice, realize potential, stimulate creativity, lift spirit, restore balance. Philosophy of compassion and kindness to all.

PERKS 

- Strong work ethic; hard work is great honor
- Tolerance promoted, diversity encouraged
- Sharing is personal and social responsibility
- One of very few religions to stress happiness

DRAWBACKS 

- Many rules; very little free will
- Leader has made claims that taint credibility
- Leaving fold may result in threats

ACTIVITIES

- Dutifully following teachings and example of guru
- Bathing before sunrise and meditating on God's name
- Singing hymns from holy book
- Putting vibrations into food to nourish soul
- Performing acts of charity, community service

PARAPHERNALIA

- White turbans and robes
- Organic vegetables and herbs, especially garlic, onions, ginger
- Yoga mats and rugs
- Five Ks of Sikhism: *kesh*, uncut hair; *kangha*, wood comb; *kara*, steel bracelet; *kachha*, cotton undershorts; *kirpan*, ceremonial dagger

HERMETIC ORDER OF THE GOLDEN DAWN

RELIGION #35

WHAT IT IS

Founded in 1888 by British Freemasons to explore occult and esoteric aspects of many traditions, including Egyptian, Mesopotamian, Greek, Roman, Jewish, Arabic. Wicca and other Neo-Pagan practices trace their roots to the Order's teachings, which are revealed gradually to qualified members only. Claims descent from European Rosicrucian societies of 1600s through 1800s.

PERKS 

- No shortage of ancient mysteries to study
- Magic tricks include transforming lead into gold
- New friends will include Neo-Pagans, Christians, Jews
- Illustrious forebears such as Aleister Crowley, Aubrey Beardsley, W. B. Yeats
- Upon progressing through ranks, get to wear robe and headdress
- Okay to worship any and all deities

DRAWBACKS 

- Lots of work and study to advance through ranks; many never even get to Second Order (3 orders total, comprising 10 levels)
- Can be very political, with infighting between temples
- Expensive ritual paraphernalia
- May decrease self-esteem if unable to transform lead into gold

ACTIVITIES

- Casting astrological charts, reading tarot cards
- Scrying (spiritual divination and vision seeking)
- Consulting Egyptian Book of the Dead and Chaldean Oracles
- Attempting alchemy
- Attending elaborate secret ceremonies

PARAPHERNALIA

- Scrying bowls
- Tarot decks
- Books on astrological chart casting
- Lamps of Hidden Knowledge (special oil lamps)
- Egyptian headdresses
- Scepters and swords
- Wand of the Kerux (sacred symbol)

QUICK RATINGS:
Conversion Difficulty: ① ② ③ ④ **⑤**
Time Commitment: ① ② ③ ④ **⑤**
Cost: ① ② ③ ④ **⑤**
New Friends: Unknown

PURPOSE OF LIFE

Study for Great Work, purification of spiritual nature in order to unite with divine self

DEITIES

Any and all, particularly Greek and Egyptian; also Judeo-Christian

KEY TEXTS

The Complete Golden Dawn Cipher Manuscript by Darcy Küntz; *The Golden Dawn* by Israel Regardie

WHERE

North America, United Kingdom

AFTERLIFE PROMISES

Reincarnate until human limitations are overcome, then unite with true self

CATEGORY

Esoteric

HINDUISM

QUICK RATINGS:

Conversion Difficulty:
① ② ③ ④ ⑤

Time Commitment:
① ② ③ ④ ⑤

Cost:
① ② ③ ④ ⑤

New Friends:
872 million

PURPOSE OF LIFE

Practice ethical living and devotion to God to resolve karma and achieve moksha

DEITIES

Brahman (the Absolute) and his many forms, including Brahma the creator, Vishnu the preserver, Shiva the destroyer (the Hindu trinity); Shakti, Krishna, Lakshmi also popular

KEY TEXTS

Vedas; Bhagavad Gita; Ramayana; Upanishads

WHERE

Worldwide, primarily India

AFTERLIFE PROMISES

Karma-based cycle of death and rebirth until moksha (release) is achieved

CATEGORY

Dharmic

WHAT IT IS

Religion tradition begun on Indian subcontinent around 1500 BCE. Worships multiple forms of same god, Brahman. Existence is cycle of birth, death, and rebirth (*samsara*), determined by karma (actions in previous life) and dharma (living in accordance with laws of nature), until sufficient growth to be released from cycle (*moksha*). *Puja* (worship) entails making offerings to gods.

PERKS 

- Ethical living emphasizes *artha* (prosperity) and *kama* (satisfying desires, including sexual)
- Aesthetics—especially depictions of gods—are lavish and fantastical
- While worship is individually oriented, with emphasis on personal spiritual experience, there are also holidays and festivals galore
- Hindu-oriented practices such as meditation and physical yoga are very trendy

DRAWBACKS 

- No beef; vegetarianism strongly encouraged
- *Vaman* (therapeutic vomiting) prescribed
- Caste system unfair
- Sacred Ganges River very polluted
- Originator of "sacred cow" concept

ACTIVITIES

- Meditating and praying, including offerings to images and icons
- Group bathing in Ganges River
- Funeral-pyre cremation of dead to encourage soul to detach and move on
- Participating in arranged marriages and elaborate wedding ceremonies
- Celebrating holy days

PARAPHERNALIA

- Altars, flowers, food for offerings
- Henna to decorate bride's hands for wedding
- *Bindis* (dots on forehead worn by women)

WHAT IT IS

Strict religion, based on nonmaterialism and sanctity of life; one sect entails complete non-ownership, even clothes (total nudity), and refraining from eating anything that didn't fall off a plant. Formed around same time and place as Buddhism (6th century BCE, eastern India) as revolt against Hinduism. Must not commit or think violent acts against living things; all, including plants, have souls.

PERKS

- Will probably lose weight
- Short commute; Jains vow not to engage in unnecessary travel
- Extremely high literacy rate and professional success; many Jains are upper middle class despite asceticism
- Knowledge that you have never harmed another living being
- Comforting belief in fixed moral rules that govern universe
- Rejects caste system

DRAWBACKS

- Rigid diet: absolute vegetarianism (though not vegan); no root vegetables, because harvesting kills plant; no broccoli, because may contain bugs that would be killed when consumed; no food in likeness of living things, like animal crackers; no alcohol; no honey
- Food and water can be eaten only during daylight
- Lots of fasting, including *santhara*, fasting to death
- Only 2 cars and 6 outfits allowed per person

ACTIVITIES

- Daily offerings (6 daily obligatory actions) and worship (performing specific mantras, prayers, meditations)
- Taking 12 vows (not lying, stealing, etc.)
- Working to rid self of both negative and positive karma
- Lots of festivals, most involving fasting

PARAPHERNALIA

- For monks and nuns, *mukhavastrika* (surgical mask or cloth), to keep insects from flying into mouth and dying
- Brooms for sweeping living things out of way before walking or sitting
- Homespun cotton cloth for straining water 3 times before drinking
- Wood home altars

QUICK RATINGS:

Conversion Difficulty:
① ② ③ **④** ⑤ (4 marked)

Time Commitment:
① ② ③ **④** ⑤ (4 marked)

Cost:
① ② ③ ④ ⑤ (1 marked)

New Friends:
4.6 million

PURPOSE OF LIFE

Revere and respect all forms of life, shedding karma through *ahimsa* (harmlessness), ultimately halting reincarnation cycle

DEITIES

No creator God; belief in perfect universal presence, with God in everything

KEY TEXTS

Other than Tattvartha Sutra, vary according to sect; most consist of teachings recorded by disciples over millennia

WHERE

India

AFTERLIFE PROMISES

After progressive reincarnations, soul becomes liberated; in between, many levels of heaven and hell

CATEGORY

Dharmic

JEHOVAH'S WITNESSES

QUICK RATINGS:
Conversion Difficulty: ① ② ③ ④ ⑤ (1)
Time Commitment: ① ② ③ ④ ⑤ (5)
Cost: ① ② ③ ④ ⑤ (2)
New Friends: 6 million

PURPOSE OF LIFE
Become worthy of eternal place in Kingdom of God through obedience to Jehovah and witnessing (proselytizing) about one's faith

DEITIES
Jehovah; God is unitary (no Holy Trinity); Jesus Christ is Lord and Savior but not deity

KEY TEXTS
New World Translation of the Holy Scriptures (version of Bible; God's literal word)

WHERE
Worldwide, especially United States, Brazil

AFTERLIFE PROMISES
Soul dies with body, but some will be resurrected for life in post-Armageddon heaven or earthly paradise

CATEGORY
Abrahamic: Christian

WHAT IT IS
Founded in 1870s by Pennsylvania businessman as the one true Christian church; others had strayed from Bible's true teachings. Civilization is in its final days; soon ultimate battle of Armageddon will take place, after which 144,000 souls (the Great Crowd, all selected before 1935) will go to heaven to rule with Jehovah and Jesus, wicked will be destroyed, others will live forever in earthly paradise.

PERKS 

- Door-to-door witnessing good exercise; makes up for not being allowed to practice yoga (seen as Hindu practice)
- No division between clergy and laity; all baptized members considered ministers
- Intimate congregations, under 200 members
- Racial equality prized
- Religious exemption from military service
- Can use birth control

DRAWBACKS 

- Unreliable predictions: Armageddon slotted for 1914, 1918, 1920, 1925, and 1941; now just "soon"
- No such thing as "Once saved, always saved," so must live faithful life continuously; worst case, can be disfellowshipped
- Most holidays, including birthdays, Easter, Christmas, considered pagan and not celebrated
- No premarital or extramarital sex; divorce permitted only in cases of adultery

ACTIVITIES

- Full-immersion baptism
- Pledging allegiance only to Jehovah; no voting or political activity, joining Boy Scouts or Girl Scouts, or "worldly" associations
- Meetings 5 times a week
- Legal battles to defend religious needs; more Supreme Court cases than any other religion

PARAPHERNALIA

- *The Watchtower* and *Awake!* for door-to-door distribution
- While witnessing, suits for men, dresses or skirts for women
- Sturdy shoes and gel insoles for pavement pounding
- Thick skin to withstand repeated rejection

JESUS PEOPLE

RELIGION #39

WHAT IT IS

Remaining incarnation of 1960s and 1970s hippie counterculture Jesus movement, which emphasized contemporary Jesus music, free love of God (*agape*), and communal living, and appealed to disenfranchised in search of meaning. Founded in 1972, Jesus People is based in Chicago and promotes communal living as basic tenet of discipleship. Youth-oriented, edgy evangelism.

PERKS

- Members debt-free after giving all assets to group; members then work for group businesses, and group fully supports members
- Cool community businesses, including publishing, record label, T-shirt printing
- Puts on Cornerstone Festival, huge 5-day Christian rock extravaganza
- Services informal; more about being part of community
- Piercings, tattoos okay

DRAWBACKS

- Nickname "Jesus freak" has been around for more than 40 years
- 8 elders decide everything, including who shall marry, when procreation shall begin, how money is spent; dissent not appreciated
- Family oriented, but man is head and woman must defer
- Cannot get assets back if you decide to leave group
- No health insurance, worker's comp, Social Security

ACTIVITIES

- Maintaining living quarters
- Sunday services and monthly Communion
- Community outreach, including running women's shelter, pregnancy center, meals for homeless, home for seniors
- Grooving to Christian rock

PARAPHERNALIA

- *Cornerstone* magazine
- Custom-designed T-shirts from in-house printing company
- Dormitory rooms for singles, private rooms for married couples
- Signed, notarized JPUSA (Jesus People USA) covenant agreeing to all terms of membership

QUICK RATINGS:

Conversion Difficulty: 3 (of 5)

Time Commitment: 5 (of 5)

Cost: 5 (of 5)

New Friends: 500

PURPOSE OF LIFE

Live in communal atmosphere to incorporate discipleship and Christian spirituality in everyday life

DEITIES

God (Father, Son, Holy Spirit)

KEY TEXTS

Bible; *The Cost of Discipleship* by Dietrich Bonhoeffer

WHERE

Chicago

AFTERLIFE PROMISES

Final judgment, followed by heaven or hell (depending on whether you're saved); redeemed will live in eternal community in God's kingdom

CATEGORY

NRM: Christian Oriented

JEWS FOR JESUS

QUICK RATINGS:

Conversion Difficulty:
① ② ③ ④ ⑤

Time Commitment:
① ② ③ ④ ⑤

Cost:
① ② ③ ④ ⑤

New Friends:
75,000

PURPOSE OF LIFE

Accept Y'shua (Jesus), live in accordance with God's laws, and prioritize direct Jewish evangelism

DEITIES

God: Father (Abba), Son (HaBen), Holy Spirit (Ruach HaKodesh)

KEY TEXTS

Bible; *Y'shua, the Jewish Way to Say Jesus* by Moishe Rosen

WHERE

Worldwide, primarily United States

AFTERLIFE PROMISES

Everlasting blessedness for saved, eternal punishment for unsaved

CATEGORY

Abrahamic: Judaism

WHAT IT IS

Founded by Moishe Rosen in 1973, composed of Jews who believe Jesus (Y'shua) is Jewish Messiah, promised to Jewish people in Old Testament. Nonmessianic Jews regarded as "unbelievers," converts as "completed Jews"; belief in Jesus necessary for salvation. Intensely evangelistic; strives to make Jesus an unavoidable issue to Jews and to draw support from Christians.

PERKS 

- Celebrate both Hanukkah and Christmas
- No need to convert to Judaism first
- Alleviates problem of whether to raise kids Christian or Jewish

DRAWBACKS 

- Both Christians and nonmessianic Jews will bear animosity toward you
- Lots of missionary work and proselytizing
- People will laugh at your T-shirt
- Cult accusations
- Not considered Jewish under Israel's Law of Return, so not entitled to Israeli citizenship
- Double the guilt: Jewish plus concept of inborn human sin

ACTIVITIES

- Communicating and evangelizing creatively (Rosen said, "It is a sin to bore people with the gospel")
- Traveling with Liberated Wailing Wall, mobile evangelistic music team
- Baptism

PARAPHERNALIA

- Star of David with cross in middle
- Informational pamphlets called broadsides (8 million hand-distributed per year)
- "Jesus Made Me Kosher" travel mugs
- Special Jews for Jesus Christmas cards, both paper and electronic versions

JOHN FRUM

WHAT IT IS

Cargo cult* on South Pacific island of Tanna. Legend of John Frum, black American soldier deity who lives in island's volcano, originated in 1930s when American troops built army base, bringing goods and jobs, fulfilling prophecy that peace and prosperity would arrive by air and sea. Followers attempt to bring back prosperity and John Frum by reenacting original scenarios.

*See page 121

PERKS 

- Men get to dress as American troops and march in formation with fake bamboo rifles
- Savior's return (John Frum's reemergence from volcano) off only by decades, not 2,000 years
- John Frum supports return to custom (*kastom*) ways, rebellion against early-20th-century Presbyterian missionaries
- Party—with Coca-Cola, cigarettes, chocolate, etc.—when John Frum returns, not Judgment Day

DRAWBACKS 

- Hard labor building piers and landing strips to entice John Frum's return
- Clashes with non-Frum Christian islanders over drinking, dancing, swearing, polygamy

ACTIVITIES

- Celebrating John Frum Day every February 15
- Decorating buildings with Red Cross symbol (many World War II supplies arrived via Red Cross)
- Wantonly spending European money both to get rid of Europeans and because John Frum will provide; also, allowing gardens to die because John Frum will provide

PARAPHERNALIA

- Flags of United States, Marines, and Georgia
- Bamboo flutes for playing "Star-Spangled Banner"

QUICK RATINGS:

Conversion Difficulty: ① ② ③ ④ ⑤ (5)

Time Commitment: ① ② ③ ④ ⑤ (5)

Cost: ① ② ③ ④ ⑤ (1)

New Friends: 2,500

PURPOSE OF LIFE

Prepare for John Frum's return with sympathetic, or imitative, magic (reenactments of original arrival); embrace native traditions and forgo the ways of Christian missionaries

DEITIES

Yasur (God), also name of sacred volcano; John Frum

KEY TEXTS

None; oral tradition

WHERE

Island of Tanna, Republic of Vanuatu

AFTERLIFE PROMISES

Spirits of dead go to live with God in heaven, where God is continually making cargo and there are no shortages

CATEGORY

NRM: Cargo Cult

JUCHE

RELIGION #42

QUICK RATINGS:

Conversion Difficulty:
① ② ③ ④ ⑤ 

Time Commitment:
① ② ③ ④ ⑤ 

Cost:
① ② ③ ④ ⑤ 

New Friends:
23 million

PURPOSE OF LIFE
Control one's own destiny by supporting government and leaders to exclusion of all other values and beliefs

DEITIES
None, but Kim Il Sung ("Eternal President") turns pinecones into bullets and walks on water

KEY TEXTS
Works by Kim Il Sung and Kim Jong Il

WHERE
North Korea

AFTERLIFE PROMISES
No heaven or hell, just productive life in North Korea

CATEGORY
NRM: Political Religion

WHAT IT IS
Official political religion of North Korea; created in 1955 by postwar leader Kim Il Sung to replace Marxism-Leninism. Juche draws on Stalinism, Neo-Confucianism, and Maoism. Asserts that individual is master of own destiny. Kim Jong Il, current leader and founder's son, has final say in all interpretations of Juche and has combined it with an "army first" policy.

PERKS 
- Sense of belonging—Juche stresses that nation-state will exist for all time, always populated by Koreans
- Spared responsibility of making own decisions
- Unique calendar begins with year of Kim Il Sung's birth
- Exclusively good news about religion (North Korea is most censored country in world)
- Many mandatory state-sponsored celebrations

DRAWBACKS 
- Dissension, free speech, interpretation of Juche philosophy all forbidden
- Only religion option in North Korea
- Must worship statues, images of Kim Jong Il

ACTIVITIES
- Participating in military parades
- Celebrating Kim Il Sung's birthday and date of death
- Practicing tae kwon do
- Bowing to 90-foot statue of Kim Il Sung in capital city
- Singing anticapitalism songs
- Loving North Korea

PARAPHERNALIA
- North Korean flag
- Pictures of leaders
- Nuclear weapons

JUDAISM

RELIGION #43

WHAT IT IS

Original Abrahamic religion, established around 2000 BCE by direct covenant between God and Abraham. God promised good life to all who followed his laws and Ten Commandments. Both culture and religion, Judaism ranges from liberal Reform movement (most American Jews) to ultra-orthodox Hasidism. Intellectual foundation; rabbis (spiritual leaders) not priests but teachers.

PERKS

- Get to be one of the chosen people
- Hanukkah presents given 8 nights in a row
- Matzoh ball soup (Jewish penicillin)
- Spice up conversation with Yiddish phrases
- Many degrees of observance and religiosity to choose from
- Rich tradition of humor and storytelling
- Independent thought, questioning, debate encouraged

DRAWBACKS 

- Mandatory circumcision if male
- Lobster and bacon not kosher
- Turns out there are actually 613 commandments
- Lots of splitting hairs over correct behavior
- Time-consuming and challenging to convert
- Jewish guilt

ACTIVITIES

- Celebrating Passover, Rosh Hashanah, Yom Kippur, Hanukkah
- Getting bar or bat mitzvahed
- Learning Hebrew
- Eating latkes, brisket, *charoset* (apple mixture meant to resemble ancient brick mortar)
- Finding love on JDate.com

PARAPHERNALIA

- Torah scrolls
- Yarmulkes
- Dreidels
- Menorahs
- Matzoh
- Sukkot huts
- Star of David jewelry
- Bagels, lox, and Sunday *New York Times*

QUICK RATINGS:

Conversion Difficulty:
① ② ③ ④ ⑤

Time Commitment:
① ② ③ ④ ⑤

Cost:
① ② ③ ④ ⑤

New Friends:
15 million

PURPOSE OF LIFE

Grow closer to God by interpreting, understanding, and obeying his rules as given to Moses and elaborated on in the Torah

DEITIES

Yahweh, all-powerful and transcendent

KEY TEXTS

Tanakh (Hebrew Bible, AKA Old Testament), especially Torah, first 5 books; Talmud

WHERE

Worldwide, primarily North America, Israel

AFTERLIFE PROMISES

Most Judaism does not focus on afterlife; some followers believe in sort of reincarnation, *gilgul*, transmigration of soul

CATEGORY

Abrahamic: Judaism

KABBALAH

RELIGION #44

QUICK RATINGS:

Conversion Difficulty:

Time Commitment:

Cost:

New Friends:
90,000

PURPOSE OF LIFE

Through study of Torah secrets, generate rather than merely receive own spiritual light and discover own Ein Sof within

DEITIES

Ein Sof, infinite omnipresence

KEY TEXTS

Torah; Zohar; Bahir; Sefer Yetzirah

WHERE

United States, Israel, Europe, Russia

AFTERLIFE PROMISES

Differing views: soul judges itself before moving on to realm of light; traditional Jewish *gilgul*; or messianic world to come (Olam-Ha-Ba)

CATEGORY

Abrahamic: Judaism

WHAT IT IS

Esoteric tradition of Jewish mysticism. Purports to reveal God's oral law—true meanings of unwritten Torah—passed down from Moses. Followers attempt to understand nature of God, pantheistically described as "no-thing without end" (Ein Sof). Teacher-driven tradition studies hidden messages of Torah, creation, and God through numerology, meditation, prayer.

PERKS 

- No commandments or prohibitions; instead, positive vs. negative energy, light vs. dark
- Solution oriented for modern lifestyle
- No need to convert to Judaism or leave current religion
- Humans are works in progress, capable of constant renewal; can work through pain and achieve freedom from our own egos, aligning ourselves with God's essence—AKA the Great Work

DRAWBACKS 

- Current trendy forms viewed as insubstantial by scholars and those of deep Jewish faith; traditionally, Kabbalah only for the very advanced
- Red string tied around left wrist to protect from negative energy of evil eye looks declassé with evening wear
- Hasn't worked very well for Britney Spears, Paris Hilton
- Hard to remember all 72 secret names of God

ACTIVITIES

- Taking Kabbalah classes
- Using Sefirot (tree of life) symbol to understand 10 aspects of God and levels of creation
- Celebrating Hanukkah as triumph of light over darkness
- Meditating on 72 secret names of God
- Finding and making *tikkun* (karmic corrections)

PARAPHERNALIA

- Talismans for protection, luck, healing, love, etc.
- Healing cups engraved with Kabbalist names
- Inspiration oil, candles, incense
- Kabbalah mountain spring water
- CDs and books on such topics as numerology, astrology, immortality, prosperity

KEMETIC RECONSTRUCTIONISM

WHAT IT IS

Literal re-creation of ancient Egyptian beliefs, culture, and practices, based on scholarly research, dating to 1970s. Followers uphold *ma'at* (honor and balance, "Perfection that was creation before it started to accumulate dust") and fight *isfet* (destructive disorder and impurity) in constantly self-renewing universe. Rituals to communicate with gods (Netjer) and venerate ancestors (*akhu*).

PERKS

- Mummification no longer practiced; photographs now suffice
- Can be practiced online
- Get to have a rootname, name of god associated with your birth month
- Cool outfits

DRAWBACKS 

- Lots of historical and linguistic study
- Moral code, the "Declaration of Innocence," has 42 rules, including not stealing the cakes of a child
- Pronunciation difficult, as many words lack vowels, e.g., *zptpy*, *shmsw*, *ntjrwy*
- Must take pre-ritual purification baths in natron, homemade combo of baking soda and salt
- Very hierarchical, with elected pharaohs and multiple levels of priesthood

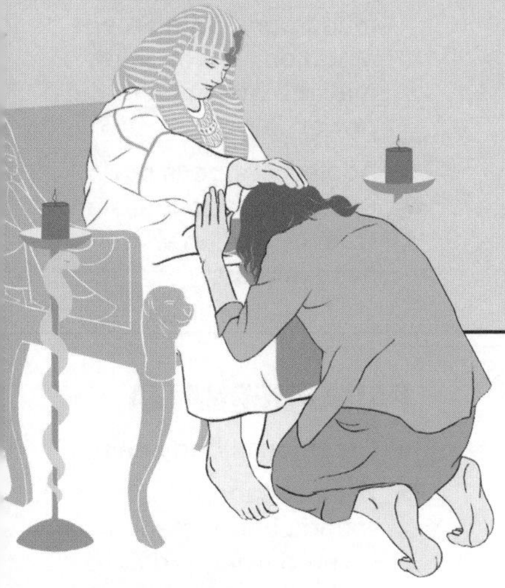

ACTIVITIES

- *Saq*, trance communication with Netjer
- Ceremonies for personal devotion, ancestor worship, rootnaming, etc.
- Using "Em hotep!" greeting

PARAPHERNALIA

- Wrist tattoos designed to look like bracelets
- Ankh pendants and scarab rings
- Clay pots for holding notes to ancestors
- Household altars, placed inside cabinet (gods prefer privacy) and containing candle, incense, and 2 bowls (one for water, one for offerings)

QUICK RATINGS:

Conversion Difficulty:

① ② ③ ④ ⑤

Time Commitment:
① ② **③** ④ ⑤

Cost:
① **②** ③ ④ ⑤

New Friends:
700

PURPOSE OF LIFE

Understand and adhere to ancient Egyptian practices and ethics (especially ma'at) in present-day society

DEITIES

Netjer, one God who manifests as individual gods such as Isis, Osiris, etc.

KEY TEXTS

"Declaration of Innocence" and Wisdom Texts, both translated from original Egyptian

WHERE

United States, online

AFTERLIFE PROMISES

Vary; some hold ancient Egyptian belief in tests that either transform spirits into akhu or send them to be eaten by monster Ammit

CATEGORY

NRM: Neo-Pagan

LAKOTA

RELIGION #46

QUICK RATINGS:

Conversion Difficulty:	① ② ③ ④ ⑤ (5)
Time Commitment:	① ② ③ ④ ⑤ (3)
Cost:	① ② ③ ④ ⑤ (2)
New Friends:	60,000

PURPOSE OF LIFE

Walk in beauty, balance, and intuition along path of Wakan Tanka; care for Mother Earth

DEITIES

Wakan Tanka, the Great Spirit

KEY TEXTS

None; oral tradition

WHERE

North Dakota, South Dakota

AFTERLIFE PROMISES

Souls spend one year as ghosts then split into 4 parts; one part follows Milky Way to afterlife, where ancestors and buffalo live traditionally, while other 3 parts reincarnate

CATEGORY

Indigenous: Native American

WHAT IT IS

One of 7 great branches of Sioux Nation. Force called Wakan Tanka breathes life, permeates and binds all, while other deities are nature based—sky, sun, etc. Until its decimation, buffalo was central to Lakota spiritual system; many rituals surrounded bravery and the hunt. Circle significant as sacred hoop, cycle of life. Seven sacred rites central to observance.

PERKS 

- Sense of seamless belonging within nature and universe, being part of dynamic whole
- Ongoing relationship with ancestral spirits
- Shamans available as bridges between spirit and human worlds
- Opportunity for purification in sweat lodge
- Ceremonies address useful ends, including healing, vision receiving, and soul keeping, all bound by smoking of sacred pipe

DRAWBACKS 

- Because faith has been exploited and misrepresented, Lakota are very wary of converts, especially New Age seekers
- Sacred Black Hills have been irrevocably scarred by uranium mining
- For women, isolation mandatory during menstruation, as condition may rob holy men of their power
- Adolescent boys must undergo arduous Vision Quests, fasting wilderness retreats

ACTIVITIES

- Sun Dance, most important spiritual ceremony, elaborate annual multi-day festival to offer bodies and souls to Wakan Tanka; consists of singing, drumming, dancing, piercing
- Smudging, cleansing of energy by burning of sage, tobacco, sweetgrass

PARAPHERNALIA

- Ceremonial body paints
- Drums, sacred for their round shape; made from revered 4-legged animals; drumbeat is spirit of animal
- Flat rocks, water, ladles for sweat lodges
- Tobacco for offerings
- Dreamcatchers, circular webs for sifting good from bad in dreams

MANDAEANISM

RELIGION #47

WHAT IT IS

Small Gnostic offshoot of Judeo-Christian belief system dating to 100 BCE. Followers believe they are direct descendants of Adam, who transmitted mystical teachings. Prophets are Adam, Noah, and John the Baptist, but not Abraham, Moses, Jesus, or Muhammad. Frequent baptism. Dualistic cosmology—good and evil, dark and light. Astrology significant.

PERKS

- Women equal to men; human soul seen as female
- Family life is top priority
- Lots of secret symbols and metaphors
- Special language (Mandaic) good for secrets
- Interest on loans is sinful
- No celibacy (but sexual license forbidden)
- On night of 6th day of 1st month, pious man may be granted anything he wishes
- Circumcision prohibited

DRAWBACKS

- Must be born to Mandaean mother
- No alcohol, tattoos, piercings, red meat
- Dipping hand in river on New Year's Day brings bad luck
- Not good for loose-lipped individuals; divulging teachings and rites is sinful
- Persecution by Iraqis and civil exclusion in Iran

ACTIVITIES

- Praying while facing north, toward gate to heaven
- Frequent, elaborate baptismal rites for purification and health
- Astrological readings
- Celebrating Springtime Panja, one of holiest holidays, with baptismal river feast
- Wearing white clothes

PARAPHERNALIA

- *Resta*, white clothing representing light of God
- White headband worn under hat by priests
- Rings (*sum yawar*) worn on little finger of right hand
- Bottles of baptismal oil

QUICK RATINGS:

Conversion Difficulty:

Time Commitment:

Cost:

New Friends:
70,000

PURPOSE OF LIFE

Follow teachings of Adam and commandments of John in order to return to Gate of Abathur to enter paradise

DEITIES

Mana Rba Kabira, Lord of Creation; *natri* (guardian spirits)

KEY TEXTS

Ginza (Book of Adam); Sidra d'Yahia (Book of John); Qulasta (Canonical Prayer-book)

WHERE

Jordan, Syria, Iran, Iraq

AFTERLIFE PROMISES

After exile on earth, souls return to realm of light, stop at various planes, then live eternally with God in paradise

CATEGORY

Esoteric

THEY'RE ALL THE SAME

It's easy to obsess over what religion to choose—after all, it's a decision with enormous consequences. Fortunately, most, if not all, religions are paths to the same destination, a fact often cited by religion cynics but actually rather useful for the aspiring adherent. In a world divided by religious conflict, those who maintain that theirs is the only true faith not only limit their choices but can also endanger others with their didactic zealotry and, in some cases, violence. Fortunately, once you scratch beneath the surface, you will find many similar spiritual underpinnings—in particular, what's known in Christianity as the Golden Rule.

ANCIENT EGYPTIAN

Do for one who may do for you, that you may cause him thus to do.

—"THE TALE OF THE ELOQUENT PEASANT," CA. 1800 BCE, EARLIEST WRITTEN VERSION

BAHA'I

Blessed is he who prefers his brother before himself.

—TABLETS OF BAHÁ'U'LLÁH

BUDDHISM

Hurt not others in ways that you yourself would find hurtful.

—UDANAVARGA

CHRISTIANITY

Do unto others as you would have them do unto you.

—NEW TESTAMENT

CONFUCIANISM

What you do not wish upon yourself, extend not to others.

—ANALECTS

ISLAM

No one of you is a believer unless he desires for his brother what he desires for himself.

—IMAM NAWAWI, FORTY HADITH

JAINISM

In happiness and suffering, in joy and grief, we should regard all creatures as we regard our own self.

—LORD MAHAVIRA, 24th TIRTHANKARA

JUDAISM

What is hateful to you, do not do to your fellow man. That is the whole of the law, the rest is commentary.

—TALMUD

NATIVE AMERICAN

All things are our relatives; what we do to everything, we do to ourselves. All is really One.

—BLACK ELK

SCIENTOLOGY

Try to treat others as you would want them to treat you.

—L. RON HUBBARD, *THE WAY TO HAPPINESS*

SECULAR HUMANISM

Humanists acknowledge human interdependence, the need for mutual respect, and the kinship of all humanity.

—DECLARATION OF HUMANIST PRINCIPLES

SHINTO

Be charitable to all beings, love is the representative of God.

—KO-JI-KI HACHIMAN KASUGA

SIKHISM

Don't create enmity with anyone as God is within everyone.

—GURU ARJAN DEV JI,
ADI GRANTH

TAOISM

Regard your neighbor's gain as your own gain, and your neighbor's loss as your own loss.

—T'AI-SHANG KANG-YING P'IEN

UNITARIAN UNIVERSALISM

We affirm and promote respect for the interdependent web of all existence of which we are a part.

—THE UNITARIAN PRINCIPLE

WICCA

An it harm no one, do what ye will.

— WICCAN REDE

YORUBA

One who is going to take a pointed stick to pinch a baby bird should first try it on himself to feel how it hurts.

—PROVERB

ZOROASTRIANISM

That nature alone is good which refrains from doing unto another whatsoever is not good for itself.

—DADISTAN-I DINIK

☞ WORLD RELIGION DAY

In 1949, the governing body of the Baha'i faith declared the first World Religion Day, to be observed annually on the 3rd Sunday in January. The holiday is now celebrated among many faiths around the globe. Following is the holiday's manifesto:

The aim of World Religion Day is to foster the establishment of interfaith understanding and harmony by emphasizing the common denominators underlying all religions. The message of World Religion Day is that mankind, which has stemmed from one origin, must now strive towards the reconciliation of that which has been split up. Human unity and true equality depend not on past origins, but on future goals, on what we are becoming and whither we are going. The prime cause of age-old conflict between man and man has been the absence of one ethical belief, a single spiritual standard—one moral code.

The history of man's cultures and civilizations is the history of his religions. Nothing has such an integrating effect as the bond of common faith. The history of religion shows that all religions had this unifying power—the power to instill in the hearts and minds of their adherents the fundamental verities, the vital spiritual standards, and thus establish a unity of conscience for motivating man toward founding great cultures and civilizations.

Thus, through World Religion Day observances, dedicated toward encouraging the leaders and followers of every religion to acknowledge the similarities in each of our sacred faiths, a unified approach to the changes that confront humanity can be agreed upon and then applied on an ever-expanding scale to permeate the very psyche of mankind, so that it can be made to see the whole Earth as a single country and humanity its citizenry.

MASAI

QUICK RATINGS:

Conversion Difficulty:	① ② ③ **④** ⑤
Time Commitment:	① ② **③** ④ ⑤
Cost:	① **②** ③ ④ ⑤
New Friends:	883,000

PURPOSE OF LIFE
Continue pastoral tradition by living and honoring ancient rituals; remain connected to one another

DEITIES
Enkai

KEY TEXTS
None; oral tradition

WHERE
Kenya, Tanzania

AFTERLIFE PROMISES
Evil people are carried away to desert while benevolent go to land rich in pastures and cattle

CATEGORY
Indigenous: African

WHAT IT IS
African group of nomadic cattlemen that believe in one God (Enkai) who has 2 manifestations: good and angry. All cattle, originally owned by Enkai, were lowered from sky for followers to oversee. Adherents continue to claim rightful ownership of any and all cattle. *Laiboni*, powerful spiritual leaders, play key role in rituals, healing, divination, offerings, and giving advice.

PERKS 
- Permanent guardian spirit stays with you even after death
- Medicine men cure with herbs
- When cow's blood is imbibed to make body stronger, okay to mix in a little milk
- Get to return to nature, living in hut made of twigs, dung, urine, skins

DRAWBACKS 
- Tending cows only acceptable occupation
- Ground may not be broken because grass is sacred for feeding cows
- Women circumcised

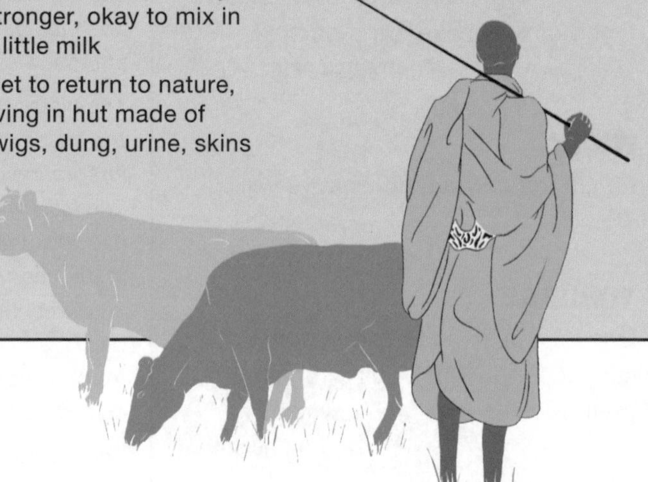

ACTIVITIES
- Blessing cows with grass
- Sacrificing cattle at rituals to be closer to Enkai
- Hunting with spears as rite of passage (men)
- Making colorful beads and jewelry (women)

PARAPHERNALIA
- Disks for ear piercing
- Hair plaits
- Heavy iron necklaces
- Wild fig (symbol of life) to make bark cloth
- Official color: red

MAYA

WHAT IT IS

Contemporary renditions of ancient practices merged with 16th-century Catholicism for distinctive blend of shamanism and Christianity. Multiple deities, both ancient gods and Christian saints, each with different roles. Emphasis on duality (night/day, life/death), nature, and ancestor veneration. Worship in churches and nature shrines. Shamanic healing and divination.

PERKS

- No more human sacrifice
- Astonishing history of architecture, mathematics (including invention of zero), timekeeping
- Shamans can cure sickness both mental and physical, often caused by angry ancestors; frequently cured by transferring ailment into a chicken, whose neck is then broken
- Can induce rain by praying to the god Chac and John the Baptist

DRAWBACKS

- Birthdays celebrated only every 52 years
- Have to make offerings to gods such as chickens, candles, liquor, incense, honey
- Lots of hiking required: mountains considered sacred areas (close to heaven); main pilgrimage to Naj Tunich painted cave requires 10- to 15-mile walk
- World to end in 2012

ACTIVITIES

- For Holy Week processions, creating *alfombras* (carpets) with Mayan symbols out of objects like fruit, vegetables, flowers
- Celebrating Day of the Dead, when ancestors return from Underworld for one-day family reunion
- Visiting cave stalagmite revered as the Black Christ, or Señor de Tila

PARAPHERNALIA

- Beautiful traditional woven cotton textiles
- *Huipiles*, women's cotton blouses embroidered with pre-Columbian designs
- *Aguardiente*, sugarcane brandy or rum to help shamans enter trances
- *Tzolkin*, 260-day sacred calendar
- Carvings and dolls of gods and saints

QUICK RATINGS:

Conversion Difficulty:

① ② ③ ④ ⑤

Time Commitment:

① ② ③ ④ ⑤

Cost:

① ② ③ ④ ⑤

New Friends:
6 million

PURPOSE OF LIFE

Follow some practices of Catholicism; also, live in harmony with rhythms of universe, explain nature's forces, satisfy gods

DEITIES

Include Hunab Ku, creator god; Kukulcán; Maximón; Chac; Christian holy trinity

KEY TEXTS

Popol Vuh; Dresden, Paris, Madrid codices

WHERE

Guatemala, Mexico, Belize

AFTERLIFE PROMISES

Unless death caused by sacrifice, childbirth, or suicide, go to Xibal (Underworld); Cizin, ruler of Underworld, known as the Flatulent One

CATEGORY

Indigenous: Native American

MORMONISM

QUICK RATINGS:

Conversion Difficulty:
① ② **③** ④ ⑤

Time Commitment:
① ② ③ **④** ⑤

Cost:
① ② ③ ④ **⑤**

New Friends:
11 million

PURPOSE OF LIFE
Show obedience to will of God and to Jesus Christ by adhering to church's commandments, sacraments

DEITIES
Three separate entities: God, perfected man with physical body; son, Jesus Christ; Holy Spirit

KEY TEXTS
Bible; Book of Mormon; *Doctrine and Covenants* and *Pearl of Great Price* by Joseph Smith

WHERE
Worldwide, primarily United States

AFTERLIFE PROMISES
Life is eternal; different levels of heaven based on life conduct

CATEGORY
Abrahamic: Christian

WHAT IT IS
Church of Jesus Christ of Latter-Day Saints, founded in 1830 by Joseph Smith, who was led by angel Moroni to buried golden plates in upstate New York inscribed with Book of Mormon (plates then disappeared). Believes Christianity corrupted after early apostles and must be restored to "latter days." No original sin. Individuals can receive revelations. Emphasis on afterlife, Second Coming.

PERKS

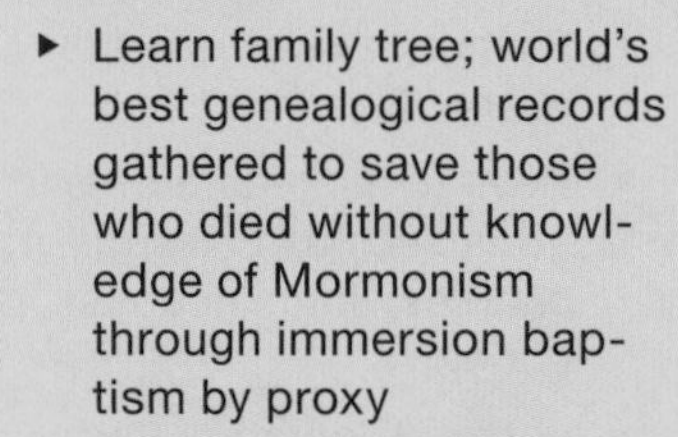

- Learn family tree; world's best genealogical records gathered to save those who died without knowledge of Mormonism through immersion baptism by proxy
- Known for business acumen and work ethic
- Save money by avoiding daily Starbucks habit: no coffee or tea allowed
- All married men get to be priests (though unpaid)
- All church leaders are prophets

DRAWBACKS

- 10 percent of income tithed to church
- Mandatory 2-year missionary service for adult males
- Men are priests of the home; women must defer to husbands
- Spouses and family members are sealed for eternity
- Homosexuality, masturbation, abortion, premarital sex prohibited
- Plural marriage (polygamy) forbidden since 1890

ACTIVITIES
- Proselytizing door-to-door and traveling abroad for missionary service
- Monthly fasting on Fast Sunday, Sunday church worship, weekly Family Home Evenings, prayer circles
- Patterning one's life after examples set by Heavenly Mother and Father
- Abundant procreation

PARAPHERNALIA
- Beehive symbol to represent industriousness
- Temple garment, sacred long johns worn by endowed adults as protection against temptation and evil and expression of commitment to Jesus Christ (AKA "angel chaps")
- No crosses (focus on resurrection rather than crucifixion)

NATION OF ISLAM

WHAT IT IS

African American Muslim movement, started in Detroit in 1930 by Wallace Fard, Allah in human form. Popularized by Elijah Muhammad, Malcolm X, Louis Farrakhan. Preaches that original humans were black, then scientist Yakub created white people, whom Allah allowed to rule for 6,000 years, until 1914. Now is time for blacks to resurrect from slavery through separatist self-reliance.

PERKS

- Sense of community pride from self-reliance, strong values
- Get new name
- While no afterlife, there is resurrection when "mentally dead so-called Negroes" come to their senses
- Black nation, God's chosen people, will inherit earth

DRAWBACKS

- If white, you're "blue-eyed devil"; also, anti-Semitism
- Cooked food only; vegetarianism recommended; no pork
- Desired goal of getting own state unlikely

ACTIVITIES

- Praying 5 times daily
- Friday-night group prayer (*Jumah*) in mosques
- Celebrating 2 Savior's Days, Elijah Muhammad's and Wallace Fard's birthdays
- Ramadan fasting
- For some, participating in Fruit of Islam, internal security force

PARAPHERNALIA

- Prayer rugs, beads
- Nation of Islam flag
- For men, cool suits, hats, bow ties
- For women, *hijabs* (head coverings), modest dress (no makeup)
- *Final Call* newspaper

QUICK RATINGS:

Conversion Difficulty:
① ② ③ **④** ⑤

Time Commitment:
① ② ③ **④** ⑤

Cost:
① **②** ③ ④ ⑤

New Friends:
50,000

PURPOSE OF LIFE

Struggle to bring into being a new world, breaking with racist past and uniting all of humanity under Allah

DEITIES

Allah, including incarnation as Wallace Fard

KEY TEXTS

Qur'an

WHERE

United States

AFTERLIFE PROMISES

No afterlife

CATEGORY

NRM: Islam Oriented

NATIVE AMERICAN CHURCH

QUICK RATINGS:

Conversion Difficulty:
① ② ③ ④ ⑤ (4)

Time Commitment:
① ② ③ ④ ⑤ (3)

Cost:
① ② ③ ④ ⑤ (2)

New Friends:
250,000

PURPOSE OF LIFE

Live moral life according to Peyote Road dogma: brotherly love, family care, self-support, avoidance of alcohol

DEITIES

Great Spirit (God); Peyote Spirit (Jesus); other spirits such as thunderbird carry prayers between humans and God

KEY TEXTS

For some groups, Bible; Native American elements via oral tradition

WHERE

North America, Mexico

AFTERLIFE PROMISES

Differing views: reincarnation, returning as spirit or ghost, or heaven and hell

CATEGORY

NRM: Native American and Entheogen Oriented

WHAT IT IS

Pan-Indian religious movement, founded as church in 1918 to unify Native Americans from different tribes; now largest Native American religious organization. Fuses general Native American spirituality with Christianity (to varying degrees) and peyotism (sacramental use of hallucinogenic peyote cactus for spiritual growth). Also stresses responsibility, family, alcohol avoidance.

PERKS 

- 10,000 years of peyote use suggests no ill health effects
- Communion breakfast served after 12-hour (8:00 AM to 8:00 PM) peyote ritual
- Combine nature spirits and Jesus into one belief system

DRAWBACKS 

- Constant government attempts to criminalize sacrament
- Sacrament tastes bitter
- Tepees can be claustrophobic while tripping
- Must be legally defined as Native American to use sacrament lawfully
- Native American faiths and Christian faiths alike disparage Native American Church as hodgepodge

ACTIVITIES

- Participating in Peyote Hunt (pilgrimage to collect sacred cactus); prior to hunt, must confess sins and undergo purification rituals; hunt may cover 500 miles
- During peyote ritual, praying, singing, drumming, reading from Bible, passing prayer cigarettes

PARAPHERNALIA

- Peyote, eaten or brewed into tea
- Prayer cigarettes, tobacco wrapped in corn husks
- Staffs of authority
- Feather fans, gourd rattles
- Tepees with sacred half-moon-shaped fireplaces

NAVAJO

WHAT IT IS

Traditional beliefs, based on creation of First Man and First Woman and progression through multiple coexisting worlds: 4 underworlds, present world, sky, and land beyond the sky. Two types of beings: Earth People and Holy People, who taught Earth People how to maintain order, balance, and harmony. All living things, including mountains and earth, have spirits and are connected.

PERKS

- Navajo among few tribes in United States who still reside on sacred ancestral land
- Divorce as simple as husband's returning to his mother's clan
- Each day brings new cycle, new lessons; dawn represents renewal and sunset chance to reflect
- Sweat lodges provide opportunities to purify mind, body, spirit, heart
- Animals and birds can serve as messengers or perform reconnaissance

DRAWBACKS 

- Difficult to convert; must have one-quarter Navajo blood to join
- No afterlife to motivate good deeds
- Misbehaving children are caught and eaten by Spider Woman (top of Spider Rock in Arizona is white because strewn with bones of bad children)
- Longtime suppression of Native American religion by American government; religious freedom only officially granted in 1978

ACTIVITIES

- More than 50 different rituals and ceremonies, with specific reasons and timing and lasting from hours to many days
- Chanting
- Creating sand paintings for use during ceremonies (destroyed afterward)
- Looking south upon awakening (south is direction of planning)

PARAPHERNALIA

- Incense to purify, heal, protect
- Cedar water and piñon needles to pour on hot rocks in sweat lodges
- Symbolic colors: white, blue, yellow, black, red
- 4 sacred stones, symbolizing 4 sacred mountains and cardinal directions: turquoise, white shell, abalone, black jet

QUICK RATINGS:

Conversion Difficulty:
① ② ③ ④ ⑤  (5 marked)

Time Commitment:
① ② ③ ④ ⑤ (4 marked)

Cost:
① ② ③ ④ ⑤ (2 marked)

New Friends:
300,000

PURPOSE OF LIFE

Tread *hozoji* (the beautiful path, AKA the Navajo way), maintaining harmony between nature, humans, deities, and the past

DEITIES

Creator, spiritual force permeating world and assuming many forms, including Sun God; Holy People

KEY TEXTS

None; oral tradition, though beliefs were transcribed in *The Navajo Texts* by ethnologist Pliny Earle Goddard

WHERE

New Mexico, Arizona, Utah

AFTERLIFE PROMISES

Little interest in afterlife; some believe soul goes to new part of universe to continue normal life

CATEGORY

Indigenous: Native American

LEFT VS. RIGHT: PATHS OF THE HANDS

Right-hand path and *left-hand path* are basic terms used to describe two dichotomous approaches to religion: in short, God-centered vs. self-centered. The terms originated with tantric practice, divided into *dakshinachara* and *vamachara*, Sanskrit words that literally mean "right-hand path" and "left-hand path." Followers of the left-hand path practiced rituals that fell outside mainstream Hindu beliefs, such as intoxication, animal sacrifice, and sex acts, while the right-hand path implied more sedate practices such as meditation, and used symbolic substitutions for the more outré rites.

In the West, "left-hand path" was first used by Helena Blavatsky, founder of Theosophy, in the late 19th century to describe religions she felt to be immoral. Followers of the left-hand path claim that theirs is the path of individuality, citing a parable in the book of Matthew: Christ returns for Judgment Day, sits on his throne, and places those who are bound for heaven on his right (the sheep, or followers) and those who are bound for hell on his left (the goats).

The terms are used primarily by followers of the left-hand path to distinguish their belief systems, rather than by the right-hand path or by religion scholars. Left-hand believers like to claim that theirs is the path for those who think and make decisions for themselves instead of following rules set down by others. Some who use the terms take a more balanced view and claim that the 2 paths are complementary, making for a balanced duality. In the broad sense, most mainstream religions could be characterized as adhering to the right-hand path.

So what will it be? Left or right? Goat or sheep? Dark or light? Compare and contrast:

LEFT-HAND TRAITS	RIGHT-HAND TRAITS
Leads inward; the only power glorified is personal power of individual.	Leads outward to higher power or deity with whom one can achieve eventual union.
Self is at center of own personal cosmology.	Self is small part of larger whole.
Trusts in human reason above emotion. Tends toward philosophical and rational analysis. Knowledge above all.	Trusts in faith above reason. Tends toward mysticism, feeling, intuition. Love above all.
Occult of hidden knowledge that can be shared only with select few.	Hidden knowledge is to be discovered, interpreted, and shared to make a better world for all.
No afterlife, so life must be lived and experienced fully.	Afterlife will be affected by deeds in this life.
Physical sensations should be explored and enjoyed.	Spiritual more important than physical; physical often denigrated.
Transformational magic performed for personal gain.	Prayer, meditation, and healing for personal salvation and for others.
Moral relativism: shades of gray.	Belief in absolutes: good and evil, black and white.

LEFT-HAND TRADITIONS	RIGHT-HAND TRADITIONS
Demonolatry	Christianity
Dragon Rouge	Druidism
Luciferianism	Hinduism
Satanism	Islam
Setianism	New Age
Shaktism	Shamanism
Temple of the Vampire	Wicca

Confused? Can't make up your mind? Thankfully, there's a Middle Path—that's how followers of Buddhism characterize their religion. Buddhism places a high value on rational thought and proof but also incorporates concepts of divine perfection to which we can aspire as an eventual reward. Practice Buddhism and, some adherents say, you really *can* have it all: chart your own moral course and still find your own individual path to the divine.

NEO-DRUIDISM

QUICK RATINGS:

Conversion Difficulty:

Time Commitment:

Cost:

New Friends:
15,000

PURPOSE OF LIFE
Adhere to ancient Celtic virtues such as honor and truth; revere nature and find spirituality in it; keep Celtic traditions alive

DEITIES
Celtic pantheon of gods

KEY TEXTS
The Mabinogion (medieval Celtic folklore); various works of history, anthropology, folklore

WHERE
United Kingdom, United States, Scandinavia

AFTERLIFE PROMISES
Reincarnation as human, animal, or plant, in either earthly world or Otherworld; ultimately reach highest realm, "the Source"

CATEGORY
NRM: Neo-Pagan

WHAT IT IS
Modern reconstruction of ancient polytheistic Celtic practices; since beliefs were transmitted orally for millennia, religion draws on scholarship of 18th-century Druid revival. Views humans as part of great web of creation, reveres nature and ecology. Promotes healing, divination, magic, creativity, and rituals honoring kinship, family, nature's rhythms.

PERKS 
- Environmentally friendly
- Rituals practiced in beautiful nature settings such as oak groves
- Fun festivals (8 per year) with home-brewed ale, mead, singing, storytelling, and lots of blessing

DRAWBACKS 
- Ample reading and research required
- Can never be sure whether practices are accurate to original
- *Druid* sounds like insult

ACTIVITIES
- Creating stone circles to worship around
- Celebrating solstices and equinoxes
- Making pilgrimages to Stonehenge
- Interpreting dreams

PARAPHERNALIA
- Sacred mistletoe and golden sickles with which to cut it down
- Cords for knot magic and measuring circles
- Celtic music

NEO-MANICHAEISM

WHAT IT IS

Revival of important religion, founded in 3rd century by Persian prophet Mani, who sought to create first universal religion, combining Christian, Zoroastrian, Buddhist, and Gnostic beliefs. Matter and darkness, not human sin, cause suffering. Humans are light spirits trapped in matter due to evil (biblical) God's creation of world. Path to salvation is through knowledge of Mani's teachings, not faith.

PERKS

- If you're anti-Christianity, you get to call biblical God evil; solves basic religious conundrum by recognizing that moral God would not have created suffering
- Can boast about explosive growth across Persian and Roman empires, western Europe, and western China in 4th and 5th centuries
- Sin not your fault; result of contact with matter
- No longer necessary to bathe in own urine

DRAWBACKS

- Emphasis on ascetic lifestyle: veganism, fasting, frequent and intense prayer rituals, some celibacy
- Struggle between good and evil is eternal; misery is inevitable
- Most of Mani's teachings were destroyed or exist only in fragments
- Must renounce world to achieve salvation
- Lonely—as few as 3 people dwell in contemporary "manistans" (monasteries or convents)

ACTIVITIES

- Observing total harmlessness in all areas of life
- Perform twelvefold bowing (prostration) prayers 4 times per day
- Singing hymns whenever possible
- Studying Mani's scriptures
- Getting baptized with oil (water is bad, product of matter)

PARAPHERNALIA

- Light-bearing foods, including melons, radishes
- Moonstones, described in ancient texts as "bright as the moon, the first of all gems"; also pearls
- White robes
- 2 sets of commandments, numbering 5 and 10

QUICK RATINGS:

Conversion Difficulty:
(1) (2) (3) (4) (5) — 1 marked

Time Commitment:
(1) (2) (3) (4) (5) — 5 marked

Cost:
(1) (2) (3) (4) (5) — 3 marked

New Friends:
1,000

PURPOSE OF LIFE
Become free of eternal cycle of death and rebirth—and thus matter—through morality and understanding

DEITIES
Father of Light; pantheon of gods, including Jesus the Splendor (not historical Jesus, who represents suffering); some include Mani

KEY TEXTS
Many text fragments

WHERE
United States, online

AFTERLIFE PROMISES
For those who attain true knowledge, leave earthly reincarnation cycle and live as light in paradise

CATEGORY
Revealed

NICHIREN BUDDHISM

QUICK RATINGS:

Conversion Difficulty: ① ② ③ ④ ⑤ (2)

Time Commitment: ① ② ③ ④ ⑤ (4)

Cost: ① ② ③ ④ ⑤ (2)

New Friends: 3.1 million

PURPOSE OF LIFE

Chant to achieve personal goals, world peace, enlightenment

DEITIES

Shu and Shoshu differ; Shu believes Sakyamuni (Siddhartha) is Eternal Buddha who foretold not-yet-arrived True Buddha (Maitreya); Shoshu believes Nichiren was True Buddha as predicted by Sakyamuni

KEY TEXTS

Lotus Sutra; Gosho, writings of Nichiren

WHERE

Primarily Japan, also United States

AFTERLIFE PROMISES

Chanting leads to nirvana on earth

CATEGORY

Dharmic: Buddhist

WHAT IT IS

Form of Mahayana Buddhism, established by 13th-century Japanese monk Nichiren. Recognized Lotus Sutra as essential truth, allowing all to reach enlightenment. Entails Three Great Dharmas: *honzon*, sacred Lotus Sutra mandala to gaze upon; *daimoku*, chanting; and *kaidan*, sacred place for *honzon*. Two main Nichiren schools, Shu and Shoshu, differ on key aspects.

PERKS 

- Chanting ensures happiness, prosperity
- Okay to chant for personal growth and gain
- Rather than relying on will of a god or Buddha, rely on self and Law of Cause and Effect: followers assured that chanting works because Nichiren tested it for 27 years before sharing it
- With Shu, get to be more mainstream and avail yourself of other Buddhist precepts that Shoshu does not follow

DRAWBACKS 

- Disagreements between Shu and Shoshu date back to 13th century
- Must chant daimoku, "Nam(u)-myoho-renge-kyo" (devotion to the Lotus Sutra), repetitively (Shoshu drops *u* after *nam*; Shu believes this is akin to dropping a Golden Buddha, as each syllable is revered)
- Followers expected to proselytize once they achieve understanding of Lotus Sutra
- Lots of practice and study

ACTIVITIES

- Gazing at Gohonzon scroll
- Attending temple ceremonies
- Morning and evening ceremonies at home
- Cleaning home altar and making offerings daily
- Studying Lotus Sutra and Gosho

PARAPHERNALIA

- Offerings of incense, prayers, and fresh flowers or evergreens for personal shrines
- *Mala* (prayer beads) for counting chants
- For Shu, statues of 4 bodhisattvas and Sakyamuni Buddha
- For Shoshu, special consecrated Dai-Gohonzon

OPUS DEI

RELIGION #57

WHAT IT IS

Opus Dei is Latin for "work of God," founded in Spain in 1928 by Josemaría Escrivá. Only "personal" (not tied to geographic area) prelature of Catholic Church. Path for devout lay Catholics to pursue Christian perfection. Strict, secretive, conservative. Most members—supernumeraries—married with careers; numeraries are celibate and may work for church and live communally.

PERKS

- Get to be in secret society, sometimes dubbed Church within the Church, Holy Mafia, or Rotary of God
- Perfect for masochists: sleep on wood board, forgo pillow once a month, pierce skin with cilice, self-flog, take daily cold shower, fast
- Male members can hang out in bars, smoke, drink to pick up recruits
- Better than mere Catholics

DRAWBACKS

- No eating between meals
- Detractors describe cult-like devotion and isolation from family members
- Rabidly antihomosexual
- Not good for independent thinkers: according to Escrivá, "You have come . . . to submit, to annihilate yourself, not to impose your own personal viewpoints"
- *Da Vinci Code* stigma

ACTIVITIES

- Jumping out of bed to kiss floor every morning ("Heroic Minute")
- Recruiting new members; recruiters referred to as "bait" or "Opie-bait"
- Conducting Plan of Life: daily Mass, daily prayer and meditation, Holy Communion, reciting rosary, using sacrament of penance, etc.

PARAPHERNALIA

- Cilices, spiked chains worn around thigh; disciplines, macramé-like cords for self-whipping
- Opus Dei–approved books (for example, Judy Blume is banned)

QUICK RATINGS:

Conversion Difficulty: ① ② ③ ④ ⑤ (3)

Time Commitment: ① ② ③ ④ ⑤ (4)

Cost: ① ② ③ ④ ⑤ (4)

New Friends: 87,000

PURPOSE OF LIFE

Pursue saintliness and divine filiation in everyday life and all endeavors

DEITIES

God (Father, Son, Holy Spirit)

KEY TEXTS

Navarre Bible; *The Way* by Josemaría Escrivá

WHERE

Worldwide, primarily Italy, Spain, Latin America

AFTERLIFE PROMISES

Standard Catholicism: die in state of grace, go to heaven; grace but venial sins, go to purgatory then heaven; mortal sins, go to hell

CATEGORY

NRM: Catholic Oriented

OSHO

RELIGION #58

QUICK RATINGS:

Conversion Difficulty:
① ② ③ ④ ⑤

Time Commitment:

Cost:
① ② ③ ④ ⑤

New Friends:
200,000

PURPOSE OF LIFE
Through meditation, find your center, learn to be alone; once totally alone, can find truth because *you* are the truth

DEITIES
God is in everyone, people are divine

KEY TEXTS
The Orange Book, *From Sex to Superconsciousness*, *Autobiography of a Spiritually Incorrect Mystic*, all by Osho

WHERE
Worldwide, primarily India

AFTERLIFE PROMISES
Death releases energy vibrations from entire life, felt by those nearby; vibrations of enlightened can linger for millennia

CATEGORY
NRM: Sex Oriented

WHAT IT IS
Movement begun in 1966 by Osho (AKA Bhagwan Shree Rajneesh), self-dubbed "anti-guru" infamous for infractions of sex, money, megalomania, drugs, cult conduct. Developed Osho Dynamic Meditation, designed to lead individuals to state of emptiness and "choiceless awareness" followed by enlightenment. Sex, "man's most vibrant energy," is another path to enlightenment.

PERKS 
- Wealth and spirituality not incompatible (asceticism is masochism)
- Meditation leads to good behavior so no need for formal code of conduct
- Existence is made of joy
- No sex restrictions after taking mandatory pre-ashram HIV test
- Active, cathartic meditation techniques (dancing, humming, hand movements, twirling, speaking gibberish, etc.) good for those who have trouble with silent meditation

DRAWBACKS 
- Negative associations with *Rajneeshi*, longtime name for followers
- Legal troubles dogged founder from Oregon to India; 1990 death possibly from drug overdose
- Ashram and following more mainstream now; less drugs, sex, etc. (however, also lighter on abusive, cultlike activities)
- Meditation can cause injury (must sign disclaimer); also, may feel initially worse as negative emotions emerge

ACTIVITIES
- Reading "No-Thought of the Day" on Osho.com
- Becoming Osho's "new man," Zorba the Buddha, combining Buddha's spirituality with Zorba the Greek's zest for life
- Following vegetarian diet
- Attending Humaniversity in the Netherlands
- Meditation camps

PARAPHERNALIA
- New names, with new titles: "Swami" for men, "Ma" for women
- For Osho International Meditation Resort and Multiversity in Pune, India, all maroon clothing, including bathing suits, robes, tennis garb
- Subscription to *Osho Times*
- Osho Zen tarot cards

PENTECOSTALISM

WHAT IT IS

Fast-growing global Christian evangelical movement, begun around 1900 in response to staid upper-class church services; followers desired less subdued, more personal experience of religion. Refers to day of Pentecost, when disciples spoke in tongues after being baptized in Holy Spirit; Pentecostals are baptized twice, once in water then later when spirit moves through them.

PERKS

- Get to experience presence of Jesus Christ through speaking in tongues, faith healing, holy laughter, falling to ground, etc.
- Exuberant services
- Miracles happen
- Clear-cut: Bible is infallible word of God
- Very popular; most contemporary of major Christian movements
- Ethnic, denominational, and socioeconomic diversity

DRAWBACKS

- Fire and brimstone
- In some churches, snake-handling fatalities
- Televangelism
- Sex and money scandals
- Moral conservatism (e.g., antihomosexuality)
- Many churches are modest storefronts that lack grandeur of stained glass and marble

ACTIVITIES

- Attending revivals; many held over course of a few days, often in tents
- Full-immersion water baptism
- Performing missionary work around the world
- Praying for prosperity in "Name It and Claim It" or "Health and Wealth" churches

PARAPHERNALIA

- Prayer cloths, prayed over by healers and applied to afflicted areas
- Tents, folding chairs
- Lozenges to soothe throats after services

QUICK RATINGS:

Conversion Difficulty: ① ② **③** ④ ⑤

Time Commitment: ① **②** ③ ④ ⑤

Cost: **①** ② ③ ④ ⑤

New Friends: 250 million

PURPOSE OF LIFE

Be cleansed of sins through baptism in the Holy Spirit in preparation for Second Coming of Jesus Christ

DEITIES

Some denominations believe in Holy Trinity, others only in Jesus Christ

KEY TEXTS

Bible, especially Acts of the Apostles

WHERE

Worldwide, primarily United States, South America, Africa

AFTERLIFE PROMISES

Ascend into heaven if saved; sinners go to hell

CATEGORY

Abrahamic: Christian

NEW AGE FOR A NEW AGE

New Age refers to a huge body of spiritual beliefs reinterpreted as alternative approaches to mainstream religion, especially Christianity. Steeped in Eastern, Native American, and Celtic influences, the movement skyrocketed during the 1960s and 1970s; the term "New Age," probably stemming from "Age of Aquarius," became popular in the late 1980s.

New Agers strive to achieve oneness with the universal life force, known to some as God. Most believe that each of us creates his or her own reality—positive energy attracts positive events and vice versa. To this end, followers take a holistic (mind, body, and spirit) approach to become as self-actualized as humanly possible and to reach their fullest potential (at least in this incarnation).

New Age is perfect for the do-it-yourselfer, as it comprises a smorgasbord of individualized activities. Due to their spiritual curiosity and commitment to self-actualization, New Agers are an education-oriented sort, frequently attending retreats and workshops. Devoted practitioners can turn their interests into lucrative careers as healers, channelers, authors, and so forth.

ASTROLOGY

Astrology, literally the "telling of the stars," interprets the movements of celestial bodies with the belief that they influence events, which is consistent with the New Age investment in nature as an active force. At least 5,000 years old, astrological belief systems developed independently around the world. Professional astrologers claim to provide accurate insights and forecasts based on birth dates, while laypersons may consult books and horoscopes for guidance.

CHANNELING

Channeling claims to connect individuals with divine figures, past lives, or spirits of the dead, usually with the help of a medium who enters a trancelike state to reach the otherworld. Once contact has been made, the spirit communicates through the channeler. The practice is sometimes combined with elements of psychotherapy or past-life regression to release blockages and heal emotional pain.

FENG SHUI

Drawn from Taoism, this ancient Chinese discipline attempts to bring harmony between people and their environments. Literally "wind-water," feng shui holds that the energy of the universe, *qi*, is carried by wind and held by water.

Believed to exert their qualities on inhabitants, spaces are examined for the ways in which they promote or block the flow of qi. Practitioners, called diviners, participate in site selection, building, and interior design using a special map and compass. To promote the well-being of inhabitants, objects are carefully situated and balanced by elements of water and reflection, and color and shape are deliberately applied.

HUMAN POTENTIAL MOVEMENT

An umbrella term advanced by Big Sur's Esalen Institute, HPM refers to a collection of therapeutic methods practiced in individual and group settings to advance self-awareness and spirituality. HPM holds that we were put on earth to achieve our fullest potential, but we have yet to tap the mind's many levels and powers. Therefore all HPM practices are designed to expand personal experience and awareness. Approaches include primal therapy, meditation, biofeedback, Gestalt psychotherapy, encounter groups, EST (Erhard Seminars Training), and hypnosis.

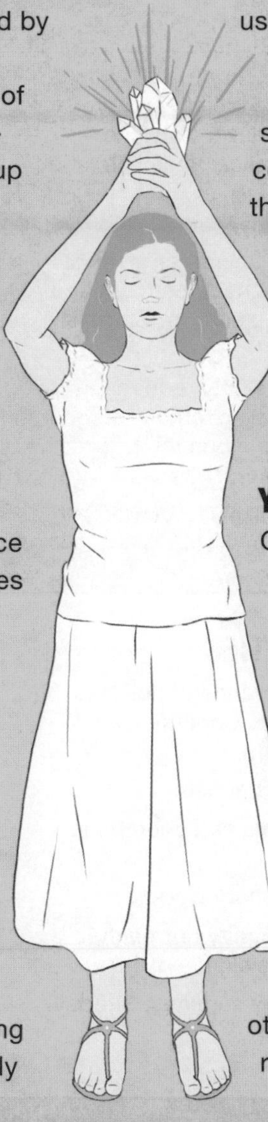

REBIRTHING

A therapeutic method that came to prominence in the 1970s, rebirthing consists of guided breathing exercises to process deeply held emotional suffering—especially the trauma caused by one's own birth. Pain is caused by the suppression of difficult memories, which, if not released, are held in the body as toxins and blockages. Called a "biological experience of God" by method pioneer Leonard Orr, the experience of reliving one's birth can take place in water or "in the dry."

TAROT

Tarot cards date to 15th-century Italy and contain symbols and archetypes used to describe character and predict the future. A tarot reader helps to interpret the cards' meaning for the seeker, or querent. Through the process of shuffling the deck, it is thought that the querent's energy is transmitted to the cards. Some believe that Tarot cards are guided by a spiritual force, while others feel their power is derived from their symbolism and its subconscious meaning to the querent.

YOGA

One of the 6 schools of Hindu philosophy, yoga (which means "yoke" in Sanskrit) seeks to free the self from the constraints of physical matter in order to achieve purity, consciousness, and bliss—a state known as *samadhi*, or liberation. The yogic process consists of eight "limbs," of which only one—*asana*—is the physical exercise most Westerners know. Breathing (*pranayama*) and meditation (*dhyana*) are 2 other aspects of yoga that have taken root in Western practice.

PROTESTANTISM

QUICK RATINGS:

Conversion Difficulty:

Time Commitment:

Cost:

New Friends:
382 million

PURPOSE OF LIFE

Seek salvation through faith in Jesus, sometimes by being "born again"; follow biblical codes of moral and ethical behavior

DEITIES

God (Father, Son, Holy Spirit), though some groups don't believe in Holy Trinity

KEY TEXTS

Bible, with emphasis on New Testament

WHERE

Worldwide

AFTERLIFE PROMISES

For most groups, saved go to heaven, unsaved go to hell; no purgatory

CATEGORY

Abrahamic: Christian

WHAT IT IS

Along with Roman Catholicism and Eastern Orthodoxy, one of 3 main branches of Christianity. Born of religious protest (hence its name) against Catholicism in 16th-century Europe, when church leaders such as Martin Luther denounced papacy, proclaiming God's will and faith in Christ (vs. good deeds or papal decrees) as sole sources of salvation and Bible as sole word of God.

PERKS 

- Many denominations to choose from, with widely varying beliefs and practices (basic divisions: evangelical, mainline, and progressive)
- Most have to perform only 2 sacraments (AKA ordinances), baptism and communion, vs. Catholicism's 7
- Faith is only requirement for heaven (catchy slogan: "Grace alone through faith alone")
- Least likely to be persecuted in West

DRAWBACKS 

- Eucharist is usually nonalcoholic
- Less pomp, circumstance, decor than Catholicism and Eastern Orthodoxy
- Being born a sinner can lead to self-esteem problems
- Church likes to involve itself in state
- Hypocrisy pitfall when "thy neighbor" not terribly lovable
- WASP repression
- Christian rock

ACTIVITIES

- Observance of holidays such as Christmas and Easter
- Water baptism
- Revivals and church picnics
- Missionary work
- Community outreach to poor, sick, needy
- Sunday services, Sunday school

PARAPHERNALIA

- Hymnals and prayer books
- Schools and universities; homeschooling curricula
- Many symbols, including cross, dove, fish, praying hands—available in all manner of tchotchkes
- Bumper stickers proclaiming religious faith
- Casseroles

WHAT IT IS

Began in 17th-century England as movement away from Anglican and Puritan structure and hypocrisy. God's Inward Light not mediated by church but revealed via direct personal experience during silent group meetings. No creed, sacred texts, rites, sacraments, clergy. Individual morality guided by conscience, informed by experience of inner light. Dedicated to pacifism and activism.

PERKS

- Who doesn't want to be a friend? Formally called Religious Society of Friends
- American Friends Service Committee won Nobel Peace Prize in 1947
- Get to use "Thee" and "Thou" because more egalitarian
- Don't have to swear oaths; would imply you were otherwise not truthful
- Committed to academic and intellectual endeavors
- No bans against drinking, divorce, birth control

DRAWBACKS

- No pomp or circumstance
- Simplicity in dress, nonmaterialism, and skepticism toward credit may turn off shoppers
- Silent meetings require patience
- No holidays

ACTIVITIES

- Weekly meetings, silent until spirit moves someone to speak
- Political and social activism, especially regarding peace, human rights, relief efforts
- Learning Quaker-speak: unique meanings for such terms as "weighty friend," "hold in the light," "lay down"

PARAPHERNALIA

- *Washington Newsletter*, monthly publication from Friends Committee on National Legislation
- Quaker hymnals

QUICK RATINGS:

Conversion Difficulty:

Time Commitment:

Cost:

New Friends:
350,000

PURPOSE OF LIFE

Experience Inward Light and live more fully in the light, making world better place as directed by conscience and concepts of simplicity, equality, integrity, peace

DEITIES

God, whose spirit is in everyone

KEY TEXTS

Bible as inspiration (not literal belief); *Faith and Practice*, annually published collective thinking on God's will for community

WHERE

Kenya, United States

AFTERLIFE PROMISES

Individuals determine own beliefs; however, no such thing as eternal punishment

CATEGORY

Abrahamic: Christian

RASTAFARI

QUICK RATINGS:
Conversion Difficulty: ① ② ③ ④ ⑤ (4)
Time Commitment: ① ② ③ ④ ⑤ (2)
Cost: ① ② ③ ④ ⑤ (3)
New Friends: 265,000

PURPOSE OF LIFE
Pursue freedom and individual path; respect all living things; promote reunification of black people in Africa (Zion); reject modern society (Babylon); worship Jah

DEITIES
Jah (God); Haile Selassie I, God's physical manifestation (Jesus)

KEY TEXTS
Sections of Bible; *Holy Piby* by Robert Athlyi Rogers; Kebra Negast, 14th-century Ethiopian holy book

WHERE
Jamaica

AFTERLIFE PROMISES
No afterlife; Africa is black heaven on earth

CATEGORY
NRM: African Diasporic

WHAT IT IS
Originated in Jamaica in 1930s. Posits late emperor Haile Selassie I of Ethiopia (original name: Ras Tafari) as Messiah (foretold by Jamaican activist Marcus Garvey) born to liberate blacks from white suppression. Ethiopia is holy land to which "downpressed" blacks from around world will return when Jah (God) finishes testing them, his chosen people. Underpinnings of Protestantism.

PERKS 
- Ritualized smoking of ganja, "wisdom weed" sanctified in Bible
- Select few will be "ever-living," alive forever in current bodies
- No need to cut or comb hair

DRAWBACKS 
- White people traditionally inferior and hated
- No pork, shellfish, unnatural foods (*I-tal* diet); some versions stricter, entirely vegetarian, or exclude alcohol and coffee
- No tattoos
- Women traditionally subordinated; birth control and abortion opposed by many followers
- Marijuana illegal in Jamaica, Ethiopia, and United States

ACTIVITIES
- "Reasoning" sessions, wisdom weed–fueled services of debates, prayer, chanting
- Days-long Nyabingi celebrations to mark Ethiopian new year
- Listening to reggae, dancing, drumming

PARAPHERNALIA
- Anything with symbolic red, green, and yellow palette of Ethiopian flag; black also significant
- For ganja smoking, ritual chalice (water pipe made from horn or wood)
- Lion to represent Haile Selassie I, Conquering Lion of Judah
- Long skirts and head coverings for women

ROMA

RELIGION #63

WHAT IT IS

Insular, nomadic people, Roma migrated from India to Europe between 11th and 15th centuries; called Gypsies because mistakenly thought to hail from Egypt. Religion combines those of host countries with Hindu and Roma worship. Focal points are avoiding *marimé* (pollution and impurity, especially from external world), evil spirits, and curses through elaborate rituals and occult practices.

PERKS

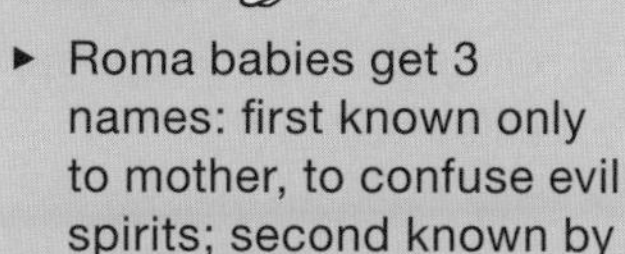

- Roma babies get 3 names: first known only to mother, to confuse evil spirits; second known by fellow Roma; third for use by *gadje* (outsiders)
- Can use curses, spells, omens, evil eye
- No dieting: weight sign of wealth, good luck; thin people believed to be poor, unfortunate
- Great music (Roma heavily influenced flamenco)
- Can make money telling fortunes to gadje

DRAWBACKS

- Impossible to convert; must be born into it
- Must be vigilant about avoiding evil spirits
- Arranged marriages, many under age 16
- No baths: stagnant water forbidden
- No pets: cats and dogs thought unclean
- Long history of persecution and discrimination
- Lower half of body viewed as impure
- Spittle considered curative

ACTIVITIES

- Cleanliness rituals to avoid marimé, involving water usage, food preparation and consumption, personal hygiene
- Curing sick, by *drabarni* (women healers)
- Conducting *kris*, community tribunals, that can result in banquets or banishment

PARAPHERNALIA

- *Trushul*, Roma cross
- Big pockets to carry mole's foot to cure rheumatism, hedgehog's foot for toothache, bread to protect against bad luck
- *Johai*, curative ghost vomit, found in garbage dumps
- To block evil spirits, ashes to plug babies' navels, wax for corpses' nostrils

QUICK RATINGS:

Conversion Difficulty: ① ② ③ ④ ⑤ (5)

Time Commitment: ① ② ③ ④ ⑤ (5)

Cost: ① ② ③ ④ ⑤ (2)

New Friends: 10 million

PURPOSE OF LIFE

Recognize *kuntari*, universal balance and order of things; live a pure, uncontaminated life, untouched by marimé

DEITIES

Devel (God), including shaktism, worship of female aspects of God; supernatural spirits, ghosts

KEY TEXTS

None; oral tradition

WHERE

Primarily Europe

AFTERLIFE PROMISES

Possible reincarnation as person or animal; living dead, *muló*, seek revenge on those who harmed them

CATEGORY

Indigenous

ROSICRUCIAN ORDER

QUICK RATINGS:

Conversion Difficulty:
① ② ③ ④ ⑤ (4)

Time Commitment:
① ② ③ ④ ⑤ (4)

Cost:
① ② ③ ④ ⑤ (3)

New Friends:
250,000

PURPOSE OF LIFE
Develop psychic abilities to attain Mastery of Life, one's full potential; achieve oneness with universal deity

DEITIES
Some believe in Universal Soul, others in tripartite God consisting of Will, Wisdom, and Activity

KEY TEXTS
Rosicrucian manifestos: *Fama Fraternitas, The Confessio,* and *The Chymical Marriage of Christian Rosenkreuz*; for some groups, Bible

WHERE
Worldwide, primarily United States, Europe, Brazil

AFTERLIFE PROMISES
Reincarnation, with ultimate goal of reuniting with God

CATEGORY
Esoteric

WHAT IT IS
Secretive Western tradition blending mysticism, metaphysics, and occult. Reportedly originated in ancient Egypt, later took root in medieval Europe. Mixes science, alchemy, philosophy, magic, and Christianity to understand life's meaning. Followers develop psychic and healing powers through rigorous study of ancient teachings. Has been linked to Masonry and Theosophy.

PERKS 
- Develop psychic abilities: telepathy, mental projection, metaphysical healing
- Get to participate in fraternal activities of Rosicrucian Lodges as well as learn secrets outsiders will never know
- Can study via correspondence coursework at home, at own pace
- Encourages doubt, open-mindedness, and not accepting anything based solely on faith
- Can practice other religions simultaneously

DRAWBACKS 
- Allegations of dangerous occultism
- Has been dismissed as elaborate hoax, with 17th-century *Fama Fraternitas* alleged as no more than satirical novel
- Intensive studies may take up to 5 years
- In some groups, use of special abilities to make money is frowned upon; membership not open to hypnotists, mediums, palm readers, astrologers
- Claims of paranormal powers unsubstantiated

ACTIVITIES
- Initiation rites upon completion of studies
- Harmonization rituals (meditating to harmonize with Grand Lodge Council of Solace)
- Participating in Rosicrucian Book Club
- Visiting Rosicrucian Egyptian Museum and Planetarium in San Jose, California

PARAPHERNALIA
- Monographs (lessons) for study
- Sanctum ritual aprons, emblems of service for members
- Incense, candles, rose and eucalyptus oil
- Rosicrucian journals, e.g., *Rosicrucian Digest*
- Ancient emblem of cross with rose in middle

SANTERIA

WHAT IT IS

Developed in Cuba as result of slave trade, synthesizing Yoruba beliefs with elements of Catholicism. Centers on keeping ancestral spirits happy and cultivating personal relationships with deities called *orishas*, enlisting their assistance in daily life with tributes, divination, animal sacrifice, and medium possession. Supreme being Olorun is source of *ashé* (life force). Colorful and ritual intensive.

PERKS

- Formerly illegal, now tolerated in Cuba
- Animal sacrifice approved by Supreme Court in 1993
- Sense of extended family with your "house" (congregation)
- Individual's association with particular orisha (determined through divination) is lifelong bond
- Initiates often aided by *eleda* (guardian angel)

DRAWBACKS

- Not for squeamish: animal sacrifice includes biting heads off chickens
- Initiation ceremonies (offerings, *aguardiente*, new clothing, sacrificial animals) can be expensive

ACTIVITIES

- *Bembés*, ceremonies inviting orishas to drum, sing, and dance with party via possession
- Making *ebo* (offerings) to your orisha and keeping *bovedas* (ancestor altars)
- Shopping at *botánicas* for ritual ingredients
- Masses invoking egún with rum, cigar, and 9 glasses of water

PARAPHERNALIA

- Aguardiente, alcoholic drink made from distilled cane juice
- *Ilekes*, sacred beaded necklaces in colors associated with orishas

QUICK RATINGS:

Conversion Difficulty:

Time Commitment:

Cost:

① ② ③ ④ ⑤

New Friends:

3 million

PURPOSE OF LIFE

Follow 11 commandments of Olorun, including refraining from eating human flesh; venerate and live in harmony with orishas and ancestors

DEITIES

Olorun, AKA Olodumare; orishas; *egún* (sacred ancestors)

KEY TEXTS

None; oral tradition

WHERE

Cuba, Florida

AFTERLIFE PROMISES

Focuses on this life, though ancestral spirits indicate spiritual plane elsewhere

CATEGORY

African Diasporic

The modern UFO movement began in 1947 with a nationally discussed sighting over Washington State. Before long, people began stepping forward claiming to have communicated with the UFOs' occupants, and some became persuasive cult leaders—the best known, of course, is L. Ron Hubbard, founder of the most famous UFO cult of them all, Scientology. While there are many nuances to the groups' belief systems, UFO cultists share the conviction that aliens exist, and most agree that these other-planetary beings select a few individuals with whom to share their messages. The best part for the savvy convert? All the UFO religions will satisfy fans of science fiction and space travel.

AETHERIUS SOCIETY

In 1954, George King, an Englishman, was contacted by the extraterrestrial Aetherius, who represented the Interplanetary Parliament of Cosmic Masters. These masters include spiritual leaders of extraterrestrial origin such as Jesus, Buddha, Krishna, and Lao-tzu. Through the practice of yoga and meditation, King was able to continue his correspondence with Aetherius, which stressed service to humanity, peace, and environmental balance. King staged many spiritual actions, including Operation Starlight, in which he climbed 18 mountains to act as a spiritual energy conduit. He devised a spiritual energy battery, which absorbs prayers and transmits healing wherever needed. Every week, Aetherians gather for Operation Prayer Power charging sessions.

INTERNATIONAL RAELIAN MOVEMENT

In 1973, a French former singer and race-car driver named Raël was chosen by the Elohim, super-advanced scientist aliens who used genetic engineering to create life on earth as a science experiment, to transmit news of humankind's origins along with miscellaneous messages. Raël, the final prophet in a long line that includes Jesus, Buddha, Muhammad, and Confucius, was subsequently brought onto their flying saucer.

In addition to the IRM's main goals of teaching the true origins of humanity and building an embassy in Jerusalem to prepare for the aliens' return, the movement actively supports human cloning and sexual freedom. Above all, however, Raëlians champion world peace, required by the aliens before their return.

UNARIUS ACADEMY OF SCIENCE

Founded in the 1950s by a California couple, the UAS believes the Chinese are from Mars and were the first to colonize Earth. Because human society has lost touch with its higher consciousness, Unarians offer teachings of the "interdimensional psychodynamics of the mind" as well as "corrective and preventive psychotherapy based upon the physics of reincarnation." An acronym that stands for *Un*iversal *Ar*ticulate *I*nterdimensional *U*nderstanding of *S*cience, Unarius contends that by 2010, 33 spaceships will bring alien teachers to make the earth a better place. Unfortunately, a similar 2001 prophecy did not come to pass.

HEAVEN'S GATE

Heaven's Gate contends that human bodies ("vehicles") are containers for soul deposits, grown like plants on the Garden Earth. A properly lived human life consists of preparing for the long journey home to eternal alien existence by fighting desires of the flesh—including voluntary castration for some male members. The 2 founders met in a psychiatric hospital and described themselves as extraterrestrials from an "evolutionary level above human" and their group as a "classroom for growing a soul." DO, one leader, determined he was the same alien spirit that had inhabited Jesus's body based on a 2,000-year reincarnation cycle. In 1997, the ascetic, insular group committed suicide in order to transport their souls to a spaceship on the Hale-Bopp comet.

CARGO CULTS

Cargo cults are a fascinating example of the logical fallacy *post hoc, ergo propter hoc*: "After this, therefore because of this," meaning if one occurrence follows another, the first must have caused the second.

Flourishing around World War II in the South Pacific, cargo cults arose among tribal societies after locals saw Western technology and goods for the first time. Soldiers came to the islands and built airstrips, after which planes arrived carrying a wealth of cargo. The islanders concluded that the gods had sent the cargo *because* the airstrips had been built, and also because of other observed rituals such as marching in formation.

With this reasoning, the islanders began building their own relics—mock landing strips and straw airplanes, for example—and mimicking troop behavior in order to make more cargo fall from the sky. When no additional cargo came, the cults faded. One remains, however: the John Frum movement, begun in the late 1930s, which continues to predict the return of the American military and its precious cargo.

SATHYA SAI BABA

QUICK RATINGS:

Conversion Difficulty: ① ② ③ ④ ⑤ (3)

Time Commitment: ① ② ③ ④ ⑤ (4)

Cost: ① ② ③ ④ ⑤ (4)

New Friends: 10 million

PURPOSE OF LIFE
Love God by performing service to needy; attain enlightenment and release from reincarnation through piety, shunning materialism, and embrace of 5 values

DEITIES
One God with many names, including those other religions use

KEY TEXTS
Vedas; Upanishads; Puranas; Qur'an

WHERE
Worldwide, primarily India

AFTERLIFE PROMISES
Reincarnation until liberation (*moksha*) from cycle through service, devotion, wisdom

CATEGORY
NRM: Hindu Oriented

WHAT IT IS
Originated in 1940 by 14-year-old Sathya Sai Baba, who announced his destiny as religious leader. Purpose is to confirm all faiths; believes the only bad religion is no religion. Guru based. Teaches 5 values: *sathya* (truth), *dharma* (right conduct), *prema* (divine love), *shanti* (peace), *ahimsa* (nonviolence). Service to needy is best way to worship God; slogan is "Love all, serve all."

PERKS 
- Baba is described as "Avatar of this yuga!" (*yuga* is multiple millennia)
- Indubitably best-looking guru in history, with astounding "crown of hair"; pictures available as screensavers
- All people are equal; castes rejected
- Diverse programs for needy, including medical care, education, water improvement
- No apocalypse on horizon; Golden Age coming soon

DRAWBACKS 
- Celibacy after age 50
- Must detach from material world
- Vegetarianism
- Hard to learn all names of God (as many as 1,008) in order to contemplate their meaning during *puja* (worship)
- Baba's "miracles" have been called into doubt, dismissed as sleight of hand; also has faced allegations of sexual misconduct
- Ashram and aura culture may not be for everybody

ACTIVITIES
- Worshipping (puja) by repeating mantras of God's name, studying texts and lectures, singing hymns, deep meditation (*dhyana*), reciting scriptures, quiet contemplation, yoga
- "Help ever, harm never": demonstrating love for all creatures
- Celebrating Baba's birthday

PARAPHERNALIA
- Holy ash (*vibhoothi*), mixed with water and applied on body before puja
- Fruits, honey, flowers, water for offerings
- Sathya Sai Baba ringtone for cell phone
- 3 ashrams in India
- *Heart2Heart*, Baba's monthly e-journal

SCIENCE OF MIND

RELIGION #67

WHAT IT IS

Early spiritual theory on power of positive thinking, founded in 1927 by Ernest Holmes. "Panentheistic" view of God—God in everything, not separate from humans or rest of universe. Universe itself is spiritual and governed by harmony, enforced by right ideas. Human ability to think and perceive own thoughts is a power to be harnessed: Law of Mind is inherent God-power within.

PERKS 

- From authorized Practitioners, learn 5-step thought process: Recognition (God is all there is); Unification (we are one with God); Realization (we already have what we seek, just need to accept it); Thanksgiving (that we already have what we want); Release (stop worrying, because it's already accomplished, or "Let go and let God")
- 24-hour prayer hotline
- Okay to use power of thought for material gain

DRAWBACKS 

- Repeating positive affirmations can get annoying
- No one else to blame if things don't work out; guilt may ensue, for example, if you can't heal yourself of illness with your own thoughts
- Religion may be confused with *The Promise* and dismissed as trendy
- Disparaged by Christians because Holmes stated Jesus was merely a good man, not son of God

ACTIVITIES

- Spiritual Mind Treatments, affirmative prayer sessions guided by Practitioners
- Sunday Celebrations, services with affirmations, meditation, and potluck
- Saying Unexpected Income prayer to open prosperity consciousness
- Making voluntary financial offerings of 2 to 10 percent of income

PARAPHERNALIA

- *Science of Mind: A Guide for Spiritual Living* magazine
- Prayer samples to help custom-script your own affirmations
- Daily online affirmations
- Books on how to use Science of Mind to stop drinking (Alcoholics Anonymous founder was early follower of Holmes)

QUICK RATINGS:

Conversion Difficulty: 1 of 5

Time Commitment: 2 of 5

Cost: 3 of 5

New Friends: 70,000

PURPOSE OF LIFE

Feel Universal Spirit and learn to practice Law of Mind to positively affect self and world through thought

DEITIES

God, AKA Infinite Intelligence, Universal Spirit, Universal Mind

KEY TEXTS

The Science of Mind by Ernest Holmes

WHERE

United States

AFTERLIFE PROMISES

Spirit is immortal; heaven is within individual and is experienced when that fact is recognized

CATEGORY

NRM: Syncretic

SCIENTOLOGY

QUICK RATINGS:
Conversion Difficulty: ① ② ③ ④ ⑤
Time Commitment: ① ② ③ ④ ⑤
Cost: ① ② ③ ④ ⑤
New Friends: 55,000

PURPOSE OF LIFE

Become clear of engrams and progress through Operating Thetan levels; help others do the same

DEITIES

Unspecified supreme being; individuals free to reach own conclusions

KEY TEXTS

Dianetics: The Modern Science of Mental Health by L. Ron Hubbard

WHERE

Worldwide, primarily United States, Europe

AFTERLIFE PROMISES

No official position; however, reincarnation supported, as some engrams come from past lives

CATEGORY

NRM: Science Fiction Oriented

WHAT IT IS

Founded by science fiction author L. Ron Hubbard in 1954. Made of body, brain, and *thetan* (spiritual being), humans must rediscover their inner thetan through auditing, an interview process using E-Meters (quasi–lie detectors) designed to identify *engrams*, negative memories and life experiences. Once clear of engrams, individuals can progress spiritually and operate at fullest potential.

PERKS 

- Very colorful cosmology
- If you progress to highest levels of church hierarchy, you may have access to Swiss bank accounts
- Training for Operating Thetan Level VIII (highest) takes place on cruise ship
- New friends include Tom Cruise, John Travolta
- Can subtly spread word through Scientology-owned groups such as anti-psychiatry Citizens Commission on Human Rights

DRAWBACKS 

- Reaching Level VIII will cost upward of $350,000
- Leaving or criticizing church may cause you to be investigated by private detectives, threatened, sued
- Cult Awareness Network reports no other group has prompted more telephone pleas for help

ACTIVITIES

- Extensive auditing and coursework
- Attending Sunday services, which include sermons and group processing
- Proselytizing
- Experiencing "exteriorization" (thetan leaving body)
- Overcoming "reactive mind"

PARAPHERNALIA

- "Bridge to Total Freedom" poster outlining levels of awareness
- Checkbooks, credit cards

SECULAR HUMANISM

WHAT IT IS

Philosophy that religious belief is not necessary to promote ethical behavior, bring out the best in individuals, or promote quality of life. Privileges search for objective truth through scientific method and reason. Humans create life meaning and purpose and should collaborate to improve world simply because it's the right thing to do. Opposes injection of religion into civic sphere.

PERKS 

- Debate encouraged; no questions off-limits
- Philosophical roots dating to ancient Greeks
- Allows focus on making this life as fulfilling as possible
- Proactive: rather than waiting for divine intervention, humans solve problems
- Universe is neutral, neither good nor bad
- Hard to disagree with basic values

DRAWBACKS 

- Subject of lawsuits, proposed legislation, and impassioned polemics by Christian right, claiming that Secular Humanism is official religion of United States and dangerous conspiracy of liberal left
- Internal controversy over whether to take religious tax exemption, thus creating target for Christian right
- No afterlife fantasies
- Official emblem, "Happy Human," resembles Honda logo

ACTIVITIES

- Political activism around commingling of church and state
- Attending humanist conferences around world
- Observing International Humanist Day
- Celebrating HumanLight or Winterval, secular alternatives to Hanukkah and Christmas

PARAPHERNALIA

- *Essays in the Philosophy of Humanism*, journal published by American Humanist Association
- *Free Inquiry*, *Skeptical Inquirer*, and *Secular Humanist Bulletin* publications
- Equinox greeting cards

QUICK RATINGS:

Conversion Difficulty:
① ② ③ ④ ⑤

Time Commitment:
① ② ③ ④ ⑤

Cost:
① ② ③ ④ ⑤

New Friends:
260 million

PURPOSE OF LIFE
Create purpose and meaning in life, take responsibility for actions, don't hurt others, work to improve world

DEITIES
None

KEY TEXTS
"A Secular Humanist Declaration" by Paul Kurtz; various manifestos

WHERE
Worldwide, primarily North America, Europe

AFTERLIFE PROMISES
None; make most of this life

CATEGORY
Non-Religious

SELF-REALIZATION FELLOWSHIP

QUICK RATINGS:

Conversion Difficulty:

① ② ③ ④ ⑤ 

Time Commitment:

① ② ③ ④ ⑤ 

Cost:

① ② ③ ④ ⑤ 

New Friends:
125,000

PURPOSE OF LIFE
Evolve one's mortal consciousness into God Consciousness through Kriya yoga

DEITIES
God, characterized as God Consciousness

KEY TEXTS
Autobiography of a Yogi by Paramahansa Yogananda; Bhagavad Gita; New Testament

WHERE
Worldwide, primarily United States, India

AFTERLIFE PROMISES
Cycle of progressive karma-based reincarnation; soul exists eternally; death is temporary state of sleep and nothing to fear

CATEGORY
NRM: Hindu Oriented

WHAT IT IS
Founded in 1920 in United States by Indian-born yogi Paramahansa Yogananda, on mission to spread Hindu techniques to West. *Kriya* yoga (meditation and breath-work) improves energy flow (*prana*) to wake up chakras, prevent decay of mind and body, and establish direct relationship with God. Affirms holiness of many prophets, especially Jesus, citing diverse paths to enlightenment.

PERKS 
- Founder's autobiography is popular, characterized as a page-turner (unusual among religious tracts)
- All paths lead to God—can convert *and* keep previous religion
- Death is laughed at, because we cannot die
- Claims practices are "scientific techniques for attaining direct personal experience of God," and that "principles of truth" exist that comprise "the common scientific foundation of all true religions"

DRAWBACKS 
- Critics say Kriya yoga practiced is not authentic, call founder's autobiography fictional, allege cultlike thought control
- Multiple yogic exercises every day
- Though "breathlessness is deathlessness," breathing exercises can be oxygen depriving
- May practice for decades without achieving blissful union with God (*samadhi*)

ACTIVITIES
- Lots of yoga, breathing exercises, chanting, meditating
- Participating in Worldwide Prayer Circle to alleviate international "inharmonies" and strife
- Attending lectures, classes, retreats
- Performing Holiday Outreach, gift donations to needy

PARAPHERNALIA
- Sandalwood prayer beads
- *Rudraksha* beads (powerful seeds) to help conduct electromagnetic current
- Incense
- Photographs of inspirational figures ranging from Yogananda to Christ
- Yogananda's "How to Live" teachings

SHI'A MUSLIM

WHAT IT IS

One of 2 divisions of Islam, around 10 percent of Muslims. Differ through allegiance to Muhammad's son-in-law Ali, who Shi'ites believe was first to profess faith in Islam to Muhammad. After Ali's assassination in 661 BCE, leadership split; Shi'ites followed Ali's sons, al-Hassan and al-Hussein, until their deaths in battle with Sunnis. Martyrdom of Ali and al-Hussein central to Shi'ite worship.

PERKS 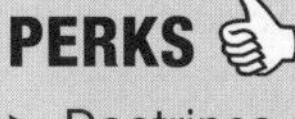

- Doctrines still open for interpretation (original Sunni doctrines sacred)
- Temporary marriages allowed, some for mere hours, getting around issue of premarital sex (Sunnis don't allow)
- Lots of same-sex bonding: prayer, socializing, other activities separated by gender
- Foreplay encouraged so wife doesn't stray

DRAWBACKS 

- 20 percent tax (*khums*; imposed only in wartime for Sunnis) plus *zakat* tithe
- Can't elect leaders: imams descend from Muhammad (Sunni leaders elected)
- Martyrdom and suffering are major themes
- Sunni persecution
- Won't see Allah in afterlife (Sunnis believe they will)

ACTIVITIES

- Praying with forehead on piece of hard clay from Karbala, site of al-Hussein's martyrdom
- Doubling up on prayers to pray only 3 times a day (Sunnis must pray all 5 times)
- Self-flagellating on Ashura, day of al-Hussein's death

PARAPHERNALIA

- *Masjids* (mosques) without domes and minarets
- Karbala and An Najaf shrines
- Pictures of al-Hussein (Sunnis display Qur'an verses)
- "Latmiya" (chant about 12 imams) ringtones (sometimes used by Sunnis to impersonate Shi'ites)

QUICK RATINGS:

Conversion Difficulty:
① ② ③ **④** ⑤

Time Commitment:
① ② **③** ④ ⑤

Cost:
① ② ③ **④** ⑤

New Friends:
187 million

PURPOSE OF LIFE

Submit to will of Allah, adhere to Qur'an, abide by Five Pillars, obey teachings and laws of imams to get to paradise

DEITIES

Allah

KEY TEXTS

Qur'an; Sunnah (Muhammad's customs); Shi'ite versions of Hadiths (Muhammad's words)

WHERE

Middle East, primarily Iran, Iraq

AFTERLIFE PROMISES

According to life deeds, suffer or enjoy peace in grave (though martyrs go straight to paradise, enemies to hell) until Last Day, when resurrected enter paradise or hell

CATEGORY

Abrahamic: Islamic

POPULARITY CONTEST

As in all areas of life, for some seekers it's important to know which are the most popular choices before making one's own decision. These are the kinds of people, for example, who select a car based on how it will reflect on them, or who buy the same clothes their friends wear. If image matters to you, consider how impressions of what constitutes a viable religion have developed.

ONLY 4 FAITHS CONSTITUTED ENLIGHTENMENT

If you'd been a European during the Enlightenment, you'd have seen the world as divided into just 4 faiths: Christianity, Islam, Judaism, and the pejorative catchall paganism. Fortunately, even though global religious freedom didn't begin to blossom until the 20th century, growing awareness of the sheer variety in world religion has caused the list of possibilities to expand ever since.

The 19th century brought increased knowledge of Asian culture, revealing to the West that Hinduism, Buddhism, Confucianism, Taoism, Jainism, Shinto, and Zoroastrianism were distinct traditions. In the 20th century, the rise of anthropology made clear that these "major world religions" were only the tip of the iceberg.

CONTEMPORARY CHOICE: VARIETY, VARIETY, AND VARIETY

Serious scholars of religion now know that any comprehensive list of faiths around the world must number at least 99—and probably in the hundreds. For example, the statisticians at *World Christian Encyclopedia* found that at the turn of the millennium, there were no fewer than 270 religions with at least 500,000 adherents.

Population isn't the only indication of a faith's importance—influence and growth rate also have to be taken into account. The relative newcomer Mormonism, for example, has made a significant mark on the United States. Those interested in the Far East will note the new religious movements that have spread in Asia, including Soka Gakkai, Cao Dai, and Falun Gong.

WHAT'S IN A LIST?

The old lists of major world religions still have value, thanks to their sheer number of followers and cultural impact. Although 500,000 adherents sounds like a lot, Catholicism and Sunni Islam each number more than 1.1 billion followers. The so-called classical religions (meaning old and established) not only have influenced one another but also have birthed influential offshoots. For example, there are more than 50 distinct flavors of Christianity and more than 30 designations of Buddhism. In addition to size, the classical world religions are, for the most part, politically powerful, institutionally stable, independent of other faiths, and dispersed over multiple nations.

But the times are changing rapidly, as this book attests. Thanks to mass migration, travel, technology, global communication, and the increased number of religious outposts far from their points of origin, nowadays all religions are, in some sense, world religions.

THE POPULAR KIDS

The approval seekers among you, of course, will say "world religion, schmorld religion—point me to where I'll find the most people to play with." Look no further than the list below.

40 MOST POPULOUS RELIGIONS					
1	Catholicism	1.1 billion	**21**	Universal Life Church	22 million
2	Sunni Muslim	1.1 billion	**22**	Soka Gakkai	18 million
3	Hinduism	872 million	**23**	Judaism	15 million
4	Nonreligious	785 million	**24**	Mormonism	11 million
5	Chinese traditional	387 million	**25**	Roma	10 million
6	Protestantism	382 million	**26**	Sathya Sai Baba	10 million
7	Ethnic tribal	264 million	**27**	Zulu	9 million
8	Pentecostalism	250 million	**28**	Vodou	8 million
9	Sufism	237 million	**29**	Baha'i	7.8 million
10	Eastern Orthodox	220 million	**30**	Confucianism	6.5 million
11	Mahayana Buddhism	214 million	**31**	Jehovah's Witnesses	6 million
12	Shi'a Muslim	187 million	**32**	Maya	6 million
13	Atheism	155 million	**33**	Transcendental Meditation	6 million
14	Theravada Buddhism	145 million	**34**	Zen Buddhism	6 million
15	African Independent Churches	93 million	**35**	Jainism	4.6 million
16	Candomble	40 million	**36**	Episcopalian	3.5 million
17	Falun Gong	30 million	**37**	Cao Dai	3.2 million
18	Sikhism	26 million	**38**	Nichiren Buddhism	3.1 million
19	Juche	23 million	**39**	Santeria	3 million
20	Tibetan Buddhism	23 million	**40**	Tenrikyo	3 million

SHINTO

QUICK RATINGS:

Conversion Difficulty: ① ② ③ ④ ⑤ (4)

Time Commitment: ① ② ③ ④ ⑤ (4)

Cost: ① ② ③ ④ ⑤ (2)

New Friends: 2.8 million

PURPOSE OF LIFE
Lead pure, truthful life of best efforts, in accordance with will of kami

DEITIES
Kami, gods and goddesses representing nature elements, ancestors, dead leaders; Amaterasu (Sun Goddess) most important

KEY TEXTS
Kojiki (Records of Ancient Matters); *Nihon Shoki* (Chronicles of Japan)

WHERE
Japan

AFTERLIFE PROMISES
Physical and supernatural worlds are one; can become ancestral kami after death or, if circumstances are bad, angry ghost or evil spirit

CATEGORY
Indigenous: Japanese

WHAT IT IS
Indigenous religion of Japan, formalized around 550 CE to distinguish from newly arrived Buddhism (the 2 faiths are now Japan's main religions). Means "way of the *kami*," spirits who rule universe. Life is governed by tradition and family; reverence for nature; purity and cleanliness; and honoring spirits. Based on rituals, ceremonies, and fulfilling obligations, not absolutes like good and evil.

PERKS 
- Sense of national Japanese identity and tradition
- Affirmations instead of commandments
- Possible to be worshipped posthumously
- Beautiful aesthetics (poetry, visual arts, architecture) based on emotion and harmony with nature
- Sake, "drink of the gods," used in many ceremonies
- Excellent creation stories
- Emphasis on cleanliness and purity makes for good housekeeping

DRAWBACKS 
- Because so culturally Japanese, hard for outsiders to convert
- Skin may grow pruny from frequent water purification; burns from being sprinkled with boiling water (*yudate*)
- Filial piety can be burdensome and oppressive
- Heavy bridal wigs have resulted in headaches and heatstroke
- If murder committed without proper respect, victim takes revenge as evil spirit (*aragami*)

ACTIVITIES
- Celebrating seasons, harvests, new year, children's rites of passage, shrine festivals
- Standing under waterfall for purification (*misogi*)
- Practicing avoidance (*imi*) of doing certain things and saying certain words due to their impurity
- Ritual sumo wrestling, humans vs. kami

PARAPHERNALIA
- Home altars with offerings such as food, money, evergreen branches tied with white strips of paper
- Tranquil shrines marked by sacred gateways and pairs of stone dogs or lions to separate sacred from secular
- Areas to store shoes at entrances of homes (for purity)

SIKHISM

WHAT IT IS

Indian religion, founded around 1500 by Guru Nanak, Hindu whom God told to spread message of truth and love transcending Hinduism and Islam. Religion evolved and matured through succession of 10 appointed gurus. Achieve enlightenment through love of others and service (*seva*), adherence to Five Kakaars, avoidance of 5 cardinal vices, and meditation on God's name.

PERKS 

- Middle or last name will become Singh (for men; "lion") or Kaur (for women; "princess")
- Personal cleanliness (bathe and wash hair morning and night)
- Opposed to caste prejudice; promotes gender equality
- No original sin
- Gurdwaras (temples) often open 24 hours

DRAWBACKS 

- Planned sovereign homeland, Khalistan, not yet a reality
- Because Adi Granth cannot be translated and contains 6 languages, hard to read reverent text
- Must learn Punjabi
- Expected to tithe 10 percent of income (*dasvandh*)

ACTIVITIES

- Throughout day, multiple occasions of praying, meditating, reciting sacred text, singing hymns
- Caring for Adi Granth as if it were a living guru, and covering head and baring feet in its presence
- Living balanced life of work, charity, and worship

PARAPHERNALIA

- After *amrit sanskar* (baptism with nectar; adult initiation), wear Five Ks (Kakaars): *kesh*, uncut hair; *kangha*, wood comb; *kara*, steel bracelet; *kachha*, cotton undershorts; *kirpan*, ceremonial dagger

QUICK RATINGS:

Conversion Difficulty:
① ② ③ ④ ⑤ (3)

Time Commitment:
① ② ③ ④ ⑤ (4)

Cost:
① ② ③ ④ ⑤ (4)

New Friends:
26 million

PURPOSE OF LIFE

Through honesty, service, and constant awareness of God, achieve liberation in life and after death

DEITIES

One God (*Ik Onkar*), AKA God, the True Name

KEY TEXTS

Adi Granth (AKA Guru Granth Sahib), Sikh holy book

WHERE

Primarily Punjab state of India

AFTERLIFE PROMISES

Reincarnation as person or animal until karma can be resolved; individual then can be absorbed into True Name

CATEGORY

Dharmic

SOKA GAKKAI

QUICK RATINGS:

Conversion Difficulty:
① ② ③ ④ ⑤

Time Commitment:
① ② ③ ④ ⑤

Cost:
① ② ③ ④ ⑤

New Friends:
18 million

PURPOSE OF LIFE

Change individual destiny positively through chanting; change world destiny positively both by improving self and by proselytizing

DEITIES

None

KEY TEXTS

Lotus Sutra; Gosho, writings of Nichiren; *Buddhism in Action* by Daisaku Ikeda

WHERE

Worldwide, primarily Japan

AFTERLIFE PROMISES

Human Revolution focuses on here and now

CATEGORY

NRM: Buddhist Oriented

WHAT IT IS

Founded in 1930s, sect of Nichiren Buddhism; name means "Value Creation Society." Anyone can achieve Buddhahood through *daimoku*, chanting "Nam-myoho-renge-kyo" ("devotion to the Lotus Sutra") to Gohonzon, inscribed scroll. Through chanting, individuals and society can achieve health, prosperity, self-improvement, happiness. Focus on worldly values and this life.

PERKS 

- Powerful: formed one of most prominent political parties in Japan, Komeito ("clean government"), now New Komeito Party, with support of millions of Soka Gakkai voters
- Provides community and sense of purpose for middle-aged Japanese housewives, who comprise much of following
- Materialism encouraged
- Will be part of Human Revolution, directing course of history

DRAWBACKS 

- Outsiders condemn cultlike activities and cite group's desire for world domination rather than stated world peace goals
- Intimidation and threats upon leaving group
- Called upon to recruit aggressively (process called *shakubuku*, "to break and subdue")
- Militant opposition to other Nichiren groups has resulted in illegal activities
- Single chant may become monotonous

ACTIVITIES

- *Gongyo*: morning and evening chanting lasting from several minutes to several hours
- Making *tozan* (pilgrimage) to temple to pray to wood Dai-Gohonzon
- Monthly world peace prayers
- Political fund-raising
- Celebrating Nichiren's birthday

PARAPHERNALIA

- Gohonzon: scroll for worship depicting Nichiren mandala, AKA "Happiness-Generating Machine"
- *Kaidan*, home altar that may house a Gohonzon
- Tea to soothe throat after hours of chanting
- *World Tribune* newspaper, *Living Buddhism* magazine

SPIRITUAL BUT NOT RELIGIOUS

RELIGION #75

WHAT IT IS

Those who hold spiritual beliefs but disparage scriptedness and hypocrisy of organized religion. Largely under age 35, adherents frequently subscribe to aspects of Eastern philosophies and believe consciousness connects all life. Personal moral and ethical codes often include environmentalism, multiculturalism, and pacifism. Also known as spiritual seekers or metrospirituals.

PERKS

- Common SBNR characteristics include free-thinking, curiosity, and open-mindedness
- Can decorate with diverse knickknacks, from statues of Ganesh to Tibetan prayer flags to *milagros*
- If online dating, one of most popular selections under "Religion" is SBNR
- Can meld religious background with current SBNR status, e.g., "I'm SBNR but grew up Jewish"
- Spiritual seeker's version of "truthiness"

DRAWBACKS

- Some say trendiness of SBNR has already peaked
- Religious individuals and institutions can become offended by idea that spirituality and religion are mutually exclusive
- Lack of organized community means fellowship is difficult to find
- Due to customized view of cosmos, in conversations you're always starting from scratch with explanations of your beliefs
- SBNR has lots of syllables

ACTIVITIES

- Steadfastly refusing to commit
- Avoiding church and temple
- Constantly seeking
- Feeling smug
- Multicultural spiritual pursuits such as yoga, tai chi, meditation
- Reading spiritual commentary rather than original texts

PARAPHERNALIA

- Internet access, especially for online dating
- Candles and incense
- Organic and fair-trade edibles, often from Whole Foods
- All-natural goods
- Jewelry with multiple religious icons, more for aesthetics than allegiance
- Prius

QUICK RATINGS:

Conversion Difficulty:
① ② ③ ④ ⑤

Time Commitment:
① ② ③ ④ ⑤

Cost:
① ② ③ ④ ⑤

New Friends:
25 million

PURPOSE OF LIFE

Feel connected to humanity, animals, earth, universe, God; find meaning in life without subscribing to dogma or creed

DEITIES

God generally perceived as all-permeating force linked to universal consciousness

KEY TEXTS

Diverse reading in various traditions of spiritual thought in order to craft own beliefs

WHERE

United States

AFTERLIFE PROMISES

Often some form of reincarnation, especially return of individual consciousness to universal consciousness

CATEGORY

Non-Religious

SPIRITUALISM

RELIGION #76

QUICK RATINGS:

Conversion Difficulty:

 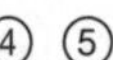

1 2 3 4 5

Time Commitment:

1 2 3 4 5

Cost:

1 2 3 4 5

New Friends:
150,000

PURPOSE OF LIFE

Allow living to access spirit world for guidance and healing

DEITIES

God, AKA Immanent Intelligence or Infinite Intelligence; Jesus seen as greatest medium of all time

KEY TEXTS

Heavenly Arcana and *Apocalypse Revealed* by Emanuel Swedenborg; *The Principles of Nature* and *The Great Harmonia* by Andrew Jackson Davis

WHERE

North America, Europe

AFTERLIFE PROMISES

Death is "being thrust into the spirit"; spirit goes to Summerland, Spiritualist heaven

CATEGORY

Spiritist

WHAT IT IS

Belief in communication with spirits due to soul's survival after body's death. Present in many religions, but as stand-alone, refers to American movement dating to mid-19th century. Primarily instigated by Fox sisters of upstate New York, whose haunted childhood home revealed their talents as mediums. As adults, they traveled globally conducting séances and making converts.

PERKS

- No hell
- No evil spirits, only ignorant ones; evolved spirits help them learn
- Contact deceased loved ones
- Can learn to channel; not an innate skill

DRAWBACKS

- Furniture damage: "departed" often move, bump, levitate objects
- Might get slimed ("manifestation of ectoplasm")
- Many believe Spiritualists are frauds
  - Dead mother may complain you don't contact her enough

ACTIVITIES

- Participating in séances (AKA sittings), channeling
- Clairvoyance (seeing the nonvisible); telepathy (conveying thoughts without speech)
- Attending Spiritualist camp

PARAPHERNALIA

- Pen and paper for spirit-guided automatic writing
- *History of Spiritualism* (2 volumes) by Arthur Conan Doyle, famous Spiritualist
- Publications such as *Parapsychology Review*

SUFISM

WHAT IT IS

Mystical aspect of Islam, with orthodox manifestations among Muslims in East and universalizing groups stemming from 1960s counterculture in West. Knowledge comes from teacher-student (*sheikh-murid*) relationship, not books. God wholly present in all of creation. Intuitive, direct communication and symmetry with God through purification, concentration, and ecstatic experience.

PERKS

- Originated as asceticism but has emphasized mysticism and pure love of God since 10th century
- If Muslim, Sufism can serve as internal expression of faith, with Islamic law (sharia) as external
- Don't have to be Muslim or follow Islam to be Sufi
- Universal Sufism, in West, incorporates Hinduism, Buddhism, Gnosticism
- Visionary states don't require drugs
- Amazing music and poetry

DRAWBACKS 

- For orthodox Islam Sufis, vows of poverty, chastity, submission required for *tariqah* (the Path)
- Multileveled process of closeness with God may not be completed in one lifetime
- Have to get teacher to accept you and your sincerity of commitment
- Point of worship is obliteration of self
- Whirling may cause dizziness

ACTIVITIES

- Performing *dhikr* (remembrance), repetition of phrases or names of Allah
- *Sama*, poetry recitals as form of worship to achieve ecstatic state
- Meditating
- Whirling; individual becomes center of mandala and moves to achieve oneness with God
- Spiritual retreats

PARAPHERNALIA

- Rosary beads for counting during dhikr
- For Islamic devout, cloak called *khirqa*, given during initiation; said to "transmit perfume of paradise"
- For Whirling Dervishes, tall camel-hair hat, representing tomb of ego
- Rumi poetry, read not as male-female romance but as human-Allah love

QUICK RATINGS:

Conversion Difficulty:

Time Commitment:

① ② ③ ④ ⑤

Cost:

① ② ③ ④ ⑤

New Friends:
237 million

PURPOSE OF LIFE

Release baser instincts and improve spiritually until pure enough to reunite with God; experience God in this life by eliminating ego

DEITIES

Allah, within whom all harmony and law originates

KEY TEXTS

Qur'an; Sunnah; Hadiths; poetry of Ibn al-'Arabi, Jalal ad-Din ar-Rumi, others

WHERE

Middle East, Indonesia, Central Asia, Pakistan, Africa

AFTERLIFE PROMISES

Experience God before death ("Die before you die"); continue to progress after death, but greater rewards for more spiritually advanced

CATEGORY

Abrahamic: Islamic

RELIGIOUS CAREERS

For most people, the experience of being a follower will provide adequate spiritual satisfaction. Others, however, may hear a higher calling or grow tired of tithing and thus seek to turn their faith into a source of income. Religion offers a wide range of career opportunities, with diverse educational requirements, salaries, and perks. As with any career decision, it pays to go into religion leadership with one's eyes wide open.

POSITION	RELIGION	PREREQUISITES	DUTIES	PAY
Waldorf School Teacher	**Anthro-posophy**	Minimum of bachelor's degree; higher degrees preferred. Certificate in Waldorf education from Waldorf teacher education institute.	Teach children and adolescents according to interdisciplinary, development-oriented, natural, artistic educational principles of Rudolf Steiner.	$28,000–$60,000 per year.
Monk or Nun	**Buddhism**	Must spend several years studying Buddhist path under teacher. After identification as full Buddhist, spend at least 5 years in "refuge" before taking monastic vows. Post-ordination, spend a few years in monastic community before going out into world.	Serve as living embodiment of Buddha's teachings and teach others. May have institutional and communal-living responsibilities.	No payment, but living expenses covered by temple. Some groups consider it virtuous for monks and nuns to beg for their food.
Priest	**Catholicism**	Must be unmarried male. 8 years of seminary, or 4 years of college and 4 years of seminary, followed by 6 months as a transitional deacon before ordainment.	Leader of Roman Catholic parish: sermonizing, counseling, teaching, administration.	Actual salary around $20,000. Fees received for performing ceremonies bring total taxable income to $33,000. Additional perks include housing, utilities, car, pension, health insurance, Social Security offset, and reimbursement for business expenses and seminary training.
Priest	**Hinduism**	Formerly had to be male and born to priestly caste; now open to all. Training ranges from 1 to 12 years and can start in childhood.	Perform all temple ceremonies and rituals as well as perform services in temple members' homes.	In India, ranges from $90 annually plus daily allotment of rice; may be supplemented by charging for home-based ceremonies and astrology. Elite priests may make $3,600.
Imam	**Islam**	Must be male and considered virtuous. Some state-sponsored training, but most aspiring imams study under other imams. Significant study into Qur'an and sharia (Islamic law).	Leader of Muslim mosque: lead prayers, sermonize, help others study and interpret Qur'an and sharia.	Salaried imams earn $20,000–$50,000. No perks.
Rabbi	**Judaism**	4–6 years of rabbinical school.	Leader of congregation: sermonizing, counseling, teaching, administration.	Starts at $50,000. Can go as high as $600,000 for superstar rabbis of wealthy congregations, including housing and other perks.

POSITION	RELIGION	PREREQUISITES	DUTIES	PAY
Missionary	**Mormonism**	Age 19–26 for males, 21–26 for females. Retired married couples also eligible. Sent to Missionary Training Center for 3–13 weeks (depending on language training) before departing for assigned location.	Spend 18 months (females), 2 years (males), or up to 3 years (retired couples) in "mission field" assigned by church, often overseas. Spread news about Mormon Church's teachings and/or perform humanitarian work for local communities.	Missionaries pay $400 per month to cover living expenses but are excused from tithing while on mission.
Minister	**Protestantism**	Some denominations require master's degrees from theological schools, while others will hire assistant pastors with bachelor's degrees (preferably in religious studies). Nondenominational churches may have religious leaders without theological training or degrees.	Leader of congregation: sermonizing, counseling, teaching, administration.	Median salary of $38,000 for solo ministers, $54,000 for congregations with multiple staff members. Can go higher than $500,000 for superstar ministers of wealthy congregations, including housing and other perks.
Priestess or Priest	**Santeria**	Multiple levels of training and initiation under elders until ceremony-intensive initiation into priesthood. After initiation, yearlong period of special practices designed to nurture: dressing in white, eating from mat on floor, covering head.	Preside over ceremonies, conduct rituals and initiations, lead spells, perform divination.	Payment for individual ceremonies, ranging from $25 to several hundred dollars.
Shaman	**Shamanism**	Must be born into shamanic family; be "called" (often while seriously ill, though illness may be caused by call, not vice versa); or undergo intense personal questing and apprenticeship.	Depends on religion. May heal, lead vision quests, channel deities, preside over ceremonies, perform divination, administer sacred psychedelic drugs.	In indigenous communities, may live on community support and payment for ceremonies. Otherwise, can charge whatever market will bear for classes, retreats, trips.
Priest	**Shinto**	Apprenticeship under Shinto priest for 2–3 years or 1- to 2-year university program.	Conduct all Shinto rituals and ceremonies, especially at shrines.	Varies; most only part-time, officiating at individually paid ceremonies.
Spirit Medium or Channeler	**Spiritualism and New Age**	Some feel medium and channeling abilities are inborn, others believe they can be developed. Must be able to contact spirit world and convince others of these capabilities.	Help others contact souls of departed. Pass messages and advice from spirit world to living.	Around $100 for half-hour individual session, $35–$50 per person for group séance.
Minister	**Universal Life Church**	Ordination through free online application.	Primarily perform weddings. Can also officiate at baptisms, funerals, exorcisms.	Can charge varying amounts for officiating at wedding ceremonies, but most work for free for friends.
Gift Shop Salesperson	**Any with stores attached to temples, churches, mosques, etc.**	No special training required; although setting is religious, job is retail. Helps to have cash-register and merchandising experience.	Sell religious charms, tchotchkes, artwork, and supplies to faithful. Sell other types of gifts to raise money for institution.	Some are staffed with volunteers from congregation. Others earn $8–$9 per hour.
Exit Counselor	**None, but called to work with followers of such religions as Hare Krishna, Unification Church, and Scientology.**	Extensive research into groups whose exitees will require counseling. Some exit counselors are themselves former members of such groups. Others have training in psychology and counseling.	Help members of groups that discourage departure and contact with outsiders to see things from a different point of view in order to break free and return to former lives.	Some volunteer their services. Others are compensated by loved ones of exitees; can run upward of $10,000 for top exit counselors or "thought-reform consultants."

SUNNI MUSLIM

QUICK RATINGS:

Conversion Difficulty: ① ② ③ ④ ⑤ (3)

Time Commitment: ① ② ③ ④ ⑤ (3)

Cost: ① ② ③ ④ ⑤ (4)

New Friends: 1.1 billion

PURPOSE OF LIFE
Submit to will of Allah (*Islam* means "surrender"), follow Qur'an, and abide by Five Pillars to get to paradise

DEITIES
Allah

KEY TEXTS
Qur'an; Sunnah (Muhammad's customs); Sunni versions of Hadiths (Muhammad's words)

WHERE
Middle East, Indonesia, Central Asia, Pakistan, Africa

AFTERLIFE PROMISES
According to life deeds, suffer or enjoy peace in grave (though martyrs go straight to paradise, enemies to hell) until Last Day, when resurrected enter paradise or hell

CATEGORY
Abrahamic: Islamic

WHAT IT IS
Representing 90 percent of Muslims, largest branch of Islam. In 7th century, God (Allah) spoke through angel Gabriel to prophet Muhammad (last in series including Abraham and Jesus); revelations recorded in Qur'an. Must follow Five Pillars: *shahadah* (profession of faith), *salat* (ritual prayer), *zakat* (tax to benefit needy), *sawm* (Ramadan fasting), and *hajj* (pilgrimage to Mecca).

PERKS 
- Allah always accessible; described as closer than one's own jugular vein
- Allah is just and merciful
- Control over admission to paradise after death: entirely dependent on your actions during life (though Satan will try to lead you astray)
- Exemption from hajj if you can't afford it
- Egalitarian: all people "equal children of Adam"
- Humans are greatest of all creatures

DRAWBACKS 
- During month of Ramadan, no eating, drinking, smoking during day
- If not in Muslim community, praying 5 times a day may prove difficult
- Must pay off credit cards monthly (usury forbidden)
- Complicated to calculate zakat (like a tithe)
- Islamic laws and states unpalatable to separation-of-church-and-state types
- Per Islamic marriage contracts, women must comply if husbands want sex

ACTIVITIES
- Studying Qur'an
- Keeping good company
- Attending mosque on Fridays to hear sermons
- Going on chaperoned dates
- Saying "Sallallahu alayhi wa sallam" (Peace be upon him) after uttering Muhammad's name; when written, abbreviate as PBUH or SAW

PARAPHERNALIA
- *Masjids* (mosques) with domes and minarets
- *Mihrabs*, spots on eastern wall to show way to face while praying
- Online zakat calculators
- *Hijabs* (head coverings) for females after puberty
- Modest, silk-free dress for men (must be covered between navel and knee)
- Prayer beads and rugs

TAOISM

WHAT IT IS

With Buddhism and Confucianism, comprises traditional Chinese religion. Practiced on its own to lesser degree. Dates to writings of Lao-tzu around 6th century BCE. Tao is natural way of universe, including cyclical rhythm and harmony of opposites; permeates all, from gods to humans to nature. Goal is to empty oneself of all but Tao through detachment, calm, and inaction (*wu-wei*).

PERKS

- May come to grasp this: "Don't meditate, don't cogitate; follow no school, follow no way, and then you will attain the Tao"
- Decor assistance from feng shui
- Fortune-telling *I Ching* great help for decision-making
- *Te* (virtue) refers to awareness of Tao and authenticity of self rather than outside dogma
- If good Taoist, you will leave no tracks

DRAWBACKS 

- Difficult to accept concept of inaction without being completely passive
- Born with certain amount of *chi* (life force); must conserve and increase it, e.g., via semen retention

ACTIVITIES

- Practicing *tai chi chuan*, seen as soft martial art or moving meditation, with many health benefits
- Qigong, breathing exercises, and meditating
- Purification rituals to restore order and harmony
- Reciting passages from *Tao-te Ching*
- Detaching from outcomes and from materialism

PARAPHERNALIA

- Talismans, strips of paper with words to bring luck and drive away evil spirits
- Yin-yang symbol
- Incense, candles, smudge sticks

QUICK RATINGS:

Conversion Difficulty:
① ② **③** ④ ⑤

Time Commitment:
① ② ③ **④** ⑤

Cost:
① ② ③ ④ ⑤

New Friends:
2.8 million

PURPOSE OF LIFE

Live without struggle or opposition, synching life rhythm with that of Tao, thus achieving immortality of pure spirit

DEITIES

Multiple deities; Eight Immortals; Three Pure Ones

KEY TEXTS

Tao-te Ching by Lao-tzu; works of Chuang-tzu and Lieh-tzu

WHERE

China, Taiwan

AFTERLIFE PROMISES

Life and death are complementary cyclical phases of being and nonbeing: "Since life and death are each other's companions, why worry about them?"

CATEGORY

Taoic

TECHNOPAGANISM

QUICK RATINGS:

Conversion Difficulty: ① (②) ③ ④ ⑤

Time Commitment: ① ② (③) ④ ⑤

Cost: ① ② (③) ④ ⑤

New Friends: 100,000

PURPOSE OF LIFE

Realize spiritual force inherent in all things, balance technology with nature, move within flow, live by "An it harm none, do what ye will"

DEITIES

Various; Eris, Goddess of Discord and Chaos, is popular

KEY TEXTS

Neuromancer by William Gibson; occult books to transform ancient spells for Internet

WHERE

Online

AFTERLIFE PROMISES

Nothing specific, although some expect to reboot

CATEGORY

NRM: Neo-Pagan

WHAT IT IS

Pagan subculture dating to 1980s that believes in connectedness of all things—new and old, nature and technology, reverent and frivolous, magical and digital—within circle of life. Sacred spaces created in imagination; next extension is computer, as elemental as earth, wind, fire, and water. Boundaries between real and virtual are fluidly blurred as rituals and spells are performed online.

PERKS 

- Popular culture considered vital, especially online gaming, Internet surfing, comic books, television shows such as *Buffy the Vampire Slayer*
- Can conduct all religious and social activities online, meeting friends on the technological astral plane
- Many followers on cutting edge of technology
- Most *neo* of the neo-paganisms
- Virtual sexuality is sacred

DRAWBACKS 

- Computer systems, accessories, software are expensive
- Sleepless nights spent in chat sessions across time zones
- Real life (RL) may suffer from too much time spent in cyberspace
- Hard to explain appeal to outsiders (AKA "mundanes")
- Dungeons & Dragons social stigma still looms large
- *Buffy* was canceled

ACTIVITIES

- Cybermancy (running electronic versions of tarot, runes, *I Ching*, astrological charts, etc.)
- Participating in MUDs, MMORPGs, MOOs, MUSHes (multiperson computer games and social networks)
- Chatting online with cybercoven
- Reading science fiction

PARAPHERNALIA

- Hard drives or webpages for compiling personal Books of Shadows
- Screensavers programmed to display mantras and chants
- Tents for Burning Man
- Lodestones to place on top of computers
- Cybercafés for group rituals
- Personal avatars

TEMPLE OF THE VAMPIRE

WHAT IT IS

Incorporated in Washington State in 1989, "only true vampire religion in the world." No blood drinking; instead, partake of humans' and animals' excess "Lifeforce." Two aspects of personality, Dayside and Nightside. First master Dayside (earthly concerns: wealth, health, career), then tackle Nightside (magic: shapeshifting, flying, immortality, communion with the Undead Gods).

PERKS

- Temple law expressly forbids any lawbreaking, including drinking blood
- Lifeforce feeding produces benefits similar to acupuncture, Reiki
- Though members are forbidden to discuss Temple with anyone, exceptions made for spouses and law enforcement
- Only form of proof is individual's own experience: Dayside motto is "Believe nothing"; Nightside motto is "Test everything"
- Get to fly

DRAWBACKS

- Very solitary pursuit; only central organization is online, so no conventional sense of community
- Suffer dark curse for unauthorized use of Temple literature, such as not buying it directly through Temple or sharing it with others
- Constant refrain of "Choose wisely" creates pressure to succeed
- Misrepresentation in television shows, books, movies about vampires

ACTIVITIES

- Constantly reassuring yourself of elite status as a Master of the Earth
- Chatting online with other members
- Progressing through 5 grades of active membership: Vampire Initiate, Predator, Priest/Priestess, Sorcerer/Sorceress, and Adept

PARAPHERNALIA

- Temple membership cards
- *Lifeforce*, monthly newsletter
- "Striking but simple" sterling silver jewelry to remind self of personal nobility and to be identified as Temple supporter
- Winged Skulls of UR to be worn during ritual communions

QUICK RATINGS:

Conversion Difficulty: ① **②** ③ ④ ⑤

Time Commitment: ① ② **③** ④ ⑤

Cost: **①** ② ③ ④ ⑤

New Friends: Unknown

PURPOSE OF LIFE

Master control over Dayside and Nightside, ultimately making connection to Undead Gods that leads to Vampiric Metamorphosis

DEITIES

Undead gods Osiris, Isis, Enki, Inanna, Rama, Krishna, Chang Ling, Quetzalcoatl; self ("I am the only God that is")

KEY TEXTS

The Vampire Bible; *Revelations*; *Bloodlines*

WHERE

United States, Australia, online

AFTERLIFE PROMISES

Achieve physical immortality if commune with Undead Gods; if not, no afterlife

CATEGORY

NRM: Left-Hand Path

TENRIKYO

RELIGION #82

QUICK RATINGS:

Conversion Difficulty: 2 (of 5)

Time Commitment: 3 (of 5)

Cost: 2 (of 5)

New Friends: 3 million

PURPOSE OF LIFE

Live Joyous Life free of disease and suffering by performing *hinokishin*, focusing on others rather than self

DEITIES

God the Parent, Tenri O no Mikoto ("Lord of Heavenly Wisdom")

KEY TEXTS

The Ofudesaki, scripture and teachings; the Mikagura-uta, songs for services; the Osashizu, code of conduct and philosophy

WHERE

Primarily Japan

AFTERLIFE PROMISES

Reincarnation, but focuses on this life; death is akin to shedding old clothes and taking on new ones

CATEGORY

Revealed

WHAT IT IS

One of earliest and largest sects of Japanese NRM movement, only one founded by a woman. In 1838, former Buddhist Miki Nakayama received vision of God the Parent common to us all. She began to carry out his wishes to save humankind through faith healing and *hinokishin*, selfless acts, thoughts, and words, which clear *hokori* (dust) in mind that prevents Joyous Life.

PERKS

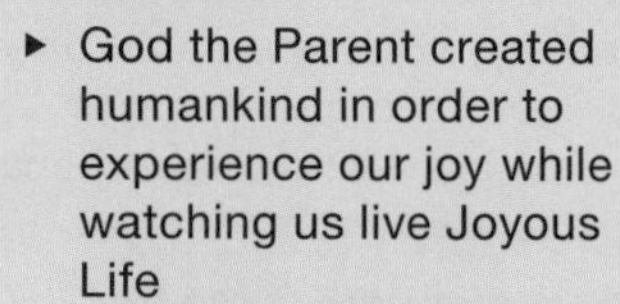

- God the Parent created humankind in order to experience our joy while watching us live Joyous Life
- Optimistic, positive goal of unifying humankind as children of God the Parent
- Encouraged to maintain individuality even while helping others
- *Hinokishin* will return us to "natural state" by "correcting use of the mind"
- Get to experience life dust-free

DRAWBACKS

- Must avoid 8 kinds of self-serving hokori: greed, stinginess, partiality, hatred, animosity, anger, covetousness, and arrogance
- Any happiness that does not bring happiness to others is not real
- Can't get too attached: bodies on loan from God the Parent; therefore, shouldn't give in to infatuation and carnal desires
- Followers sometimes criticized for doing good deeds just to generate publicity

ACTIVITIES

- Monthly services at Tenri headquarters (where God resides), involving dancing in masks around large post symbolizing human creation and spiritual maturity
- Daily reflection to clear dust in mind before it becomes *innen* (stains)
- Providing disaster relief, caring for lepers, faith healing

PARAPHERNALIA

- Amulet, piece of red cloth from clothing of Nakayama (AKA Oyasama, Mother of Humanity), to keep mind pure
- 3 sacred packs of rice to give pregnant women to assure worry-free birth
- Musical instruments for religious services: wooden clappers, gongs, cymbals, drums, bamboo flutes

THEOSOPHY

WHAT IT IS

Movement crystallized in 1875 with founding of Theosophical Society in New York City. Influenced by Spiritualism and Hinduism; inspired New Age movement. Cumulative wisdom (Secret Doctrine, AKA Theosophy) found in every religion by those who know how to look. All existence is one, all cycles according to natural laws, and consciousness progresses through different levels.

PERKS

- *Theosophy* means "divine wisdom" in Greek
- Knowledge of comparative religion will make you a hit at cocktail parties
- You have 7 parts: body; astral body (template for physical form); passions and desires (*kama*); life energy (*prana*); mind (*manas*); individual spirit (*buddhi*); and universal spirit (*atma*)
- Mahatma Gandhi said, "Theosophy is Hinduism in theory, and Hinduism is Theosophy in practice"

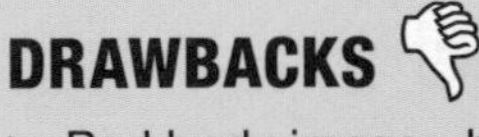

DRAWBACKS

- Bad body image—humans are sparks of divine trapped in material world, cut off from spiritual home
- Devout renounce sex, meat, alcohol, and smoking as unconducive to spiritual existence
- Founder Helena Blavatsky's writings sometimes inconsistent; was accused of fraud
- Role in starting New Age movement may not be appreciated by some

ACTIVITIES

- Interfaith prayer sessions for world peace and to recognize commonality of all religions
- Investigating nature's unexplained laws
- Weekly meetings, which include lectures, meditations, readings
- Yoga for spiritual growth and physical health
- Interpreting dreams

PARAPHERNALIA

- Books by and about Blavatsky; also, on spirituality and comparative religion
- Incense, candles, *mala* prayer beads (from Hinduism) to aid with meditation, which helps connect with transcendent consciousness
- *The Quest* magazine

QUICK RATINGS:

Conversion Difficulty: ① (of 1–5)

Time Commitment: ③ (of 1–5)

Cost: ② (of 1–5)

New Friends: 40,000

PURPOSE OF LIFE

Promote universal brotherhood of human race; study comparative religion, philosophy, science; explore unexplained in nature and latent human powers

DEITIES

Universal Oversoul, with which each individual soul is identified

KEY TEXTS

The Secret Doctrine by Helena Blavatsky

WHERE

Primarily United States, United Kingdom

AFTERLIFE PROMISES

Death is rite of passage; spirit learns lessons of previous life, rests for millennium or so, then reincarnates

CATEGORY

NRM: Esoteric

THERAVADA BUDDHISM

QUICK RATINGS:
Conversion Difficulty: ① ② ③ ④ ⑤   
Time Commitment: ① ② ③ ④ ⑤    
Cost: ① ② ③ ④ ⑤ 
New Friends: 145 million

PURPOSE OF LIFE

Become *arhat* (worthy one, perfected person who will not be reborn) by eliminating all cravings, desires, attachments (self-liberation)

DEITIES

None

KEY TEXTS

Pali Canon, AKA Tripitaka (contains 3 sections, or "baskets": monastic discipline, teachings, and metaphysical doctrines)

WHERE

Worldwide, primarily Southeast Asia

AFTERLIFE PROMISES

Karma-based rebirth until enlightenment (unlike Mahayana, no Bardo stage) and nirvana

CATEGORY

Dharmic: Buddhist

WHAT IT IS

Oldest school of Buddhism; means "Doctrine of the Elders." Most orthodox of 3 main types of Buddhism (vs. Mahayana and Vajrayana). Around 500 BCE, a former Hindu, Siddhartha Gautama (AKA Historical Buddha), realized suffering was part of life. Meditated under tree, reached state of nirvana, then taught Buddhist cornerstones: Four Noble Truths and Noble Eightfold Path.

PERKS

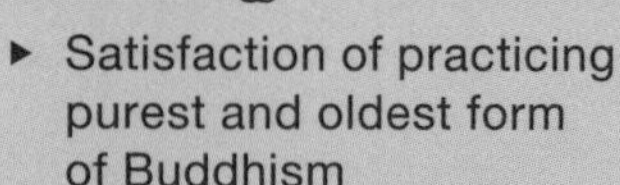

- Satisfaction of practicing purest and oldest form of Buddhism
- Unlike Mahayana, emphasis on self-salvation (vs. helping others achieve salvation); highly individualistic
- Good for cerebral types: focuses on wisdom (vs. compassion of Mahayana)
- Three Trainings—ethical conduct, meditation, and wisdom—help with self-salvation
- Light on ritual and wallet

DRAWBACKS

- Almost impossible to achieve enlightenment as layperson; life of *sangha* (monks) and adherence to Ten Precepts (no sex, money, etc.) not compatible with contemporary life
- While Vipassana (insight meditation) results in permanent change, results are only temporary with Samatha (calming meditation)
- Tripitaka is 20,000 pages
- May step in yak dung during walking meditation

ACTIVITIES

- Following Five Precepts (Ten for monks)
- Providing food and other necessities to sangha in exchange for spiritual guidance and blessings
- *Uposatha*, group worship on 4 monthly Moon Days
- Monastery retreats
- Accumulating merit
- Lots of meditating

PARAPHERNALIA

- Symbols such as Bodhi tree (AKA Tree of Wisdom, under which Gautama meditated), lotus, Buddha's footprints, 8-spoked wheel (represents Noble Eightfold Path)
- Simple temples (Mahayana temples are elaborate)
- Personal shrines with incense, candles, flowers, Buddha statues, meditation cushions

TIBETAN BUDDHISM

WHAT IT IS

Form of Vajrayana (tantric) Buddhism, distinguished by shamanistic influence of indigenous religion, Bön; monastic tradition; supernatural beings and magic; concept of reincarnating lamas (bodhisattvas). Practice incorporates traditional Buddhist precepts with emphasis on student-teacher knowledge transmission, ritual, life and death cycle, universal love and compassion.

PERKS 

- Emphasis on happiness and peace; Dzogchen meditation seeks peace beyond peace
- Get *yidam* (personal deity) that stays with you for life as focus of your worship
- More outward, communal worship than other forms of Buddhism
- Ceremonies are lively events, with music and chanting
- Rich in color, symbolism, art
- Trendy

DRAWBACKS 

- Chinese government persecution; Dalai Lama leads from exile in India
- Memorization of mantras
- Difficulty of universal love and compassion

ACTIVITIES

- Chanting prayers
- Performing *mudras* (sacred hand gestures) during meditation
- Promoting Tibetan rights
- Taming mind to free it in order to love others
- Practicing 6 yogas of Naropa, inner work to realize that reality is just projection

PARAPHERNALIA

- Images and statues of deities
- Colorful prayer flags
- Mantra-inscribed prayer wheels
- Butter sculptures

QUICK RATINGS:

Conversion Difficulty: ① ② ③ ④ ⑤ (3)

Time Commitment: ① ② ③ ④ ⑤ (3)

Cost: ① ② ③ ④ ⑤ (2)

New Friends: 23 million

PURPOSE OF LIFE

Use divine energy (tantra) of universe to realize own Buddha nature and act as spiritual guide for others

DEITIES

Many, including Five Dhyani Buddhas, Eight Wrathful Deities, goddess Tara, Four Heavenly Kings

KEY TEXTS

Tibetan Buddhist Canon: Kanjyur; Tenjyur; Bardo Thodol (Tibetan Book of the Dead)

WHERE

Worldwide, primarily Nepal, Bhutan, Tibet, Mongolia

AFTERLIFE PROMISES

Karma-based rebirth cycle with emphasis on Bardo, stage in which living help deceased make transition

CATEGORY

Dharmic: Buddhist

WHAT THEY SAID

It can be difficult to sound intelligent when talking about religion, particularly if you're trying to justify an unconventional choice or change someone's mind. As a seeker, whether religious, spiritual, agnostic, or atheist, you will come across individuals who will attempt to dissuade you from your path. Not to worry, there's no need for original thought—people have been saying smart things about religion for thousands of years. Just memorize a few of these pithy ruminations and pull them from your mental back pocket whenever necessary.

Religion is probably, after sex, the second oldest resource which human beings have available to them for blowing their minds.

—SUSAN SONTAG

You can do very little with faith, but you can do nothing without it.

—SAMUEL BUTLER

In the affairs of this world men are saved, not by faith, but by want of it.

—BENJAMIN FRANKLIN

Faith is much better than belief. Belief is when someone else does the thinking.

—R. BUCKMINSTER FULLER

I do not feel obligated to believe that the same God who has endowed us with sense, reasons, and intellect has intended us to forgo their use.

—GALILEO GALILEI

I think that the leaf of a tree, the meanest insect on which we trample, are in themselves arguments more conclusive than any which can be adduced that some vast intellect animates Infinity.

—PERCY BYSSHE SHELLEY

The first and last lesson of religion is, "The things that are seen are temporal; the things that are unseen are eternal."

—RALPH WALDO EMERSON

The many great gardens of the world, of literature and poetry, of painting and music, of religion and architecture, all make the point as clear as possible: the soul cannot thrive in the absence of a garden. If you don't want paradise, you are not human; and if you are not human, you don't have a soul.

—THOMAS MOORE

The man who regards his own life and that of his fellow creatures as meaningless is not merely unfortunate but almost disqualified for life.

—ALBERT EINSTEIN

Only barbarians are not curious about where they come from, how they came to be where they are, where they appear to be going, whether they wish to go there, and if so, why, and if not, why not.

—ISAIAH BERLIN

I do not consider it an insult, but rather a compliment to be called an agnostic. I do not pretend to know where many ignorant men are sure—that is all that agnosticism means.

—CLARENCE DARROW

When we blindly adopt a religion, a political system, a literary dogma, we become automatons. We cease to grow.

—ANAÏS NIN

Doubt is part of all religion. All the religious thinkers were doubters.

—ISAAC BASHEVIS SINGER

Difference of opinion is helpful in religion.

—THOMAS JEFFERSON

You can safely assume that you've created God in your own image when it turns out that God hates all the same people you do.

—ANNE LAMOTT

In the matter of religion, people eagerly fasten their eyes on the difference between their own creed and yours; whilst the charm of the study is in finding the agreements and identities in all the religions of humanity.

—RALPH WALDO EMERSON

In religion and politics, people's beliefs and convictions are in almost every case gotten at secondhand, and without examination.

—MARK TWAIN

Those who say religion has nothing to do with politics do not know what religion is.

—MOHANDAS K. GANDHI

Many have quarreled about religion that never practiced it.

—BENJAMIN FRANKLIN

Religion is a candle inside a multicolored lantern. Everyone looks through a particular color, but the candle is always there.

—MUHAMMAD NAGUIB

God made so many different kinds of people. Why would he allow only one way to serve him?

—MARTIN BUBER

Religion enables us to ignore nothingness and get on with the jobs of life.

—JOHN UPDIKE

It may be that religion is dead, and if it is, we had better know it and set ourselves to try to discover other sources of moral strength before it is too late.

—PEARL S. BUCK

Mankind have banned the Divinity from their presence; they have relegated him to a sanctuary; the walls of the temple restrict his view; he does not exist outside of it.

—DENIS DIDEROT

Every day people are straying away from the church and going back to God.

—LENNY BRUCE

I do benefits for all religions—I'd hate to blow the hereafter on a technicality.

—BOB HOPE

If you gain, you gain all; if you lose, you lose nothing. Wager, then, without hesitation, that He exists.

—BLAISE PASCAL

Making fun of born-again Christians is like hunting dairy cows with a high-powered rifle and scope.

—P. J. O'ROURKE

TRANSCENDENTAL MEDITATION

RELIGION #86

QUICK RATINGS:

Conversion Difficulty:	1
Time Commitment:	3
Cost:	2
New Friends:	6 million

PURPOSE OF LIFE
Through meditation, harness full energy, creativity, and intelligence, as well as make world better place

DEITIES
No official deity; Maharishi has stated enlightenment is path to God (eternal being existing in many forms)

KEY TEXTS
Science of Being and Art of Living by Maharishi Mahesh Yogi; for advanced study, Bhagavad Gita and Rig Veda

WHERE
Worldwide, primarily United States, United Kingdom, India

AFTERLIFE PROMISES
None; goal is heaven on earth through meditation

CATEGORY
NRM: Hindu Oriented

WHAT IT IS
New Age movement, started in 1958 by Maharishi Mahesh Yogi, and based on Hindu-inspired meditation techniques. Followers meditate twice daily using mantras of single Sanskrit words. Goal is to achieve Transcendental consciousness to align with natural law of universe, then progress to Cosmic, God, and Unity levels of consciousness, representing "full awakening."

PERKS 
- Followers profess immediate positive impact on well-being and say even if you don't believe in it, it works (like gravity)
- Invisibility and levitation (Yogic Flying) abilities attributed to masters
- May cut crime rates and foster social harmony (Maharishi Effect)
- Over 600 scientific studies cited to back up claims
- Maharishi's nickname was "the Giggling Guru"
- Many celebrity followers

DRAWBACKS 
- Mantras supposed to be unique and secret, but former members say people get same ones based on age, sex, etc.
- Yogic Flying disputed as jumping in lotus position
- Cult accusations

ACTIVITIES
- Initiation: pay $2,500, bring fruit and flowers as offerings, and receive instruction and mantra from teacher
- Meditating 20 minutes, twice a day
- Getting degree at Maharishi University of Management, in Iowa
- Political activism through group's Natural Law Party

PARAPHERNALIA
- Maharishi's line of ayurvedic supplements, enemas, etc.
- *Global Good News*, online publication

TRANSCENDENTALISM

WHAT IT IS

Early Transcendentalism rejected religious doctrines of mid-19th-century New England in attempt to reform philosophy, literature, culture, and religion. Spirituality stems not from creed or knowledge but from individual intuition. Divinity found in humanity and natural world; God is Universal Soul, all-pervading. Hugely influential; marks beginning of distinction between spirituality and religion.

PERKS

- Optimistic about human divinity and potential for utopian social change
- Self-reliance is useful
- Basic texts are sublime classics; can experience faith in fiction, poetry, *and* philosophy
- Claim lineage to forward-thinking movements, such as Beat Generation, feminism, civil rights, New Age, environmentalism, Cultural Creatives movement
- Get to experience God in nature

DRAWBACKS 

- Mostly to be found as influence in other arenas
- Despite assertion that divinity comes from intuition, not knowledge, will have to do lots of reading to understand original Transcendentalism
- No holidays or icons
- Farming, composting, homeschooling, nature communing, etc. are time-consuming

ACTIVITIES

- Promoting social change; fighting injustice, conformity
- Advancing environmentalism; shunning materialism
- Contemplating, especially in nature
- Creating art with authentic self-expression
- Seeing divinity, dignity, beauty in everything around you

PARAPHERNALIA

- Recycling and composting bins
- Solar panels
- Natural-fiber clothing (if cotton, pesticide-free)
- Cloth bags for groceries
- Hybrid cars
- Well-read volumes of Emerson, Thoreau
- Journals, art supplies
- Yoga mats

QUICK RATINGS:

Conversion Difficulty:

Time Commitment:

Cost:

New Friends:
1

PURPOSE OF LIFE

Improve society through self-reliance; transcend materialistic world, following divine guidance within yourself, to find "an original relation to the universe" (Emerson); realize God is everywhere, within everyone

DEITIES

God, AKA Universal Soul, Oversoul, or Divine Soul, connects everything

KEY TEXTS

Nature and *Essays* by Ralph Waldo Emerson; *Walden* by Henry David Thoreau

WHERE

United States

AFTERLIFE PROMISES

None

CATEGORY

Non-Revealed

UNIFICATION CHURCH

QUICK RATINGS:

Conversion Difficulty: ① **②** ③ ④ ⑤

Time Commitment: ① ② ③ **④** ⑤

Cost: ① ② ③ **④** ⑤

New Friends: 50,000

PURPOSE OF LIFE

Achieve true love, not selfish love (fornication), through creation of True Families; pay for sins by fasting, fund-raising, and recruiting; unite Christianity—and whole world—into Moon's true faith

DEITIES

God, Moon (Jesus was just good man who died before completing work)

KEY TEXTS

Divine Principle by Sun Myung Moon; Bible

WHERE

Worldwide, primarily South Korea, United States

AFTERLIFE PROMISES

Heaven for saved, hell for unsaved; departed souls can be contacted from earth

CATEGORY

NRM: Christian Oriented

WHAT IT IS

Founded by Rev. Sun Myung Moon in South Korea in 1954 after Jesus told Moon he would be new messiah to complete Jesus' unfinished business: marrying and procreating. Moon charged with redirecting humankind to God's will by promoting blessed marital unions and sex only for procreation to produce "children born without sin." Moon, wife, and children comprise first True Family.

PERKS 

- No more blind dates: church pairs singles; supposedly Moon himself makes all matches by reviewing photographs
- After marriage, no need for birth control
- Can be employed by any of hundreds of church businesses, including political, recruiting, media
- Moon exceedingly well connected with politicians and celebrities

DRAWBACKS 

- Moon was jailed for tax evasion; also accused of sexual impropriety, excessive spending, fraud
- 10 to 100 percent tithing
- Despite church's best efforts, followers still called Moonies

ACTIVITIES

- Mass marriage ceremonies, known as the Blessing Ceremony, which may involve thousands; 5 steps involved, including 40-day abstinence period post-marriage
- Observing day you joined church as your birthday
- Bowing before altar with Moon's picture at 5:00 AM on Sunday mornings (ritual pledge service)

PARAPHERNALIA

- *Washington Times*, newspaper owned by church
- Posters of True Family, Moons and some 40 offspring, grandchildren, etc.

UNITARIAN UNIVERSALISM

WHAT IT IS

All-inclusive, politically liberal, socially conscious movement, begun in Boston in 1961 with merger of Universalist Church of America and American Unitarian Association. Non-creedal approach; followers look to reason, conscience, personal experience, and diverse wisdom traditions for insight. God is everywhere and in everyone. Embraces all beliefs, including atheism and agnosticism.

PERKS

- Humans considered good
- All races, religions, political affiliations, sexual orientations welcome
- Trendsetters: UUs have performed same-sex marriages since 1960s
- Strong history of civil rights activism
- Despite free-thinking and relaxed atmosphere without set liturgy, strong sense of community and many holidays, traditions, ceremonies
- No conversion practices

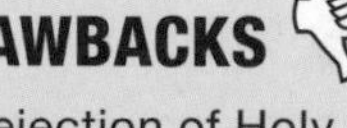

DRAWBACKS

- Rejection of Holy Trinity viewed as heretical by traditional Christians; support for same-sex marriages may incur hostility from religious conservatives
- Sometimes difficult to affirm worth of all human beings and live ethically
- Public service and activism time-consuming
- No afterlife assurance
- Nickname among followers is UUs (pronounced YOO-yooz); also, UUism

ACTIVITIES

- Sunday services
- Child dedications for babies, coming-of-age ceremonies for teens
- Flower Communion (in spring; congregants exchange flowers to reaffirm individuality)
- Water Communion (in fall; congregants bring and combine water to reaffirm community bonds)

PARAPHERNALIA

- Chalice (wide-lipped cup), lit at beginning of worship services to symbolize spiritual quest and unity of members
- Hymnals of the "Living Tradition"
- Posters of Principles and Sources, 7 principles by which UUs live and 6 sources from which UUs draw

QUICK RATINGS:

Conversion Difficulty:
① ② ③ ④ ⑤

Time Commitment:
① **②** ③ ④ ⑤

Cost:
① ② ③ ④ ⑤

New Friends:
800,000

PURPOSE OF LIFE

Recognize worth of every person; pursue justice, equity, compassion; search for truth and meaning; respect interdependent web of existence

DEITIES

Unspecified God everywhere and in everything, but belief not required

KEY TEXTS

No one religious text held as dominant, but Bible often used for teaching

WHERE

North America

AFTERLIFE PROMISES

Individuals determine own beliefs; however, no such thing as eternal punishment

CATEGORY

Syncretic

UNITED NUWAUBIAN NATION OF MOORS

QUICK RATINGS:

Conversion Difficulty:	① ② ③ ④ ⑤ (4)
Time Commitment:	① ② ③ ④ ⑤ (3)
Cost:	① ② ③ ④ ⑤ (2)
New Friends:	500

PURPOSE OF LIFE

Use Right Thinking, Right Knowledge, Right Wisdom, and Right Overstanding to break *Kingu* ("Spell of Ignorance") propagated by religion, media, schools

DEITIES

Anu, Most High

KEY TEXTS

Writings of Dr. Malachi Z. York

WHERE

United States, primarily Georgia, online

AFTERLIFE PROMISES

Physical body recycles into ground then enters atmosphere as particles; women breathe particles into bloodstream, become pregnant, and flesh is thus reanimated

CATEGORY

NRM: Alien Oriented

WHAT IT IS

Colorful group, founded by former Black Panther Dr. Malachi Z. York, Supreme Grand Master. Under York's leadership, changing beliefs have derived from Islam, ancient Egypt, Native Americans, Judaism, Masonic ritual, Christianity, and outer space. York himself hails from planet Rizq but is now serving 135-year sentence on earth for racketeering and child molestation.

PERKS 

- Sometime soon, spacecraft will bring 144,000 Nuwaubians back to Rizq for rebirth
- Only doctrine is respecting Mother Earth and living by York's teachings
- Cool, syllable-altering language called Sound Right Reasoning (*Caucasian* becomes *carcass-ian*, *television* becomes *tell-lie-vision*, etc.)

DRAWBACKS 

- Even though group has claimed to be Native American (and thus sovereign from United States), must be African American to join
- Disco is creation of devil
- Group's Georgia compound (Tama-Re, or Egypt of the West) was sold to developer
- May have to move to Liberia if York is released

ACTIVITIES

- Burying afterbirth when baby is born so Satan cannot make clone
- Campaigning for founder's release
- Keeping track of York's many names and changing beliefs

PARAPHERNALIA

- New outfits each time belief system changes (previous articles have included fez hats, nostril rings, tunics, and shoes called Romeos)
- Special Nuwaubic fonts
- *The Truth* magazine

UNIVERSAL LIFE CHURCH

WHAT IT IS

Nondenominational church, founded in 1959 by Rev. Kirby J. Hensley. Hensley never learned to read or write, sought to form ministry for all people. More than 50 congregations; two main branches, original ULC in Modesto, CA, and ULC Monastery in Seattle. No doctrine; each person finds own path. Promotes diversity and religious freedom. Best known for mail-order ordination services.

PERKS

- Ordination online—for free—makes you a minister who can marry and bury; potentially lucrative ($100 to $800 per ceremony)
- Option to pray and confess online
- All living people are part of Universal Life, according to Hensley, so whole world is your flock
- Congregations can incorporate their own flavor, e.g., ULC Pagan Ministries
- All 4 Beatles were ULC ministers

DRAWBACKS 

- Must be a real person to be ordained; if you have unusual name, such as Seymour Butts or Ben Dover, may be required to submit proof of identity
- Must know local laws about what ministers can and can't do
- Not considered a true church by some, but rather a money-making scheme (IRS tried to revoke tax-exempt status but failed)
- May be too unstructured for certain followers

ACTIVITIES

- Discussing ULC, philosophical and legal issues, ministering in online forums
- Promoting spiritual progress and freedom, especially the First Amendment and civil rights
- Annual ULC conventions
- Marrying, burying, baptizing, etc.

PARAPHERNALIA

- Ministry-in-a-Box: includes minister's manual; certificate of ordination; wallet ID card; certificate of Doctor of Divinity; 15 certificates for weddings, house blessings, etc.; ULC clergy badge; laminated clergy parking placard
- Minister's Car Kit: includes license-plate covers, bumper stickers, and more

QUICK RATINGS:

Conversion Difficulty:
1 2 3 4 5

Time Commitment:
1 2 3 4 5

Cost:
1 2 3 4 5

New Friends:
22 million

PURPOSE OF LIFE

"To do that which is right" and "to live and help live," providing "a fuller life for everyone"; Eternal Progression (undefined)

DEITIES

Many references to God, though different faiths, atheism, agnosticism embraced

KEY TEXTS

All sacred texts viable; prayer references often come from Bible

WHERE

North America, online

AFTERLIFE PROMISES

Eternal Progression and reincarnation of soul until nothing separates it from the divine

CATEGORY

NRM: Mail-Order Oriented

URANTIA BROTHERHOOD

QUICK RATINGS:

Conversion Difficulty: ① ② ③ ④ ⑤ (1)

Time Commitment: ① ② ③ ④ ⑤ (4)

Cost: ① ② ③ ④ ⑤ (1)

New Friends: 1,500

PURPOSE OF LIFE

Understand all by reading book; follow internal Thought Adjuster (divine spark within); continue eons-long progression toward perfection and unity with God

DEITIES

God the Father, AKA I AM; Jesus, one of many Eternal Sons; Infinite Spirit

KEY TEXTS

The Urantia Book by Urantia Foundation

WHERE

United States, Europe, amazon.com

AFTERLIFE PROMISES

Development continues in 7 Mansion Worlds on way to paradise with help of angels to guide and teach

CATEGORY

NRM: Revealed

WHAT IT IS

Follows teachings from *The Urantia Book*, published in 1955, 2,097 pages channeled from supernatural beings through "SS" (Sleeping Subject), who spoke book's truths while slumbering. Transcribed by former Seventh-Day Adventists and doctors William and Lena Sadler. Explains true nature of universe and humankind's place in it, history of Urantia (earth), and Jesus.

PERKS 

- Everything you need to know lies between covers of one (very long and, many say, difficult to understand) book
- Book out of copyright, available for free on Internet
- May appeal to fans of science fiction, as cosmology (view of universe) is quite imaginative, with many inhabited worlds and levels of space
- No services, code of behavior, creed, clergy
- We are all children of God

DRAWBACKS 

- Must base life on book of unknown origin containing untranslated terms from unknown language
- No holidays, not much fellowship
- Despite its supernatural channeling by unnamed Sleeping Subject, book has faced persistent allegations of plagiarism
- Hard to believe claims that original humans were red, orange, yellow, green, blue, and indigo
- Followers inelegantly called *agondonters*

ACTIVITIES

- Reading *The Urantia Book*
- Rereading *The Urantia Book*
- Participating in book study groups, in person and online
- Spreading book's teachings by word of mouth
- Attending meetings, seminars, conferences about book

PARAPHERNALIA

- *Urantia News*, biannual publication of Urantia Foundation
- Urantia Foundation silver membership pins
- Outreach tools such as "How to Tell People About the Urantia Book Without Telling Them About the Urantia Book"
- Cornflakes (main founders were Kelloggs)

Though it may seem uncharitable to think about the cost of participation in a religion, it's practical. For everybody, no matter how wealthy, money is a finite resource, so it's critical to determine whether a religion will fit into your budget over a lifetime.

RELIGION	MONEY SPENT ON	TOTAL
Scientology	Coursework, auditing, internships, literature, recordings, and E-Meter necessary to get up to Operating Thetan Level VIII	$350,000
Mormonism	Expenses during mission ($400 per month), 10 percent annual tithe	$208,400
Catholicism	Collection plate (1 percent of income), Catholic school ($4,000 per year; 3 children)	$156,000
Islam	Mosque membership ($60 per year), *zakat* (income tithing; 6.25 percent), increase in food costs for *halal* diet, hajj (pilgrimage to Mecca)	$136,207
Healthy Happy Holy	Yoga classes ($80 per month), white clothing ($300 per year), retreats ($1,500 per year)	$110,400
Wicca	Introductory courses ($1,060), books, paraphernalia, and perishables for spells ($840 per year), travel to gatherings and Renaissance Faire attendance ($895 per year)	$70,460
Judaism	Conversion costs ($1,200), annual synagogue membership ($1,200 per year), increase in food costs to keep kosher	$62,442
Atheism	Reading materials, lifetime membership in Atheist Alliance International ($1,000), annual convention attendance ($600 per year)	$25,250
Zen Buddhism	Meditation cushions, *sangha* meal donations for blessing ($100 per year), voluntary donations to monastic order ($25 per month)	$25,020
Temple of the Vampire	*The Vampire Bible* (hardcover $35), active membership ($10 per month)	$4,835

NOTE: Recurring costs calculated based on 40 years of religion membership. Tithing based on median American household income of $50,000.

VEDANTA SOCIETY

QUICK RATINGS:

Conversion Difficulty:

Time Commitment:

Cost:

New Friends:
65,000

PURPOSE OF LIFE
"Liberation for oneself and service to mankind"; lift veil of *maya* (ignorance) that keeps us from knowing God and *atman* (one's true self)

DEITIES
Brahman, Supreme Reality, worshipped in different forms

KEY TEXTS
Bhagavad Gita; Vedanta Sutras; Vedas; Upanishads

WHERE
Worldwide, primarily India, United States

AFTERLIFE PROMISES
Atman reborn into new body until attains God realization (AKA Self-realization) and experiences *moksha* (release)

CATEGORY
NRM: Hindu Oriented

WHAT IT IS
Hindu belief system, with mission of applicability to all cultures, not just India; founded around 1900. From the Hindi words *veda* (knowledge) and *anta* (goal), refers to search for knowledge of God and our own divinity. Faith in multiple avatars (God in human form), including Christ, Muhammad, Buddha. Stresses same truth in all religions, service to others, and unity of existence.

PERKS 
- No sin or evil, only mistakes and ignorance
- Free to visualize the divine in any way that feels right
- Everyone has a divine nature and potential to realize it
- Get to recognize oneness rather than separateness
- Nonmonastic members don't need to abstain from alcohol, meat, sex
- Opposes caste system
- Historical friends include Aldous Huxley, Greta Garbo

DRAWBACKS 
- Service oriented, focus on eradication of poverty; may be time-consuming
- Eating beef discouraged; cows not sacred but highly regarded, like pets; better to have milk for long time than eat meat once
- Can't enter monastic life if older than 35
- May need to revisit views on yoga: goal not washboard abs but growth, development, fulfillment
- Need to find right swami

ACTIVITIES
- Overcoming *maya* and separateness via purification through 4 yoga paths: *karma* (selfless work), *bhakti* (love and devotion), *raja* (meditation and psychic control), and *jnana* (knowledge)
- Receiving meditation instruction through teachers and on retreats
- *Puja* (worship) services for variety of occasions

PARAPHERNALIA
- *Prabuddha Bharata*, journal published since 1896; quarterly *American Vedantist*
- Items to symbolize elements: *arati* lamps (fire); conch shells (water); flowers (earth); *chamaras* (yak-tail fans; air)
- Bells to ring during worship to invoke eternally reverberating *OM* of universe

VODOU

WHAT IT IS

Haitian blend of Catholicism and Yoruban, Dahomean, and Kongo traditions of slaves. *Vodun* means "spirit" in African language Fon, and Vodou is based on belief that everything is spirit: humans are living and visible, while others are unseen, including *lwa* (spirits), *mystè* (mysteries), *anvizib* (invisibles), *zang* (angels), and ancestors. Elaborate rituals revolve around serving God and spirits.

PERKS

- Get to hang on to your spirits: spirits often grouped in families and passed down through generations
- Only white magic (brings good results and healing) practiced, except by *malfacteurs* wielding "left-handed Vodou"
- No longer need to practice in secret; sanctioned as official religion in Haiti in 2003
- Can marry and have sex with your spirit
- Community oriented

DRAWBACKS 

- Might be possessed by hot spirit: cool (Rada) spirits came from Africa, while hot (Petro) originated in New World and carry rage of enslaved
- Must keep Iwa happy because everything that happens to you is in their hands; little free will
- Can't take shortcut to initiation: some priests charge thousands for truncated ceremony, but not viewed as authentic
- Must speak to your ancestors daily

ACTIVITIES

- *Tambors*, parties with drumming, dancing, and singing to invite Iwa to possess initiates
- Multiple levels of initiation
- If "owned" by multiple Iwa, negotiating harmony between them
- Celebrating Ghede spirits (responsible for death, fertility, and humor) in November

PARAPHERNALIA

- Elaborate altars
- Sacred bead-adorned rattles presented to *mambos* (priestesses) and *houngans* (priests) upon initiation into priesthood
- Special bags for holding ingredients for *wangas* (spells)
- Sequined flags representing Iwas

QUICK RATINGS:

Conversion Difficulty:

① ② ③ ④ ⑤ 

Time Commitment:

① ② ③ ④ ⑤  

Cost:

① ② ③ ④ ⑤  

New Friends:
8 million

PURPOSE OF LIFE

World is alive with spirits; individual must find harmony with them, particularly the ones who "own his or her head"

DEITIES

Bondje, Christian God, from *bon dieu*; Iwa (spirits); ancestors

KEY TEXTS

None; oral tradition

WHERE

Haiti

AFTERLIFE PROMISES

Spirit may be captured in *govi* (clay pot) and live on as ancestor, or may be escorted by Papa Baron (guardian of dead) to world of Iwa

CATEGORY

African Diasporic

IT'S THE END OF THE WORLD

If you're looking into religion, you're inevitably going to hear that the end of the world is coming—but when and how? Some religions, such as Buddhism, view time as cyclic in nature, but the Abrahamic traditions have always incorporated some sort of end-of-days vision.

BRAHMA KUMARIS

At the end of time, 900,000 faithful Brahma Kumaris followers will be reborn in a new Golden Age, and the cycle will start all over again.

CATHOLICISM

Jesus will come to judge the living and the dead, sentencing them to heaven or hell. All souls in purgatory will be released to join the heaven-bound.

ISLAM

The Day of Judgment will be preceded by a 30-year period of pain and debauchery. Jesus will then appear on earth and urge Christians to convert to Islam, and there will be a war between the unconverted Christians (led by the Antichrist) and the Muslims (led by Jesus and Iman Mahd, a descendant of Muhammad). On the last day, the Final Trumpet will sound and only the true faithful will survive to live in peace and prosperity until Al-Qiyámah, the Resurrection.

JEHOVAH'S WITNESSES

At the end of days, 144,000 of the elect will join God in heaven while the rest will either be destroyed in Armageddon or live on in an earthly paradise ruled by the 144,000.

JUDAISM

The Messiah (a descendant of King David) will come to earth to bring about world peace, gather the Jews in Israel, resurrect the dead, and direct the rebuilding of the Temple in Jerusalem.

MAYA

According to the Mayan sacred text, the Popul Vuh, we are currently living in the Fifth (and possibly final) Age. Mayan calendars reckon time only up to December 21, 2012.

PENTECOSTALISM

True believers will experience rapture and simultaneously ascend to heaven. Seven years later, after the Great Tribulation, Christ will return to earth to rule over a millennium of peace before the Final Judgment, when he will sentence everybody to heaven or hell.

ZOROASTRIANISM

Zoroastrians believe history consists of 1,000-year periods, each ending in warfare and destruction, until the final period, when a king named Saoshyant will come to reign in peace and purity forever. Note: This was all supposed to have happened in the year 2000.

WICCA

WHAT IT IS

Largest sect of Neo-Paganism; arose in mid-20th century. Based on pre-Christian Anglo-Saxon and Celtic practices but with embrace of all polytheistic, pre-Christian faiths, such as Norse, Greek, Egyptian, Hindu. Central tenets include reverence of nature, invocation of ceremonial magic (witchcraft), and worship of the Goddess and other deities (often manifestations of natural forces).

PERKS

- Practice in covens or alone ("solitaries")
- Men and women equal, all sexualities welcome; can pursue feminist offshoot, Dianic Wicca
- More experiential and symbolic than intellectual
- Spells often rhyme
- Opportunities to socialize "skyclad" (naked)
- Rituals are outdoors and sometimes culminate in dancing, cakes, ale
- Burning at stake extremely rare nowadays

DRAWBACKS 

- No harnessing energies of universe for personal gain
- "Witch" still carries negative, Satanic stigma (only 20 percent "out of closet" about their practice)
- Accoutrements can get expensive

ACTIVITIES

- Training for "a year and a day," then initiation and dedication ceremonies for newer followers
- Casting circles (sacred spaces) by invoking powers of 4 directions
- Rituals, spells, and earth and Goddess worship
- Celebrating eight *sabbats* (holy days), including solstices and equinoxes

PARAPHERNALIA

- Books of Shadows to record spells
- Pentagrams, pentacles
- Chalices, cauldrons, crystals, candles, herbs

QUICK RATINGS:

Conversion Difficulty:
① ② **③** ④ ⑤

Time Commitment:
① ② **③** ④ ⑤

Cost:
① ② **③** ④ ⑤

New Friends:
200,000

PURPOSE OF LIFE

Observe Rule of Three (any energy put into universe will return to you threefold); honor nature; follow "An it harm none, do what ye will"

DEITIES

Triple Goddess, trinity of maiden, mother, crone; her consort, Horned God; many deities from other traditions

KEY TEXTS

Include *Witchcraft Today* by Gerald Gardner; *Drawing Down the Moon* by Margot Adler

WHERE

North America, United Kingdom

AFTERLIFE PROMISES

Reincarnate eternally or until enlightenment; before rebirth soul rests in Summerland

CATEGORY

NRM: Neo-Pagan

YORUBA

RELIGION #96

QUICK RATINGS:

Conversion Difficulty: ① ② ③ **④** ⑤

Time Commitment: ① ② **③** ④ ⑤

Cost: ① **②** ③ ④ ⑤

New Friends: 856,000

PURPOSE OF LIFE

Realize *ori inu* by drawing on *ase* of gods, family, and nature; because life is gift from Olodumare, express gratitude, graciousness, politeness

DEITIES

Olodumare, ultimate deity, AKA Olorun; 401 orisas

KEY TEXTS

None; oral tradition, Odu Ifa, contains all Yoruba wisdom

WHERE

Primarily Nigeria

AFTERLIFE PROMISES

3 levels of existence: soul of baby in heaven before birth, human on earth, then appear before Olodumare for judgment after death

CATEGORY

Indigenous: African

WHAT IT IS

Indigenous beliefs of Nigerian Yoruba people, AKA Ifa. Via slave trade, root of many African diasporic religions, including Santeria and Candomble. Universe has 2 halves: *aye* (realm of living) and *orun* (realm of spirits), which includes *orisas* (deities) and ancestors. *Ase* (life force) runs through all. Each person born with *ori inu* (personal destiny); divination is key to staying on path.

PERKS

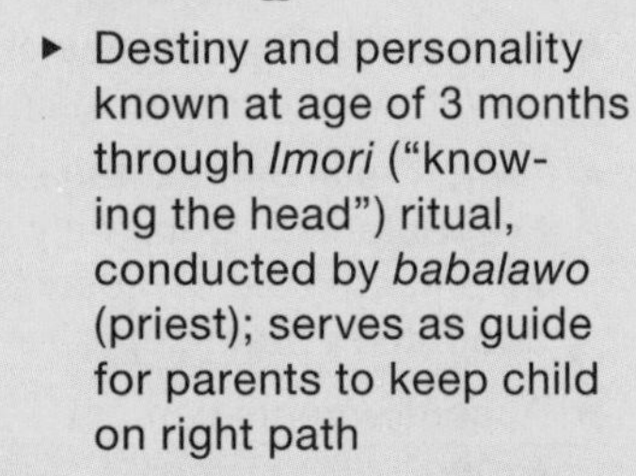

- Destiny and personality known at age of 3 months through *Imori* ("knowing the head") ritual, conducted by *babalawo* (priest); serves as guide for parents to keep child on right path
- When path is unclear, can consult with babalawo for divination (interpretation of signs involving 16 sacred palm nuts)
- Elders respected
- In rituals, emphasis on storytelling, improvisation, play

DRAWBACKS

- Though baby chooses its own destiny before birth, in later years this may feel confining
- Parental consent necessary to wed
- Female circumcision
- Taboos on premarital sex and sex during lactation
- Women shave heads at end of mourning periods
- While diasporic forms of Yoruba are increasing in popularity, original in Nigeria is decreasing due to Islam and Christianity

ACTIVITIES

- *Tambor* celebrations: altars built with offerings to orisas, then drumming and dancing to orisa-specific rhythms
- Weaving, beadwork, pottery, metalsmithing, carving
- *Egungun* festival for ancestors, with men in colorful costumes and masks to represent ancestral spirits

PARAPHERNALIA

- Divination tools: palm nuts, *opon* (tray), *opele* (chain), *iroke* (tapper), *agere* (bowl)
- Sacred 3-piece *bata* drums and other percussion instruments for music that has influenced jazz, blues, gospel, salsa
- Carved statuary, headdresses, staffs

ZEN BUDDHISM

WHAT IT IS

Form of Mahayana Buddhism. Adheres to basic Buddhist precepts, incorporating elements of Taoism and yoga. Brought to China by Indian monk, Bodhidharma, around 6th century BCE; later spread to Japan and Korea. Focuses on true Buddha nature (all humans possess; must be revealed through practice) and "consciousness only" meditation (*zen* means "meditation").

PERKS

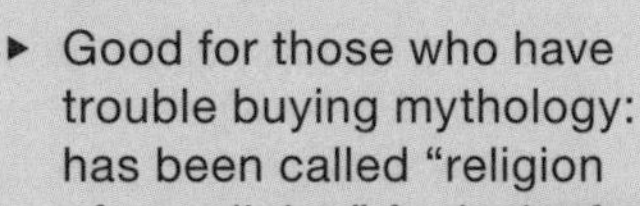

- Good for those who have trouble buying mythology: has been called "religion of no religion" for lack of dogma, doctrine, deities
- Can attain satori through *koans*, mental paradoxes to fatigue mind and jolt student into awareness
- Guidance from Zen master: teacher-student relationship central to temple-based training system
- Values spontaneity and naturalness in all things

DRAWBACKS

- Zen meditation (*zazen*) involves "just sitting," with goal to achieve absolute stillness and emptiness to realize true self; can require many hours in this state; founder practiced wall gazing, facing wall at temple for 9 years
- May be prodded with *kyosaku* (waking stick) if you sleep while meditating
- Can't brown-nose your way to salvation: about moment-by-moment awareness rather than good deeds

ACTIVITIES

- Attempting to give *roshi* (teacher) satisfactory answers to assigned koan
- Attending temple meditation sessions
- Helping care for temple
- Forms of meditation other than sitting, such as raking sand, arranging rocks, *kinhin* (walking zazen)
- Intensive meditation retreats

PARAPHERNALIA

- *Kanshos* (bells rung at beginning and end of zazen)
- Images of Laughing Buddha, considered in Zen to be the future Buddha
- *Zafus*, round, pleated black meditation cushions
- Black robes worn by monks during services
- *Oryoki* bowls for food offerings to monks

QUICK RATINGS:

Conversion Difficulty: ① ② **③** ④ ⑤

Time Commitment: ① ② **③** ④ ⑤

Cost: ① **②** ③ ④ ⑤

New Friends: 6 million

PURPOSE OF LIFE

Awaken to own Buddha nature, and thus enlightenment, through meditation and *satori* (sudden enlightenment)

DEITIES

No deities; prominent *bodhisattvas* (enlightened beings who delay nirvana to help others) include Manjusri, Jizo, Samantabhadra

KEY TEXTS

Pali Canon, AKA Tripitaka; Mahayana Sutras; teachings of Zen masters

WHERE

Primarily Japan, China, South Korea, Vietnam

AFTERLIFE PROMISES

Freedom from rebirth and attainment of nirvana upon enlightenment

CATEGORY

Dharmic: Buddhist

ZOROASTRIANISM

QUICK RATINGS:

Conversion Difficulty: ① ② ③ ❹ ⑤ (4)

Time Commitment: ① ② ③ ❹ ⑤ (4)

Cost: ① ❷ ③ ④ ⑤ (2)

New Friends: 180,000

PURPOSE OF LIFE
Maintain *Asha* (truth, world order, eternal law, righteousness), fighting evil with "Good thought, good work, good deeds" mantra

DEITIES
Ahura Mazda, Supreme Being, source of all good

KEY TEXTS
Avesta (Book of the Law); Younger Avesta; Gathas (hymns); Yasna; Pahlavi literature

WHERE
India, Iran

AFTERLIFE PROMISES
Paradise for good, hell for sinners; souls cross bridge to judgment; if unfit, fall off bridge to realm of Angra Mainyu (source of all evil)

CATEGORY
Revealed

WHAT IT IS
World's oldest monotheistic religion, founded by Iranian prophet Zoroaster (AKA Zarathustra) after revelation from Ahura Mazda (God) in 6th century BCE. Influenced Judaism, Christianity, Islam. Survived rise of Islam in Iran, with some followers (called Parsis) migrating to India. Central tenet is dualistic battle between good and evil; humans free to choose, so salvation depends on actions in life.

PERKS

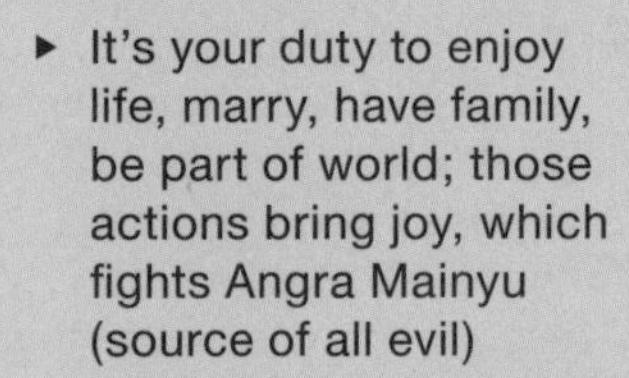

- It's your duty to enjoy life, marry, have family, be part of world; those actions bring joy, which fights Angra Mainyu (source of all evil)
- Hell only temporary for sinners, but they must first be purified by ordeal of molten metal

DRAWBACKS

- Death impure, so bodies placed in roofless *daxma* ("tower of silence") for vultures to eat
- Entirely responsible for own actions, though can confess and repent
- Some purification rituals entail drinking or applying *gomez* (bull's urine)

ACTIVITIES
- Praying 5 times a day
- Feeding sacred fires in temples 5 times a day (fire symbol of original light of God)
- Many joyous festivals

PARAPHERNALIA
- 4-eyed dogs (dogs with spots over eyes) to attend death rites
- *Kustis*, sacred cords knotted 3 times, wound 3 times around waist; *sudrehs*, sacred shirts

RELIGION #99

WHAT IT IS

Indigenous religion of South African tribes, descended from Zulu, patriarchal figure whose name means "heaven." All misfortune caused by angry spirits and *abathakathi* (sorcerers); *amadlozi* (ancestors) worshipped and invoked for protection. Causes of problems diagnosed by *sangoma* (diviners); restitution made with offerings, often of cattle.

PERKS

- Respect highly valued; children taught manners at young age, elders revered
- Can use nonverbal language of beads—white for love, blue for loyalty, red for desire, yellow for wealth; jewelry often patterned to convey story, such as romantic interest
- Beautiful tradition of a cappella harmony, popularized by Ladysmith Black Mambazo and Paul Simon in *Graceland*
- Misfortune never your fault

DRAWBACKS

- Cleanliness stressed; several baths per day not uncommon; variety of dishware used
- Small, nasty, magic, potentially lethal creatures lurk under bed; sleep with bed elevated on red bricks for protection
- Very patriarchal: women do lion's share of work
- Polygyny (multiple wives) practiced
- Can't be prudish: women often go topless, men wear only *amabheshu* (cowhide aprons)

ACTIVITIES

- For boys, stick fighting
- Dancing, singing
- Basket weaving, spear and shield creation, beadwork
- Puberty rituals: for girls, separation from group for days, then reintroduction with celebration and animal slaughter; for boys, initiation ceremonies with warrior dress

PARAPHERNALIA

- Beads and bread for offerings; bones, seeds, shells for divination
- *Ugubus*, stringed instruments played with bow
- Herbs to treat disease, prescribed by *izinyanga* (medicine men), including wild dagga plant, used only by Zulus over 40, and bark for pre-ritual cleansing via vomiting

QUICK RATINGS:

Conversion Difficulty:

① ② ③ ④ ⑤

Time Commitment:

① ② ③ ④ ⑤

Cost:

① ② ③ ④ ⑤

New Friends:
9 million

PURPOSE OF LIFE

Honor ancestors through daily offerings; raise children well and respect elderly; practice *ubuntu*, moral principle of doing right thing

DEITIES

Unkulunkulu, creator god, but ancestors are primary targets of worship

KEY TEXTS

None; oral tradition, often sung

WHERE

Primarily South Africa

AFTERLIFE PROMISES

No hell (those who anger ancestors punished on earth); after death, spend 2 to 12 months in "in-between place," then go to underworld as ancestor

CATEGORY

Indigenous: African

RETURNING YOUR RELIGION

Though most religions present no obstacles if unhappy followers wish to leave the fold, some work aggressively to prohibit such departures. They prepare for this long before a prospective defection by exerting tremendous control and pressure, by taking over the individual's finances, and by influencing the way the individual thinks about the world. When the adherent expresses a desire to leave, the religion may go so far as to physically prohibit the exit or threaten retribution. Part of being a savvy convert includes knowing when you're headed for trouble and, if you land there, how to get out of it. Do note that it's much easier to avoid joining a hard-to-leave religion than to extract yourself later, but if you come to the conclusion that you're in with a bad group, try to find your way to safety.

WARNING SIGNS

- The leader has absolute authority but little culpability. The leader is only one who knows God's will and may even claim to be divine.
- Inquiry and uncertainty aren't tolerated and are often derided as evidence of weak faith or outside influence.
- The group's finances are secret.
- Everything outside the group is characterized as scary, faithless, and sinful. Paranoia is fostered.
- The group's identity and goals are synonymous with the individual's. Homogeneity is encouraged.
- Followers feel they must constantly prove their worthiness.
- Different standards exist for followers than for leadership.
- Leaving is equated with evil and sin. Followers who leave are shunned and disparaged.

GETTING OUT

- Don't mention your worries or intentions to group members.
- Plan to make your exit when the group sends you into the community to make money or proselytize.
- Identify a safe haven, whether homeless shelter, hotel, or homes of friends or relatives.
- Once you've made your way to the safe haven, slowly divest yourself of the faith's paraphernalia and books. This may prove difficult, as such groups excel at instilling feelings of guilt and uncertainty in their members.
- Seek counseling for help with readjustment, reclaiming your life, and understanding how this religion, despite its problems, met certain needs for you. Determine how to get those needs met in a healthier way.

If you can't manage to leave on your own, it may be necessary to contact a friend or family member for help, or to slip a note to a stranger when you're out performing group tasks. In the note, be sure to include information identifying whom the note should be forwarded to, where you can be found, and the best time and place to meet you.

What happens next could include some type of rescue to extract you from your environment, followed by an intervention such as exit counseling or deprogramming. However, these activities are more likely to be independently initiated by loved ones worried for your well-being.

DEPROGRAMMING

Deprogramming attempts to wrest the follower out of the religion's beliefs and thought patterns and to break the follower's allegiance. This occurs in a neutral environment, away from outside contact, against the follower's will. Because it uses many of the same manipulative methods as cults—sleep deprivation, brainwashing, imprisonment, physical restraint—deprogramming has lost support since its peak in the 1970s and early 1980s.

EXIT COUNSELING

Exit counseling, by contrast, is a voluntary process that the individual is free to stop at any time, whether or not the intention is to return to the religion. Exit counseling attempts to guide the follower to his or her own conclusions—and ultimately to the decision to leave the group. Techniques include:

- Engaging in dialogue about why the person joined the group.
- Sharing information about others who have left the religion.
- Showing videos about mind-control techniques used by religious and political organizations.
- Exposing the follower to doubt-inducing facts about the religion that had been withheld by the religion's leadership.
- Highlighting conflicts and inconsistencies in the follower's beliefs and the religion's statements or actions.
- Ongoing follow-up.

HOW TO START YOUR OWN RELIGION

PART 1: THE RELIGION ENTREPRENEUR

EVEN AFTER EXPLORING ALL 99 RELIGIONS PROFILED IN this book, you still may be unsatisfied. While one aspect of a particular faith may resonate with you, others may fit uncomfortably. The prospect of blending your beliefs as a sole practitioner—a metrospiritual, for example—doesn't appeal to you because you want to worship with a group and put your message across publicly. Finally, you just may have that indefinable

Planning on availing yourself of nubile young followers?
DO choose a mate who shares your vision.

leadership drive that leads a few committed souls to start up new businesses—and religions. (Or, best of all, both at the same time.)

"Find a need and fill it" can characterize not just the commercial side of life but the spiritual as well. As you've toured the possibilities contained in this book, you've no doubt seen the yearning out there for higher fulfillment and understanding—and that's your audience. The likelihood that you're the only one who can't quite fit into pre-established faiths is slim, yet few will take the call to create a new home for the spiritually disenfranchised.

In religion, we're taught to follow, not lead. But if you're questioning what you see out there in the religion marketplace, you're already exhibiting signs of leadership. Now it's time to take the next step and explore whether you have what it takes to bite the Bible and do it—start your own religion. That's right—maybe *you* have the answers you seek. Whether you've formulated a new spin on an old belief or come up with answers to age-old questions that haven't been considered yet, or even if you just enjoy having attractive young men or women fawning at your blessed feet, you might be someone who functions better as shepherd than as sheep. The select few are those who've sat in the back of their houses of worship and thought, *I can do better.* If this sounds like you, read on to see if you actually have what it takes.

STARTING A NEW RELIGION: AS MANY MOTIVATIONS AS POSSIBILITIES

Coming up with new ways to approach religion is as American as Christianity. The United States was founded by worshippers fleeing religious persecution, and even though these freedom seekers punished other

Want to make sure dissent is nipped in the bud?
DON'T be afraid to lay down the law (after creating it).

believers for demanding the same thing, the marketplace stayed open (at least relative to other countries). Americans have been exercising their religious freedom by modifying existing schools of thought and creating original ideologies ever since, qualifying this country as the greatest hotbed for the creation of new religion that the world has ever known.

We currently find ourselves enjoying a global boom for the religious entrepreneur. Most of the worshipper growth is occurring in independent churches and new religious movements (NRMs). Current estimates place the number of "alternative" religions in the world at anywhere from 500 to 10,000—and this book leans toward the latter figure.

One of the reasons new religions are difficult to count, however, is that so many fail early on. While serving a higher purpose and fulfilling a spiritual need, new religions are subject to the same realities as new enterprises everywhere: cutthroat competition, lackluster sales, poor location, bad management, and PR snafus. No matter how original your manifesto, a few managerial missteps can shutter your spiritual kingdom forever.

New religions also contend with the pressures of public scrutiny: prying relatives, overzealous deprogrammers, IRS audits, and government raids. In the end, religions come and go, but a few do survive long enough to become mainstream—or at least financially successful. Further along in this chapter, you'll find a nuts-and-bolts guide for getting your religion started, but before you make the decision to go forward, it's important to examine your motivations.

No one motivation is right or wrong; however, it's vital that you be ruthlessly honest with yourself—in a way that you may not be with your followers—when searching deep within to identify the reasons for your

Looking for fame, fortune, and a manifesto?
DO write a book that will be a bestseller *and* required reading for followers.

drive. Every entrepreneur has strengths and weaknesses; what distinguishes an entrepreneur's successes is the ability to recognize one's own weaknesses and compensate for them, whether by modeling the enterprise to take advantage of one's strengths, anointing complementary staff members, or working to substantially improve personal deficits. For a leader, the keys to building a robust tax-exempt organization lie in maximizing competencies and shoring up shortcomings.

Religion entrepreneurs tend to be motivated by one or any of the following:

Motivation	Potential Strengths	Potential Weaknesses	Compensation Techniques
Message from higher power(s)	Persuasive to others. Can authentically claim direct spiritual connection or lineage. Belief in self derives from seamless connection between beliefs and self.	Higher-calling leaders are the artists of the religion world; they may not excel at administrative aspects of running a religion, such as overseeing staff, structure, and money. May become disillusioned when others don't believe. Thin-skinned.	Find functionary who can be trusted and, as visionary, focus on writing and preaching. Or, educate self on business practices. Could choose to keep following small so organizational issues less of a concern.
Rebellion against an existing church's dogma or leadership	Something to rebel against lends conviction and heightens energy levels. Built-in congregations for worshipper poaching ("sheep stealing"). No need to reinvent ideology; instead, more of a revision.	Movement led by negativity, by maligning something else; worshippers seek positivity, too. Easy to get blinded by object of rebellion. Can incur wrath of original institution, increasing outside pressure.	Search within self to determine whether motivation is solely anger based vs. truly wanting to establish an alternative; if anger only, reconsider endeavor. Emphasize the positive, what worshippers are moving toward rather than solely away from. Get good attorney early on.

Need something to fill their heads during downtime?
DON'T forget the music . . . and the chants and mantras.

Motivation	Potential Strengths	Potential Weaknesses	Compensation Techniques
Quest to reconcile multiple faiths into one	Open mind, capacity for diplomacy. Often intellectual, with focus on religion studies.	Can be wishy-washy or overly cerebral. Ability to see many viewpoints may compromise decisiveness as leader. May be viewed as derivative.	Followers seek structure and authority; work hard on manifesto before soliciting followers so that messages are clear and appear original. Don't acknowledge sources; instead, invent new names for old practices. Demonstrate decisiveness after listening to multiple viewpoints.
Pure leadership drive, thirst for power and/or money, or tendency toward con artistry	Ambitious, willing to work hard. Natural capabilities as leader. Can fool people and lead them on.	May lack message, power of authentic spiritual conviction. Will possibly be seen as fraud. Flock may rebel against abused authority.	Get a message, learn it, and project it persuasively, whether or not you believe it. Look for signs that worshippers are doubting you, then pull back a bit. Maintain aura of mystery so others can't examine you too closely. Open bank accounts in Cayman Islands.
Rebellion against government, culture, or other races	Vast pool of anger to tap into. Many inequities to cite in support of message. "Us vs. Them" mentality breeds loyalty. Since only 6.1 percent of land in United States is populated, plenty of room for establishing insular compound.	As with any rebellion, must guard against anger-only message, providing "path to," not just "path away." Will undergo government scrutiny, especially if firearms are involved.	Concoct positive message for followers amid conspiracy theories, cultivating their "Us" pride while demonizing "Them." Isolate followers from all outside influences. Buy guns in small quantities, then hide in multiple locations. Don't break law for unimportant things. Get good attorney early on.

Hoping to enlist a publicist and make some waves?
DO choose a name for yourself that looks good in headlines.

DO YOU HAVE WHAT IT TAKES? THE CHALLENGES (AND BENEFITS) OF STARTING A RELIGION

Fact: 80 percent of new enterprises fail within the first 5 years. What will help ensure that you're in the other 20 percent that succeed? All successful religions have 2 common denominators: a charismatic leader and a message people want to hear.

Charisma

Though you may believe that your main product is your message, the more important contributor to your potential success is actually personal charisma. That *je ne sais quoi* doesn't have to be visible to anyone but your followers (in fact, your charisma may not be detectable to *anyone* on the outside), but it is essential that your followers feel it. Otherwise, you're going to have a difficult time getting people to believe in you, follow you, invest their time and money, depend on you for salvation, and so forth.

The term *charisma* came into common use in the 1920s through the sociologist Max Weber, who had taken the Greek term, meaning "gift of grace," and redefined it as "a certain quality of an individual personality by virtue of which he is set apart from ordinary men and treated as endowed with supernatural, superhuman, or at least specifically exceptional powers or qualities." Charisma doesn't have to present loudly, however. Just think of those magnetic people who speak quietly so that you have to lean in to hear them, thus focusing more attention and importance on their words. In its colloquial meaning, charisma doesn't have to be superhuman, either. Here are some charismatic qualities that will prove helpful to the aspiring religion leader:

Not sure where your next revelation is coming from?
DON'T reinvent the wheel. Revive an ancient religion!

- Inspirational to others
- Magnetic personality
- Confident
- Good communicator, dynamic when speaking in public
- Persuasive and charming
- Appearance of trustworthiness
- Able to manage impression one makes as well as stage-direct and promote personal appearances
- Embodies proclaimed vision, believes self to be uniquely qualified to deliver message
- Sex appeal

Your future followers need to believe that you, and only you, can deliver whatever it is you say you can—and deliver *them,* as well. There are thousands of NRMs to choose from, but they're going to choose yours, and your ability to build your own inimitable cult of personality will play a significant role in that success.

Message

There's no doubt that a strong message makes a religion compelling and offers followers something to believe in. Whether or not *you* believe your message isn't as important as you might think, though the ability to *convey* authentic faith is critical.

Perhaps you already have your message, and that's why you're reading this. Many guiding religious concepts come from revelations. Whenever you receive one, be sure to write it down, as these will ultimately comprise your religion's teachings. Faith healing and divination abilities not only will convince followers of your spiritual authority but also can be used to underscore the contents of your message and obtain an audience's trust.

Following are some questions to help you craft your message. Think carefully as you answer, because your responses will lead the way to composing your manifesto.

Wary about giving away the milk and honey for free?
DO dole out knowledge, requiring greater financial commitment for each nugget.

YOUR MESSAGE: CREATING A CALLING OTHERS WILL HEED

1. Will you base your religion on existing dogma (e.g., a breakaway sect—or, in business jargon, a franchise) or will you start from scratch?

2. Do you have an existing model for your religion, a blueprint into which you can drop your spiritual thoughts?

3. How is your religion similar to or different from others offered in the marketplace?

4. What is your religion's cosmology (view of the universe)? Who created it, when, and out of what? Who rules it? What has happened to it, what is happening to it, and what will happen to it?

5. Why are we here? What does it mean to be human? What is the relationship between human and deity? Do humans have souls? What's the definition of a soul, and is it separate from the body?

6. What happens before we are born and after we die?

7. Is your vision tied to an impending event such as Judgment Day, the arrival of a UFO, or the total annihilation of the earth by an errant comet? (Be careful about linking your religion to a specific date; while such an event may be a valuable marketing tool, you lose credibility if the event doesn't happen.)

8. What will you promise? Examples: salvation, enlightenment, purity, world peace, peace of mind, a return to basics, passageway to heaven.

Worried about contradicting yourself or explaining the Rolls-Royce?

DON'T create a paper trail, unless it helps with your tax-exempt status.

9. What will your followers worship? Examples: a particular deity or deities; nature elements such as the sun, moon, solstice, or equinox; idols; aliens; you.

10. What is the state of the world today? How does your religion position itself in reference to that point of view?

11. To practice your religion, can followers live within the world as it is, or is it important to form insular communities or even live communally, far away from anybody else? Can followers watch television and read the newspaper?

12. What's your position on sex? Examples: complete celibacy, marital sex only, free love, sex only with you, opposed to birth control, pro-choice.

13. What main activities will be practiced? Examples: prayer, meditation, singing, dancing, fund-raising, evangelism, proselytizing.

14. What holidays will your religion celebrate? Examples: existing holidays of source religion, deity birthdays, seasons, rites of passage, your birthday.

15. What would you like followers to call you? Examples: first name (perhaps newly adopted), traditional religious title such as Reverend, Father or Mother, Master, Swami, Guru, Exalted Leader.

16. How should followers dress and groom themselves? Examples: modest clothing, all-black clothing, all-white clothing, burkas, shaved heads, random tufts of hair.

17. What will you call your religion?

Already have tattoos, piercings, or a poor sense of style?
DO establish a look that will puzzle outsiders and bond your flock.

Writing Your Manifesto

Once you've answered most of these questions—and probably a few others you've conjured on your own—you're ready to write your spiritual manifesto. While charisma is critical in face-to-face encounters and public appearances, the ability to put across your ideas in writing not only will affirm and clarify your beliefs, it also will allow you to communicate far beyond your personal reach. Just as some aspiring religion leaders grow nervous at the prospect of public speaking, so do others fear the writing process. Both are necessary to being an effective religious leader, and if you can just get over the initial hurdle of actually starting, you'll probably find that the words flow. When writing your manifesto, do the following:

- Record your religion's cosmology, dogma, core beliefs, rituals, and practices.
- Try to be as poetic as possible in order to win followers.
- Copy the final draft onto something that can be worshipped, such as vellum, pigskin, or a scroll.
- Highlight particularly memorable quotes for use as chants or mantras and in marketing materials.

If you've made it this far, you can feel relatively confident that your spiritual beliefs are sufficient for starting your religion. However, starting and running a religion involve so much more than mere beliefs. Because you will grapple with difficulties greater than any you've previously faced, it's important that you understand what you're getting into.

Challenges Encountered by the Religion Entrepreneur

As you birth your religion, you must be prepared to face a world that may not even realize it needs another religion. Competition and adversity will come from all sides—a society increasingly driven by technology, tabloids,

Struggling with low self-esteem?
DON'T be discouraged by doubting Thomases—banish them!

and antidepressants; a government suspicious of new religious activity; religion establishments that don't appreciate threats to their power and membership. Along the way, you may doubt your message or feel that it lacks a unique point of view—and you may even doubt yourself. In these entirely natural moments, just remind yourself of your strength of mission and conviction. It's not easy to start a religion, and it may take some time for yours to catch on. Keep in mind that every religion in history has started at the grassroots level, against considerable odds.

No entrepreneur truly understands the extent to which a new endeavor will take over his or her life. For the first 5 years (at least), you will eat, sleep, and breathe your new religion. Here are some questions to ask yourself in determining whether you're ready for this commitment and intensity:

- Have you always wanted to start a religion?
- Is your message a deeply held core belief?
- Can you develop a flow of ideas to keep your message fresh over time?
- Does your family share your vision, or will your new idea separate you from them? Do they support the commitment this represents?
- Can you withstand solitude? It's lonely at the top. As a religion leader, you won't have a peer, someone with whom you can share everything. Indeed, no one person other than yourself should know *everything*. Part of your power will also come from maintaining distance from the flock, cultivating an air of mystery so they'll never see that you're just another human being.
- Do you like being "on"? You will face the constant pressure to perform as well as maintain open lines of communication with the higher power(s).
- Have you fully considered the responsibilities of leading a flock, such as working on holidays, always being the last to close up the temple, and making difficult, sometimes unpopular, decisions? Accountability for the salvation of others is 24/7/365.
- Are you prepared to address conflict? Religious leaders have been persecuted by governments, imprisoned, and even killed by angry mobs, while the press often excoriates left-of-center religious beliefs.

Basing your finances on the end of the world?
DO have a backup plan for apocalypse dates that come and go.

As the spokesperson for your religion, you'll get praise when things go right, but you'll also get blamed when things go wrong, and no matter how things go, your personal life will be a thing of the past.

Benefits of Religion Leadership

When all is said and done, there's nothing more fulfilling and satisfying than spreading a message, gathering followers, and leading them to the destination of your choice. While many of the opportunities presented by religion leadership arise only after the initial start-up work has been done, they are considerable enough to motivate many aspirants:

- You'll be respected and revered. People may even take notes when you speak!
- If you're a faith-driven, largely altruistic religious leader, you'll be doing something you believe in, and you'll feel that you are helping people achieve their highest potential.
- You'll have the satisfaction of building something from nothing.
- You'll have the opportunity to right wrongs you've seen in other religions or institutions, doing it the way you see fit.
- You'll learn and experience more than you ever imagined possible.
- After a while, you won't have to lead by example. You could choose to enforce chastity for your flock but live the swinger's life yourself, even selecting a few special followers to be specially sanctioned for direct connection with your "higher power."
- You'll be able to demand volunteer work from your followers to spread the word, build the church, and keep the organization running—without having to pay salaries!
- While followers are out fund-raising, you'll get to mind the store—which, after you've assessed your growing coffers, may involve taking a relaxing soak in the hot tub or watching movies in your personal theater.
- You'll have the power to perform weddings and break up marriages.
- No person or institution will be looking over your shoulder to question your authority or message.

Brimming over with a lot to say?
DON'T limit your message to the written word.

- You'll encounter limitless opportunities to have your ego inflated.
- You might go down in the history books.

Successful religions aren't just pie-in-the-sky dreams, however; they're not-for-profit (at least in the eyes of the IRS) businesses that require structure, funding, marketing, and managed growth. You could have the best ideas and faith in the world, but if you don't look at your religion like a business, you'll be preaching to empty, rundown pews.

PART 2: STARTING, RUNNING, AND GROWING YOUR RELIGION

Every entrepreneur, whether religious or secular, must be self-educated to some extent. You may not be a reader, but books are one of the best sources for informing yourself on how to manage each stage of your religion. Your library should consist of both business and spiritual books. Of course, different religions will involve varying degrees of intellectualism. If your approach is syncretic, you may be avidly reading key texts and commentary on many religions. If you operate more on instinct and intuition than on knowledge, spiritual books might not be relevant for you. For all religion entrepreneurs, however, it's immeasurably helpful to absorb books on business as well as have key advisers such as attorneys and accountants. In the following sections, you'll find a basic overview of key phases in founding your religion, but as you find yourself facing particular challenges, you'll want to seek out the right in-depth information to answer the inevitable questions as they come up.

Manifesting a vision that's incompatible with populated areas?
DO invest in land, be it farm, compound, or underground bunker.

STRUCTURING YOUR RELIGION

As you begin to put your dreams into action, you'll want to dot *i*'s and cross *t*'s for each phase of development: legal structure, funding, physical location, staffing, marketing, flock management, and growth.

Before you determine the best legal structure for your religion—partnership, corporation, limited-liability corporation, etc.—and whether you'll go for tax-exempt status, you'll require an attorney. You may only need your attorney to help with ongoing structural issues, but it's common to seek legal assistance for the following types of challenges:

- Obtaining a legal waiver allowing you and your followers to consume spiritually necessary mind-altering drugs
- Fighting lawsuits alleging mind control of followers, sexual harassment, or financial mismanagement
- Defending your tax-exempt status
- Responding to government intrusions onto your compound

Likewise, an accountant will help you set up your books so that money can be tracked as it comes in and goes out. The right accountant can also help you hide money via mind-numbingly arcane accounting maneuvers, offshore accounts, and self-serving investments and purchases.

Funding Your Religion

Depending on your plans for overhead and your own need for income, it's possible to start a religion for very little money. However, it's important to assess how much your start-up will require, what your monthly "burn" rate will be to keep your organization running, and what growth plans you envision until the money really starts rolling in. In putting together your initial budgets, consider the following:

Time to shame people in public or punish their transgressions?
DON'T do the dirty work yourself.

Funding: Where will the money come from?

START-UP

- Personal savings or family money
- Investors
- Loans

RUNNING EXPENSES

- Personal savings or family money
- Investors
- Loans
- Tithing
- Membership fees
- Member assets (sale of followers' houses, cars, etc.)
- Collection plates
- Coursework (providing necessary education for followers)
- Services (foretelling the future, exorcisms, etc.)
- Video, CD, book, and T-shirt sales
- Flower sales
- One-on-one fund-raising (panhandling)
- Street performances

Start-Up Expenses and Overhead: How much money will you need?

- LOCATION. Where will you house your religion empire? Will you start in your garage until the empire grows, or will you buy land to start an ashram? Will there be rent or a mortgage?
- PHYSICAL PLANT. What are your space requirements? Square footage? Office space vs. worship space? Multiple homes? If you purchase land or an existing building requiring renovation, or even need to modify your garage, what will the onetime construction costs be?
- LIVING SITUATION. What will you need to support communal living? Often such compounds cost more in start-up mode but pay off as followers, thus housed, can devote all their time and energy to making money for the religion.
- TECHNOLOGY AND FURNISHINGS. What will you need to fill your space and keep it running? Computers and software, telephones and copiers?
- UTILITIES AND RUNNING EXPENSES. Calculate what you'll be paying for phones, heat, insurance, taxes (or not), etc.
- PAYROLL. How will you cover your living expenses during the start-up phase? Will you be paid? Create an organizational chart for your religion's growth. Will these be unpaid positions, or will you have to pay a few individuals?

Got an amazing idea that's easy to capitalize on?
DO be leery of imitators, infiltrators, and sheep stealers.

- OUTREACH EFFORTS. Will necessary marketing and proselytizing incur any costs?
- PERKS. What would you like to have when the religion becomes profitable? A mansion, swimming pool, or private jet? Though it may be early to contemplate such luxuries, if you don't project your dreams into the universe, they may never come true.

Intellectual Property

Before you unleash your religion on the world, make sure you're protected from those who aren't original enough to think up their own religions. Whether or not you use an attorney, don't forget to do the following:

- Trademark the name of your religion (after you've determined that your first-choice name doesn't infringe on any other existing trademarks).
- Develop and trademark a recognizable logo.
- Copyright your manifesto and any other writings.
- Reserve as many URLs as possible based on iterations of your religion's name.

Once you feel confident that the initial structure of your religion is in place, you've got a reasonably workable go-forward business plan, and you're protected from copycats, it's time for the fun stuff: spreading the gospel and acquiring your flock.

MARKETING AND SELLING YOUR RELIGION: FINDING FOLLOWERS

The best religious ideas in the world won't catch on if you don't have a strategy to get them from your mouth (often serving as God's mouth) to people's ears. In the 21st century, there are so many more ways to reach potential followers than merely going door-to-door or chanting on a street corner, and the better you employ all the techniques at your disposal, the more followers you'll attract.

Seeking to instill groupthink and groupspeak?
DON'T be afraid to coin new terminology and phrases.

Identifying Your Target Market

In order to most effectively popularize your religion, you'll want to profile your ideal follower. This not only will help you locate these individuals, it also will assist in customizing your pitch. For some new religions, it may be worthwhile to understand your competition: Do they pose a threat? Are they potential sources for new followers? What do they do right, and where do they miss the mark? Do you want to define yourself as similar to or different from them? Stay on top of market trends, whether by attending competitors' services or by subscribing to trade publications.

Contemplation of the perfect follower will indicate how you might find such individuals. Following are some typical characteristics sought by religion leaders, as well as suggestions about recruiting locations:

- **Young and impressionable:** College campuses, youth social organizations, typical hangouts such as commercial downtowns and 7-Eleven parking lots.
- **Older and wealthy:** Tony social circles, funerals, hospitals, retirement homes, yacht clubs, existing churches and religious services, advertisements in demographically appropriate publications.
- **Individuals with latent racial prejudices to exploit:** Racially segregated neighborhoods, neighborhoods that were once racially segregated but now are experiencing an influx of people thought to bring property values down, existing churches, skateboard parks.
- **Living on the streets and in need of help:** Homeless shelters, under freeway overpasses, in sewers and subways, public parks.
- **Sinners crying out to be saved:** Bars, massage parlors, gambling enclaves, convenience stores, jail.
- **Lonely singles:** Laundromats, cafés, singles events such as speed dating, advertisements on Internet dating sites, answering personals ads.
- **Ready for a return to orthodoxy:** Stand in the back of churches and temples and eavesdrop on followers' conversations. Cherry-pick the ones who complain about loose morals, overly modern clergy, etc.

Looking for a win-win marketing profit center?

DO sell products identifiable with your group—at a good markup.

Perfecting Your Pitch

When it comes to explaining your religious vision to potential followers, it's vital that you hone it into a persuasive, compelling pitch that can be delivered quickly to your target followers. Also, decide whether you want to appeal to the masses or to just a select few; this will determine how much you need to dilute and simplify your message as opposed to keeping it more abstruse and specific.

To create your pitch, first review your manifesto for relevant excerpts, then address the following:

- What are you going to offer potential converts?
- How soon will followers be enlightened or saved?
- How direct a connection will followers have with God?
- Do you have any special powers?
- How effective are your sermons?
- What about the state of the world—and potential converts' lives—makes your religion timely and necessary?
- Do you provide adequate holidays?
- Will there be more than one location so that followers will be able to transfer to other branches?
- Whether or not it's true, make sure that potential converts know they can cancel at any time.

After you provide the information with which potential converts can make the decision to join your religion, they should always end up believing that joining your religion was *their* idea. If they don't feel ownership of and accountability for their choice, they'll end up resenting your authority and may not do your bidding without protest.

More into parchment than silicon?

DON'T fear technology—use it for credit card donations and cyber-services.

Marketing Materials

Proselytizing religions have pamphlets and literature at the ready, not to mention utilizing all the 21st-century media to convey their message. Over time, you'll be transforming your original written pitch—lengthening, shortening, bullet-pointing—for different settings. Have some pictures taken of yourself, staged with garb, props, setting, and photographic effects to present you as a worship-worthy leader. Film footage of yourself preaching to blissed-out extras. Record your manifesto and other writings onto audio files. Then prepare some of the following:

- **Wardrobe.** The ardent follower wants to stand out, and wants a leader who does as well. Why not design a unique wardrobe and look for your religion?
- **Newsletter or magazine.** Communicating with existing and potential followers on a regular basis is an excellent way to keep your religion top-of-mind.
- **Website.** Internet presence is critical to the growth of 21st-century NRMs; indeed, some exist *only* on the Internet. Your website should convey your message visually and in writing, and should also transmit audio and video footage of yourself in action.
- **Paraphernalia.** Think inside the box about such items as prayer beads, shawls, mats, deity statues, milestone souvenirs, T-shirts, books, recordings, and videos. All should have your religion's logo boldly proclaimed. Paraphernalia is also an excellent source of revenue.

Promotion Plan

Once you have your marketing strategy and materials in place, you'll be ready to go into promotion mode to spread the word. Overall, you'll need to determine what works best for your religion, whether it's one-on-one encounters, presentations in group settings, word of mouth, planned publicity, advertising, self-promotion, or press coverage. Here are some approaches both time-honored and cutting edge:

Serving gods that require a little more from you?
DO learn local laws on animal sacrifice and sacrament cultivation.

- **Publicist.** A good publicist is worth her weight in Qur'ans. Because she will have press contacts and resources to help you get cost-free coverage, a publicist often obviates the need for paid advertising.
- **Advertising.** Choose publications, programs, or websites that you think draw potential followers' eyeballs, then determine an advertising plan that suits your budget.
- **Free literature distribution.** Not only is this a good job for new converts (the more they explain the message to others, the more they will internalize it themselves), but it also gets the message out quickly, directly, and inexpensively. Offer something free, especially food (e.g., dinner at the ashram), to increase the likelihood that you'll get follow-up interest.
- **The Internet.** While the Web is a useful tool for many NRMs, it has also made the search for dedicated followers that much more competitive. You can use pay-per-click advertising and search-engine optimization to bring people to your site. You can search for potential followers in chat rooms and personals ads. Distribute a video on YouTube or create a MySpace page. With a creative approach, the Internet can serve almost any promotional purpose.
- **Airwaves.** Start a cable-access television show, an Internet video series, or a podcast to broadly disperse your message.
- **Buzz and word of mouth.** Performing such good deeds as disaster relief, social work, and rain dances is sure to garner notice. Public displays of divination and faith healing also get people talking.
- **Self-promotion.** Until your religion is well established, *you* are your religion. Write books incorporating your message. Establish a musical group in which you're the lead singer. Position yourself as an expert on something and pitch your perspective to news programs. Do something outlandishly publicity worthy such as walking around as naked as God made you.
- **Flock promotion.** Consider allowing your group to become known for something. Can your followers make furniture? Play the tambourine? Bake? Raise bees? The most successful religions are able to bring in money while building a brand. This kind of cross-promotion endears you to the local community and makes good financial sense. Followers are also more likely to make a full-time commitment if they have work that gives them a sense of accomplishment and an outlet for their creativity.

Already contemplating your legacy?
DON'T forget to save personal artifacts for worship after you're gone.

As the saying goes, be careful what you pray for! If you're victorious in just a few of your marketing efforts, you'll have a flock to tend to in no time. At the beginning of this process, it probably seemed like an insurmountable project to get your religion off the ground. The bad news? Running your flock can be just as challenging as starting it. The good news? You're about to learn how to handle many of the challenges that will come your way.

MANAGING YOUR FLOCK AND YOUR ORGANIZATION

As with romance, getting someone is one thing, but keeping the relationship is entirely another. Once your group begins to grow, your primary responsibilities will consist of keeping followers engaged and believing, cultivating group dynamics that serve your purposes, and managing the organization. Overall, you've got to guide the religion's culture and allow it to solidify; someday the religion will be able to perpetuate itself, and that's when you can step back and enjoy the fruits of your hard-earned spirituality.

Keeping Their Interest

Your followers joined your religion because of your initial message. While it goes without saying that you'll need various parables, aphorisms, and teachings for variety, there may be moments when you feel followers slipping away or questioning their commitment. In these moments, try any of the following methods to bring them firmly back to the fold:

- **Renew their sense of purpose.** Maybe your followers are simply bored and need a new goal. This would be a good time to request an increased financial commitment to separate the dabblers from the lifers and will ensure a heightened sense of investment in the community (the more they've invested, the more they'll want to make the religion work). Communal projects such as building or repairing group facilities can also help unite the group.

Want to keep followers from looking to outside influences?
DO provide an active social calendar from dawn to dusk.

- **Change the group's sexual dynamics.** Experts agree that one of the best ways to eliminate a person's sense of individual ego and self is to control his or her sex life. Whether, in the name of religion, your followers renounce marriage and family, have sex for the good of the group, or have sex with you, they will unconsciously feel more loyal to the mission.
- **Listen to your flock.** Sometimes your followers are the best source of feedback on what they need from you and your religion. The trick in soliciting their commentary is maintaining your authority while allowing them to feel like they're contributing, or listening without them knowing it.
- **Put followers to the test.** Without challenges from you, their leader, followers may grow complacent. Test their loyalty by ordering them to do something outside their comfort zones, whether it's shaving their heads, cutting off contact with their families, or executing suicide bombings. Once they've performed their task, they'll have a renewed sense of commitment to you (even if it's in the afterlife).
- **Give followers an enemy.** Fuel the paranoia that got followers to come on board in the first place. Re-emphasize the threat of the outside world: abortion, homosexuals, black people, immigrants, Britney Spears, capitalism. This will remind them why your message resonated in the first place. The more scared they are of the outside world, the more they will cling to you.
- **Update your message.** The best way to introduce new concepts is by receiving a new vision from God. Share it sparingly to maintain mystery while giving followers just enough to keep them coming back.

Cultivating Beneficial Group Dynamics

For any religion to succeed, individual egos must be subordinated to the identity of the group to some extent—or, in certain cases, completely. In everything you do, promote group unity over individual voices. For some religions, this will extend easily from the group's cosmology—for example, the idea that we all comprise one consciousness. For others, unity will be driven more by shared beliefs. Absolute loyalty to an especially charismatic leader also brings people together. Finally, paranoia about the outside world and fear of going outside the group are very effective binding agents.

Fighting a tendency to mumble like Moses?
DON'T forget to enunciate, especially when creating sound bites.

Many dynamics that promote group unity and loyalty to you are contradictory statements that prescribe doing one thing while not exactly neglecting to do its opposite, including these useful techniques:

- Make followers dependent on you, but allow them to feel it's their choice to be dependent.
- Censor outside influences, but lead followers to believe they don't want to know what it is you're censoring.
- Quash dissent without making followers feel oppressed.
- Rule as you wish while professing to have an open-door policy.
- Run things with an iron grip, but appear to share some authority.
- Be mysterious yet accessible.
- Create the rules, but don't provoke followers to rebel against you.
- Tell followers they can leave anytime, but subtly make them fear leaving.
- Allow followers to have relationships with one another, but never let their bonds grow tighter than their loyalty to you.
- Cultivate group cohesion while undermining group strength.
- Make followers feel that your love is unconditional, but threaten them with banishment from the group, commonly known as shunning, if they cross certain taboo lines.

Above all, a religion leader has his pulse on the group dynamic. The flock is everything, and it takes only a few bad birds to make the rest fly away. What the religious leader doesn't know about her group will inevitably come back to weaken her position and thus the religion.

Tending to the Organization

In the heady early days of a new religion's growth, it's all too easy to neglect the pesky housekeeping tasks that keep the candles burning and the altars dust-free. Until your flock is of sufficient size and commitment to

Trying to make your religion feel contemporary and fresh?
DO enlist young, energetic followers to spearhead recruitment activities.

take these responsibilities over, it's up to you to make sure the necessary tasks get done. Mosque facilities are only as good as their foundation, and the structure that you create today will support growth in the future. Here are a few tips for ensuring solid footing:

- **Maintain organized membership information.** A solid mailing list of both converts and those who have considered joining your religion will allow you to track the size of your organization and provide an audience for your marketing materials.
- **Avoid creating problems with surrounding communities.** If a religion is controversial to outsiders, it's far more likely that legal problems will ensue. You can proactively offer your flock's services to the community, promote and support popular causes, or donate to local politicians and charities. Encourage followers to behave well in public. Obey the law when not behind closed doors. Be sure to file believable tax returns. If you're going to engage in red-flag activities such as stockpiling weapons or selling drugs, be sure it's worth the risk, and then do it as discreetly as possible.
- **Track finances carefully.** Money is the lifeblood of your organization. Every cent must be accounted for. This is a job you must not delegate until absolutely necessary, and when you do delegate it, divide responsibilities so that no one but you can know your religion's complete financial outlook.
- **Cultivate your managerial and leadership skills.** Now that you have a running religion, your abilities to manage and inspire people will be put to the test—and more likely than not, you will be deeply humbled by the challenges you face. Continue to read books on leadership, management, and psychology to brush up on your skills.

With a solid flock in place, your religion is well on its way to outlasting the 80 percent of enterprises that fail. The religion leader, however, rarely lacks ambition, and once you have things running smoothly, you're going to start contemplating the next step: growth.

Called for a path of televangelism?
DON'T forget to budget for clothing needs and hair implements.

YOU DID IT: TIME TO GROW?

It's common for first-time religion entrepreneurs to believe that any growth is good growth. The idea that a religion can become too successful too quickly is anathema to someone in the early planning phases who has yet to acquire a flock. The dreams you've had of followers who share your vision, volunteer for your missions, and donate to your organization have most likely ranged from proselytizing alone on a street corner to sitting on a throne surrounded by sexy young disciples—with no comprehension whatsoever of the intervening transition.

Challenges of Growth

Paradoxically, success that occurs too quickly is generally more challenging than failure. Such growing pains can manifest themselves as follows:

- **Disparity between level of interest and level of cash.** While you know that your religion is compelling enough to see significant growth, you don't have the cash flow to support the journey from alpha to omega.
- **Poor distribution of labor.** You can't do everything, and you haven't yet divided responsibilities among the flock.
- **Increased overhead.** If you grow to fit demand, that means you have to continue bringing in new followers and writing new books—anything to increase revenue—to meet those growing monthly expenses.
- **Outstripped management abilities.** Your flock, too large for you to manage alone, becomes unmanageable, and you haven't had time to implement a management structure beyond yourself. Additionally, if the organization grows faster than your learning curve, you may find yourself in over your head.
- **Public attention and government scrutiny.** As you grow, you will receive more press, not all of it flattering, and the IRS will be sure to take more of an interest in your finances.

Ready to have people fight over their place in your group?
DO create buzz by limiting followers to first-come, first-saved.

Do You Really *Want* to Grow?

It's important to remember that not every religion needs to grow. If you're happy with 100 followers on a self-sustaining compound, why franchise? Your role and your overall job satisfaction will change if you grow. Some gurus were born to inspire and manage millions; others prefer the intimacy of one-on-one leadership. Before strategizing about how to cope with growth, you need to determine your long- and short-term goals:

- What's your ideal job description as a religion leader? Be vigilant about putting aside others' ambitions for you, or ambitions for yourself that come from the desire for external acclaim. What are you happiest doing?
- Do you enjoy intimate spiritual encounters or the thrill that comes from preaching to thousands?
- Are you at heart a DIY kind of person, or would you prefer to stand on the sidelines and direct others? Can you let go enough to create the kind of management structure that growth requires?
- Do you want to act locally or change the world?
- Would you enjoy constant travel to make appearances and visit compounds all over the world, or do you prefer to stay put?
- Do you get stage fright from public speaking? Do you sweat when wearing heavy makeup for television appearances?
- Do you want to be able to pluck nubile young followers at will?
- Is money important to you?

It's easy to get carried away with ambition, so be honest with yourself about what you want and what makes you happy. If *you're* happy, your followers will be happy. Although flock members may not be able to detect a spiritual fraud, they can certainly sense when a religious leader isn't pleased with the organization's direction.

Worried they'll see right through you?
DON'T encourage reading, family contact, or other viewpoints.

Planning for Growth

Once you've formulated your goals for the growth of your religion, you can begin to plan it. Deliberate, steady growth is infinitely easier to manage than surprise growth that comes in fits and spurts. Basically, you want to be the one managing growth rather than the other way around. Here are some arenas to address when contemplating your religion's expansion:

- **Recognizing your own style and limitations.** As your religion's founder, leader, and possibly deity, your management style should set the tone for the organization. This does not mean that you are infallible (even though followers should think you are). Keep them believing in your perfection by being shrewd about your own limitations and creating a structure around you that will maximize your strengths and cover your weaknesses. At the same time, don't allow growth to pull you away from the style that originally drew people to you.
- **Creating a management structure.** All leaders need trusted lieutenants to do the heavy lifting and dirty work (it's vital that a religion's leader not be associated with such negativity). Some religion leaders have difficulty relinquishing control to loyal followers. If you want your religion to grow, there's no other way to make it happen. In most religious organizations, with the exception of independent contractors such as attorneys and accountants, promotion occurs from within. You can choose one of two directions for the management structure of your religion: functional or dysfunctional. The pejorative connotations of "dysfunctional" are not relevant here; instead, "dysfunction" refers to a technique of keeping management just strong enough to run the organization for you, but off-kilter enough not to take it over from you. If you choose leaders who are good enough but not the best, or those who are unlikely for their posts, and then make sure these leaders don't get along with one another, they'll be too concerned with competence, status, and infighting to stage a coup. For functional management, however, always choose the best person for the position and cultivate a culture of teamwork and cooperation. Appointing quality lieutenants will be most important when you expand beyond your original location, as these surrogates will need to instill the religion's values and culture in a new congregation that has not had the benefit of direct, full-time contact with you. When ordaining ministers, be sure to look for humility as well as religious know-how, as a cocky minister is one of the most likely candidates to breed dissent within the organization.

Hoping they'll hang on to your every word?
DO keep your message fresh with new "revelations."

- **Maintaining control.** As you empower others to lead within the organization, you risk their wresting control away from you. Keep your eyes open for this phenomenon; many religion leaders don't notice rebellion until it's too late. Ways to prevent mutiny include compartmentalizing information so that only you know everything and others' knowledge is limited to their area of oversight. Dysfunctional leadership, outlined above, is another technique. Make sure that no other leaders are authorized to perform your miracles. Select leaders who are functionaries rather than visionaries to avoid small pockets of personality cults arising beyond you. Finally, keep your skills and talents sharp so that followers never want to pledge their allegiance to another leader.
- **Evolving your role.** As you relinquish managerial control, continue to grow the skills and talents that only you can manifest. When others begin taking over the day-to-day running of your religion, pulling away from the flock can be a valuable tool in elevating your status. Once the groundwork has been laid and management is in place, you want people to talk *about* you, not *to* you. Maintain communication with the flock through your inner circle and your writings, public appearances, recorded messages, and vibrations.
- **Succession planning.** Unless you and your flock have a suicide pact, provisions must be made for someone to take over for you after you're gone. Marrying another leader within the religion has traditionally ensured a smooth transition. Otherwise, watch your trusted lieutenants to see who might make a good follow-up leader after you've gone to the great beyond. Under no circumstances, however, should you let him know that you've got your eye on him, as he may try to take over before you've exhaled for the last time.

Growing the Flock

Bringing your flock through growth primarily depends on 2 things: recruiting new followers and maintaining the loyalty of existing followers. Here are some ways to do both:

- **Formulate an active and ambitious recruitment plan.** Who will be responsible for bringing in new followers? Missionaries? Satisfied followers? Celebrities? This is your religion's sales plan, and it's one of the most important areas for the religion leader's concern. Set quotas and goals for your recruiters, with corresponding rewards and punishments.

Fantasizing about franchising worldwide within 5 years?
DON'T become a victim of your own success.

- **Stay in touch with what your existing flock needs.** Your current followers are your best marketing tool. No matter your level of mystery and distance, you must find a way to keep your finger on the pulse of your followers' unconscious needs and make sure they're met in a way that benefits your religion.
- **Innovate.** Create new practices as needed. Stay on top of current trends to keep things fresh for followers and increase enrollment—for example, implement Flying Yoga coursework or institute successive levels of membership with corresponding financial commitments.
- **Invent crises.** Reinvigorate a complacent following by fomenting paranoia and fear and by focusing them on an impending problem and mission. Instability serves as an excellent diversion for your followers.
- **Review your image.** Many mature NRMs have image problems from their early days. If there are holdover practices, such as sex with minors or polygamy, that you need to discontinue or de-emphasize, do so. Renaming your religion is an excellent way to distance yourself from early negative publicity. As you grow, managing controversy may become one of your key strategic activities as leader. By the time the unmarked Suburbans show up outside your compound, it will be too late.

REVIEW YOUR GOALS

Periodically, you should reexamine both your growth strategies and your spiritual manifesto to see if you're still on track. Are you sticking to your beliefs? Do your followers understand what's at stake? Are you all on the same page? Is it time to overhaul the manifesto, or is it time to get back to basics? Are you where you want to be? You can always pull back from growth and return to fundamentals, or you can deputize one of your lieutenants, stage your own martyrdom, then disappear to Mexico. Your happiness and your religion's progress are up to you.

Targeting a less wealthy pool of potential followers?
DO consider paraphernalia costs when creating rituals.

PART 3: GO WITH GOD(S)!

Starting your own religion can be the most fulfilling way of expressing yourself and realizing your dreams. With those privileges, however, comes a weighty responsibility. Your followers have put their salvation in your hands. Your commitment to establishing and growing a stable organization is essential for their smooth transition to a better life, both on earth and beyond. They've put their trust in you, and it's your responsibility to see that their faith and the money they've raised is put to good use.

Some religion leaders are in it for themselves—the power, the acclaim, the ego boost, the money. Others truly want to do good. Those who begin their religions out of altruism can be agents of social change outside their immediate kingdoms—performing charitable acts and bringing new ideas into the public conversation (historic examples include the abolition of slavery, equal rights, and holistic healing). Religious leaders not only have the potential to guide their followers, they also can affect the zeitgeist of their generation. Regardless of whether you are a self-interested or altruistic religious leader, or whether you are crazy or sane, focus on being the best you can be, and the success of your religion will follow.

Outsiders may not understand everything you do—your secrecy, tests of loyalty, rituals, communal living, penchant for homeschooling, or attitude toward sex. They may point and laugh at your uniforms and hairstyles, question your financial activities, or exclude you from community events. When external pressure intrudes, remember that all new ventures go through rough patches. The trick is to keep your eyes on the prize and have confidence in what the outsiders will never understand: that you were called to lead.

Drawing on a pool of preexisting dogma?

DON'T forget to study. One false sutra quotation and your credibility will be shot.

As your religion grows, perhaps you'll start a newspaper, recruit movie stars, sell products to outsiders, or provide the cavalry for the next disaster. In time, society will forget what's strange about your organization and embrace what they understand—your conservative values, strong work ethic, or political power—and you'll experience a spiritual tipping point where the misunderstood becomes the mainstream. You'll finally be part of the fold.

Best of luck with your new religion. God(s) willing, you might make it into the next edition of this book.

INDEX BY CATEGORY

RELIGION	PAGE	NOTES

RELIGION	PAGE	NOTES

RELIGION	PAGE	NOTES

RELIGION	PAGE	NOTES

RELIGION	PAGE	NOTES

NOTES

RELIGION	PAGE	NOTES

RELIGION	PAGE	NOTES

RELIGION	PAGE	NOTES

GODSPEED